DATE DUE

AP 7 '99		
AP 28 '99		
MY 12 '99		
NO 22 '99		
DE 15 '99		
JE 7 '00		
DE 29 '00		
JR 2 7 '01		
MY 23 '01		
DE 19 '01		
MY 2 3 '07		

DEMCO 38-296

R

Gender Issues
in Elder Abuse

Lynda Aitken
and
Gabriele Griffin

SAGE Publications
London • Thousand Oaks • New Delhi

This edition first published 1996

SAGE Publications Ltd
6 Bonhill Street
London EC2A 4PU

SAGE Publications Inc.
2455 Teller Road
Thousand Oaks, California 91320

SAGE Publications India Pvt Ltd
32, M-Block Market
Greater Kailash – I
New Delhi 110 048

British Library Cataloguing in Publication data

A catalogue record for this book is available from the British Library.

ISBN 0 8039 7522-8
ISBN 0 8039 7523-6 (pbk)

Library of Congress catalog card number 96–070414

Typeset by Photoprint, Torquay, Devon
Printed in Great Britain by Biddles Ltd, Guildford, Surrey

Lynda Aitken would like to dedicate this book to Bill, the archetypal Scots male, who supported her forays into gender issues and whose brief illness and untimely death coincided with much of the preparatory work for this volume. This book is also dedicated to Jamie and Bruce who continue to struggle with the concept of having a mother who is a feminist – not always a laughing matter.

Gabriele Griffin would like to dedicate this volume to Andrea, Christiane, Katrin and Jochen who are far from contemplating their own ageing, and to CS who was party to a lot of comments on 'work in progress'.

Last but not least, we would like to acknowledge our mothers Kay Maker and Hanna Zielke – still bowling and cycling after all these years!

Contents

Acknowledgements

We would like to thank Northamptonshire County Council Social Services Department for supporting Lynda Aitken in undertaking her MA in Women's Studies and the research that was part of it; June Stevenson for typing her dissertation on outdated technology; the care-at-home social workers who gave up their time to talk to Lynda Aitken about situations of elder abuse; colleagues on the multi-disciplinary working party who were responsible for conducting the study detailed in Chapter 5 and who produced the Northamptonshire Guidelines on Elder Abuse; the Social Work Team at Northampton General Hospital for their continual support; and Philip Douglas, Aitken's Operations Manager, who usually remembered to ask how things were going.

We would also like to thank Karen Phillips, editor at Sage, for her support with this project; Jane Marshall, the always friendly, obliging and proactive Faculty Librarian from Nene College and all those who let us talk about this project and offered support and advice along the way.

Introduction

The aim of this book is to highlight the fact that gender is a significant factor in elder abuse. By this we mean that the structural inequalities which inhere in the socio-cultural and economic differences between women and men impact directly on questions of elder abuse. Elder abuse has been a concern in medical and sociological research for more than twenty years (e.g. Thomas, 1977; Stearns, 1986; Steinmetz, 1988; Social Services Inspectorate, 1992; Bennett and Kingston, 1993; Biggs et al., 1995) but the gendered findings which this work has produced (e.g. Baker, 1975; Eastman, 1984) have only been recognized and considered as such in the very recent past (e.g. Wilson, 1994; Whittaker, 1995). Predictably perhaps, it has taken *women*, ourselves included, to focus on gender as an important issue in elder abuse. For despite the many achievements of the various feminist movements which have helped to effect changes in the conditions of women's lives, it is still largely women who are concerned to challenge gender inequalities, especially within heterosexual contexts. Any publisher's catalogue will confirm this. The reasons are fairly obvious: they have to do with the systematic structural disadvantages to which women continue to be exposed and which, in order to be changed, require changes in attitude that are difficult to achieve and resources that men are still largely in control of.

In asserting the importance of gender in the context of elder abuse we adopt a materialist feminist stance which operates from the premise that the gender ascribed to any individual will directly affect their lives (Hennessy, 1993). It has been the unique achievement of feminism and feminist practices/theories to establish that gender impacts on and structures people's lives. We wish to explore how this happens in the context of elder abuse. In trying to understand how gender issues affect elder abuse we do not want to reproduce the gender stereotypes which in our view inform much of the research done in the field and which, for instance, can assume that women are nurturant and caring while men commit acts of physical violence. Thus Linda Grant (1994) writes, 'We may imagine that the rape of elderly women is a rare, horrible and peculiarly unnatural crime, but it is not. Looking at newspaper cuttings covering the past two or three years, it becomes clear that the rape of older women is not only commonplace but that the number of reported incidents are increasing.' The 'image' of a young man raping an elderly woman fits pervasive notions of (a) young men as (sexually) aggressive and older women as helpless victims, and (b) men as aggressors and women as objects of aggression. While this is undoubtedly the case (Dobash and Dobash, 1992; Kingston and Penhale, 1995), it does not constitute the whole truth. Our expectations – and by 'our' we mean non-feminists as well as feminists – to find particular patterns of abuse in line with conventional gender role definitions may lead us to overlook or ignore abusive situations which do not coincide with prevalent gender stereotypes. Thus the discussions both of women violating and abusing each other, and of women abusing men have yet to be had. We address this issue further in Chapters 4 and 5.

Our interest in gender issues in elder abuse has several different sources. These are related to

- our professional concerns;
- our ideological positions as feminists;
- our own situation as women.

We support Stanley and Wise's contention that 'it is one's *own* experience which should form the basis of both theory and practice. Experience, theory and practice should exist in mutual and immediate relationship with each other' (1993: 89).

The Issue of Care

One of the threads running through this volume is the issue of care as a context for elder abuse. This is not just because historically that context has been identified as one in which elder abuse occurs (Eastman, 1994b; Homer, 1994). On a very basic and personal level, we both think that we may have to care for an older relative at some point in our lives and that we ourselves may in turn become the recipients of care. We have both lost fathers and have older mothers, at present still living on their own but potentially in need of care at some point in the future. We passionately want our mothers to be well looked after but feel ambivalent about the role of becoming a carer. We know other women who have become seriously stressed by caring for their ageing parents, especially in cases where ageing has been accompanied by severe degrees of physical and/or mental decline (see also Homer, 1994). This raises anxieties about, for example, our ability to cope with having to care without resorting to abuse or neglect in however mild a form as well as about our own vulnerability once we become the objects of care. We are very clear that our expectation to care is associated with gender roles in Western heteropatriachal society which attribute 'caring' to women without really investigating how caring we – as women – are, or can/should be expected to be. We are also aware that a lifetime's experience of women being constructed as vulnerable and of being exposed to various forms of harassment and minor crime means that we will experience our vulnerability in old age in specific and gendered ways (see Pain, 1995).

One of us, Lynda Aitken, has to deal with elder abuse within the context of care in her professional role as a Social Services manager. The empirical research which informs this volume was conducted as part of Aitken's involvement in setting up guidelines for dealing with elder abuse. Aitken is a social worker, working in a hospital setting, where her day-to-day responsibilities include making care arrangements for patients. Many of these patients on both acute and geriatric wards are older. There is, in addition to this age dimension, an important gender dimension as regards both patients and potential/actual carers. The majority of these older patients are female. Aitken's team of social workers deals with many carers, predominantly female, in arranging discharges from hospital. Within the family, responsibility for caring for older people tends to rest with the partner or spouse (unless the older person is single or widowed) or with a daughter, daughter-in-law or son. The alternative to support for an older person by family members is care – at home or in a residental setting – by a largely female workforce of low-paid or volunteer carers.

Aitken's day-to-day observations regarding the intersection of age and gender in the context of care acquired a new dimension in the light of changes in the legislation affecting elders in Britain in the 1990s. Aitken's peer group of colleagues in Social Services are managers of older persons' homes and domiciliary services for elders. She became interested in raising the awareness of her colleagues in health and social services concerning the problems of elder abuse with the coming into force of the National Health Service (NHS) and Community Care Act of 1991 on 1 April 1993. This Act may be seen as an attempt to ration resources for elders and other vulnerable groups of people. Residential care had become a growth industry in the 1980s and early 1990s, costing increasingly large amounts of public money (Hugman, 1994: 46–57). The new Act was meant to shift resources from residential care to care in the community, in other words to the family and the 'free' services of female family members, thus effectively privatizing the care of older people and solving the problem of the increasing financial burden of care on the state. It is worth noting that this Act came into being and force under a male prime minister, John Major, who subsequently became (in)famous for his misfiring 'back-to-basics' campaign, intended to reassert the values of the bourgeois nuclear family and lashing out against single mothers, the unemployed and other disadvantaged groups. As Macdonald and Rich had pointed out: 'Men used family as a way of controlling individual women, and thereby of colonizing women as a class' (1984: 102).

It was within this context that Aitken was asked to help set up a working party to develop guidelines for professional staff for dealing with abuse of vulnerable adults, later modified to mean guidelines for dealing with elder abuse. In order to establish such guidelines, some research was by questionnaire (discussed further in Chapters 2 and 5) to discover what Social Services' staff's experience of elder abuse was. Aitken subsequently did interviews with some of these staff to broaden the information base established by the questionnaires. The intention behind this research was to raise participants' awareness of elder abuse both as regards prevalence and type, to establish what participants' training needs were and to glean views which would inform the establishment of the guidelines on elder abuse. The research on which this volume is grounded is therefore informed by Aitken's professional commitment to enabling her staff as well as other professional staff to deal effectively with elder abuse as they encounter it. It offers a view on gender issues in elder abuse from the perspective of a social worker involved in dealing with care issues for older people. While we fully acknowledge (and discuss in Chapter 2) that this is not the only perspective from which one might view elder abuse, we think it is one of the necessary ones because social workers constitute a point of intervention in abuse scenarios and need to be informed both about the issues and about how to deal with them.

Problems of Categorization: Family Violence vs Care or the Either/Or Syndrome

It is possible (as we do in Chapter 2) to present the history of the 'discovery' of and research into as well as action on elder abuse as a successive, linear story of increasing complexity but also of greater and greater 'truth'. This mimics the history of science, which is one of discovery and refutation. For instance, Mervyn Eastman's (1984) portrayal of the abuser as the stressed, middle-aged daughter looking after a dependent older mother has been 'succeeded' by texts such as Homer and Gilleard's (1990), which characterized the abuser as a male with alcohol-related and other problems. Similarly, there has been a debate about the relative importance of cycles of violence within families whereby abused children in turn abuse their parents in old age versus carer stress in the occurrence of elder abuse. Following Pillemer and Wolf (1989), McCreadie (1994) cites five factors which family violence theorists consider important in the abuse of older people:

1. The pathology of the individual.
2. The 'cycle of violence' in which violent behaviour is transmitted from one generation to another.
3. The pattern of dependency in the relationship between the abused person and the abuser.
4. The social isolation of families.
5. The amount of *external stress*, i.e. stress arising from factors such as unemployment. (McCreadie, 1994: 17)

This model of representing factors influencing abuse by identifying and separating out specific issues may lead one to assume that any one of these factors is a necessary and sufficient condition for abuse to occur. We would argue that a more holistic view is needed whereby the interrelationship of these factors is properly acknowledged as well as the notion that different factors can play a role in any one type of abuse and across a range of abusive situations. Thus the five points made above in relation to family violence could easily be made, and have been made, in relation to abuse in care-giving situations. Importantly, in any event, it is frequently a family member who is both the main carer and the abuser (Eastman, 1994b; Homer 1994).

The tendency in all these discussions is to present them in either/or terms, to suggest that one explanation is more adequate than another. The intention is, of course, to produce a watertight framework for analysing elder abuse but the effect is to reduce the complexity of the situation to a single factor which is actually unlikely to be the one necessary and sufficient ingredient which will determine whether we are dealing with elder abuse or not. This is particularly the case in the context of categorizing abuse itself, commonly divided into groups such as physical abuse, sexual abuse, emotional abuse, financial abuse, verbal abuse, etc. as if elder abuse could easily fit into these categories. It ignores the fact that abuse may not be easily classifiable and that any one person may be the object of more than one type of abuse. We would therefore argue that instead of constructing the either/or scenarios or successive revelations typically encountered in the social sciences literature on elder abuse, we need to think of elder abuse in terms of and/as well as. There is, for example, no reason to assume that stressed middle-aged daughters do not occasionally abuse their aged mothers for whom they care. But this is not either a necessary or a sufficient reason for elder abuse to occur. It is just one reason. Similarly, to show that only some people who were abused by their parents in turn abuse them when the parents have become older themselves does not – because it does not occur in all such cases – mean that cycles of violence within a family do not play a role in elder abuse. They may well *in some cases*. Resisting dichotomous thinking, one of the central tenets of much feminist work (e.g. Cixous, 1981; Code, 1991; Stanley and Wise, 1993), seems to us to be important in keeping the debate about elder abuse open and inclusive; it is also more likely to reflect the reality of what occurs.

The Marginalization of Older Women in Society

Part of that reality is the marginalization of older women in Western society across a vast range of situations, some of which we shall address in this volume. Gabriele Griffin teaches Women's Studies, a discipline which one might expect to grapple with the issue of ageing in women, especially since Women's Studies in Britain frequently caters for so-called 'women returners' – older women who have either been outside the academy or never entered it prior to doing Women's Studies. Yet the situation in the discipline in Britain mirrors that in society at large – we are at present not aware of any Women's Studies courses which offer modules on women and ageing. Only very gradually, and as 'age' has hit them, have feminists such as Simone de Beauvoir (1972), Betty Friedan (1993) and Germaine Greer (1991) begun to address the matter of women growing old. But these are relatively isolated and individual voices in the feminist arena. It may be that the emphasis on 'experience' (Stanley and Wise, 1993) in second wave feminism has made feminists focus very closely on their specific life stages and immediate experiences, thus leading to a lack of engagement with issues not pertinent to their own situation. This is certainly an accusation which has been made by some women (hooks, 1984).

While the existence of elder abuse is now acknowledged by many professionals working with elders, it tends to remain hidden from the general public. The media have shown relatively little interest in the subject of elder abuse. The focus of newspapers and general reporting is, on the whole, the criminal action of young muggers, with headlines such as 'Thugs Attack Woman, 83' (*Northampton Chronicle and Echo*, 6 November 1992: 1) and 'O.A.P.s tied to Bedpost' (*Northampton Chronicle and Echo*, 11 May 1992: 1). The national press in Britain and papers in the United States have picked up on the rare but newsworthy 'elder abandonment' (also known as 'Granny dumping'). One feature in the *Guardian* (1993) quoted a study of the phenomenon of granny dumping which claimed that it occurred once a year in one hospital out of three (Weale, 1993: 13). The cases of elder abuse, if statistics were systematically kept across the range of services where elder abuse might come to light (and such statistics are only very incompletely available), are, we suspect, far greater than this for almost every general hospital. According to Anna Blundy, 'Through the year about half the patients admitted to casualty departments are aged 75 or older. At Christmas this rises to about 75%' (1995: 9). An abandoned old lady with a note pinned to her coat, a badly mugged old man – these are cases which will hit the headlines. A frail eighty-year old with 'pepper-pot' bruising (indicating forcible restriction) on her chest or an old man whose daughter commandeers his Attendance Allowance to pay her bus fares are less likely to be reported in the press. One reason for this silence may be that few cases of elder abuse in Britain result in criminal prosecution, partly because of the difficulties associated with defining elder abuse (McCreadie, 1991) and because of the degree to which it has to happen before it will come to any agency's notice, partly because those abused can be reluctant to come forward out of shame or for fear of losing their home or because they are too impaired to do so (Homer and Gilleard, 1990).

Another reason for this silence may be that our society is reluctant to admit that familial violence exists. Somehow it may seem easier to comprehend a tearaway high on drugs or solvents beating up an old lady for her pension money than it is to picture a sixty-year-old daughter tying her mother into a chair so that she can go to the shops. The family and the private world are still in many respects taboo areas for public investigation. This rebounds fairly and squarely on women, many of whom (especially old women) have only a private life within the family home. A further aspect of the silence surrounding elder abuse may be an element of collusion when the abuser is a stressed female carer. After all, many of the 'professional' carers who may have an investigative role in elder abuse are women, too. It is important to note here, however, that the question of who precisely abuses and why (to which *one* answer is: 'a stressed female carer') has been subject to some enquiry and, as we shall discuss in Chapters 3, 4 and 5, the image of the abuser which early studies of elder abuse projected has been modified in the light of subsequent findings.

The majority of abused older people are women. But old women are 'invisible'. Most have private lives only; few live extensively in the public domain. Their abuse goes on behind the closed doors of the home or the institution. Without adequate access to the public domain, it is difficult for older women to draw attention to the abuse they endure. At the same time, they may also have 'good' additional reasons not to declare the abuse, to remain with the abuser and endure abuse, such as the fear of being put into a home or a sense of shame about being the object of abuse. There is a clear need to work towards the empowerment of older women (Browne, 1995).

The Elderly, Elders or 'Older'? Issues of Terminology

In the first version of the manuscript for this book we used the expression 'the elderly' and 'elderly' as an adjective freely, partly because 'elderly' appears extensively in the literature on elder abuse and thus creates a connection between the concerns of that literature and ours, and partly because we wanted to distinguish between adults in general and people in their seventies and eighties specifically. The anonymous reader's report we received suggested that we 'delete all references to the elderly' as this phrase was 'dehumanizing, de-individualizing, segregationist and ageist'. An alternative is to refer to 'older people' or 'elders', which is what we do in this text. Biggs et al. (1995: 2) explain their use of 'older people' and 'elders' as follows:

> 'Older people' conveys the fact that we see our chosen subjects as people, that is, citizens with the same human and civil rights as the rest of the adult population. It also conveys their special status in life course terms, the older group of citizens who may also have particular requirements. 'Elders' is used more or less interchangeably with 'older people', and its use is intended to emphasize the positive aspects that old age can confer. Whilst terms such as 'elderly', for example as in the 'elderly population', may occasionally be used, we consider that this term is best avoided if it reinforces the view of older people as a homogeneous bloc of the population. This is both depersonalizing as well as inaccurate as a description of older people at the turn of the century.

Although we decided to use 'older people' and 'elders' in this volume we have some reservations about the usefulness of these terms which need to be indicated. It seems to us that 'older people' as a phrase not only perpetuates the – sometimes necessary – homogenization of older people in the same way that 'the elderly' does but, more importantly, we think that 'elderly people' refers to a group of people within a more clearly defined age range than 'older people' which, depending on one's perspective, can encompass anyone from their late thirties or even earlier onwards. Talking of 'older people' can therefore homogenize an even larger and thus still more diverse group of the general population than the phrase 'elderly people' does. Biggs et al. (1995) appear less concerned with the age range than with the question of the subject or citizen status of older people. Their argument about the 'special status in life course terms' associated with 'particular needs' is less easy to follow as 'older people' simply extends the range talked about and thus widens the life course statuses and diversity of needs of the older people under discussion.

There is a further, gender-specific issue here: as we discuss in Chapter 1, in life course terms the proportion of women to men changes with increasing age; very elderly people are in fact predominantly older *women*. The phrase 'older people' obscures this fact. This is also the case with the word 'elders', which we found somewhat problematic even as we used it. This is because we associate 'elders' with what the *Oxford English Dictionary* describes as 'a member of a "senate", governing body or class, consisting of men venerable for age, or conventionally supposed to be so'. In other words, the term 'elders' points, from our perspective, to a gendered group (men) of people who are held in high esteem and have an office as well as status. It is a phrase rarely used in Western white culture where older people, specifically older women, are not held in high esteem and tend not to have central and elevated functions within society. But this is predominantly the group of people we are talking about in this volume. We think that to use the term 'elders' in some respects almost acquires an ironic dimension whereby that term serves to highlight the discrepancy between what it commonly denotes and who we are actually talking about. It is not, however, a laughing matter.

While we use the expressions 'older people' and 'elders' we do so with some reservations. Both terms can be regarded as 'segregationist' and 'ageist'. As soon as we talk about a specific group of people within a particular age range such accusations can be levelled. But it has to be recognized that the identification of the group of people we are talking about is a necessary part of a meaningful discussion about elder abuse.

Thinking in Numbers – The Feminization of Old Age and Its Conditions

The well-rehearsed fact that there are proportionally more women in the general population the older it gets has not led researchers on elder abuse to conclude that elder abuse is predominantly an issue affecting women. In Chapter 1 we examine the feminization of old age and its conditions in order to highlight how these factors lead to a situation where older women are likely to be abused. The large number of older women in contemporary Western societies, their relative poverty and the absence of a public health policy which addresses their needs are all examined. We discuss older people's changing lifestyles and household arrangements, including those of people from minority groups within Britain, to suggest that the policies which inform how Social Services target care provision do not take adequate account of older people's actual needs, and this may be one reason why we have difficulty in assessing the prevalence of elder abuse.

Gender Issues in the History of the Research on Elder Abuse

In the second chapter we argue that while the history of the reseach on elder abuse points to the gendered nature of that phenomenon, this has only very recently been acknowledged and then, predictably, by *feminist* researchers in the field. Much of the research on elder abuse has been done by men; it focuses on prevalence rates as a way of establishing the legitimacy of concern about elder abuse and of constructing histories of individual pathology in both abuser and abused as one dominant explanation for the occurrence of elder abuse. We suggest that much of the research either ignores and obscures gender issues in elder abuse or else replicates gender stereotypes in the ways in which it is constructed and conducted.

Ageism and Sexism – Discrimination in/of Old Age

In the third chapter we examine the impact of ageism, particularly in relation to women, of sexism and other kinds of discriminatory attitudes and structures such as class and race on elder abuse. We argue that the construction and representation of women in Western society conduces to power imbalances which facilitate older women's abuse by insisting on women's, specifically older women's, inferior status. This discrimination is augmented where ageism and sexism are complicated by racism, both individual and institutional. The latter is expressed in the limited available knowledge of the experiences of elders from diverse cultures living in Britain.

Paid to Care – Gender Issues in Elder Abuse in Institutional Settings

Relatively little is known about elder abuse in institutional settings, a fact all the more worrying in the current socio-political and economic climate in which publicly funded and therefore scrutinized homes for older people are being supplanted, in part, by domiciliary care agencies which at present escape such scrutiny, precisely because they are supposed to be encouraged to enable the government to carry out its care-in-the-community policy. We suggest additionally that the lack of research and knowledge regarding elder abuse in institutional settings is associated with the gender specificities of the setting where a largely female client group is looked after by a predominantly female workforce who are on the whole low paid. We maintain that elder abuse in institutional settings is in the main about abuse of women by women, a scenario which defies gender stereotypes and is therefore either addressed through the pathologizing of the individual – a move commonly used in relation to women who are regarded as transgressing gendered boundaries – or not addressed at all. Importantly in this context, we argue that the tendency to identify with the perpetrator rather than the victim of elder abuse has been used as a way of 'exonerating' abusers along gendered lines.

Who Cares? A Gendered View of Care and Elder Abuse in Domestic Settings

This situation is slightly different in the context of elder abuse in domestic settings where the notion of the daughter or daughter-in-law abusing the older mother has been widened by the recognition that cross-gender abuse may and will occur. This is corroborated by the Northamptonshire research findings which underpin this chapter and which include abuse of mothers by sons, of wives by husbands and vice versa. In this chapter we explore the shifts which have happened in how domestic elder abuse is constructed, setting this in the context of findings from interviews with social workers in Northamptonshire which reveal their level of knowledge and attitude towards elder abuse at a particular point in time. We analyse the findings of a research project done in Northamptonshire in the early 1990s which correlated the gender of the abuser and the abused with the type of abuse which was committed, thus revealing the need to evolve a differentiated rather than monocausal model for understanding elder abuse.

This book brings together the research and writings which have been produced in response to the growing recognition that elder abuse occurs and that gender issues are a significant factor in this occurrence. It reflects our view that social reality and cultural representation conjoin to construct and reinforce the conditions which facilitate and perpetuate elder abuse, thus suggesting that changes in how elders are treated in Western society can only be brought about by an understanding that individual cases of elder abuse point beyond themselves towards the gendered structural inequalities which inform the abusive situations that need to be confronted.

1

Thinking in Numbers – The Feminization of Old Age and Its Conditions

'Advances in medicine have led to a dramatic increase in the numbers of people reaching 100 years of age (known as centenarians). In 1951 there were 300 in the UK; by 1991 there were 4,390, all but 500 of whom were women' ('Counting the Cost of Caring': 12). Thus the *Guardian* on 20 September 1994, during Age Concern week. 'Counting the Cost of Caring', the title of the *Guardian*'s article and perhaps the major reason why age has become a concern, has implications for the general population and in more than economic terms, although the latter tend to determine public discourses on ageing.

Older populations are now beginning to appear in contexts where, once upon a time, they were hardly in existence. Thus a recent article in the *Guardian* detailed the problems that are arising in the UK regarding an older population in Britain's prisons: 'Problems in caring for inmates now in their 80s have led to the planned pensioners' wing at Kingston prison' (*Guardian* 18 October 1994: 1). The proportion of old people relative to young ones in the overall population in Western society has changed during this century. The fall in the general birth rate, longer life expectancy and the two world wars in which large numbers of young men were killed mean that the proportion of older people, specifically of older women, within the total population has grown. Women's mortality rate has decreased and women in Britain live on average five years longer than men (Arber and Ginn, 1991: 9). And even though women's longevity relative to that of men is decreasing (see Table 1.1) so that in future we may not expect so many more women to outlive men, for the foreseeable future women still outnumber men in increasing proportion relative to age.

As the numbers of older people increase, so do the opportunities for their abuse. But these opportunities have to be considered in context. Elder abuse does not occur in a vacuum. Rather, it has to be viewed within the social, economic and ideological structures which older women and men inhabit and which constitute the conditions for elder abuse. In this chapter we discuss a number of differences

Table 1.1   *Death rate per thousand population for women and*
men over 55, by age group, England and Wales, 1971–89

		55–64	65–74	75–84	85+
1971	Men	20.1	50.5	113.0	231.8
	Women	10.0	26.1	73.6	185.7
	Sex ratio M/F	2.01	1.93	1.54	1.25
1981	Men	17.7	45.6	105.2	226.5
	Women	9.5	24.1	66.2	178.2
	Sex ratio (M/F)	1.86	1.89	1.59	1.27
1989	Men	14.8	39.5	95.7	195.7
	Women	8.8	22.6	60.3	162.4
	Sex ratio (M/F)	1.68	1.75	1.59	1.21
% decrease	Men	26.4	21.8	15.37	15.6
1971–89	Women	12.0	13.4	18.1	12.5

Source: Arber and Ginn, 1991: 109

among elders in which gender plays a role. In brief, we wish to highlight that

- there are increasingly higher numbers of older women in the general population than men the further up the age scale we go;
- these women tend to be poorer than men, which affects the economically based decisions they can make;
- these women's health needs are not considered in public health policies with the effect that those needs are not sufficiently catered for;
- the combination of poverty and ill health helps to foster dependency and thus exploitability;
- many older women live by themselves, which affects the kinds of abuse they may be the objects of;
- Social Services target services at the single occupant household which means that abuse in cohabiting households can escape notice;
- we have yet to investigate the specific issues which may arise for elders from diverse ethnic backgrounds in Britain, given the specificities, including those of gender distribution, of these populations.

Altogether, these factors offer a context in which to consider the occurrence of elder abuse.

The Feminization of Old Age

Local and national Census data reveal a higher proportion of older women among the older population than men and thus a feminization of old age. For instance, the vast majority of over eighty-four-year-olds (see Table 1.1) are women. These data are roughly comparable with those from other studies (e.g. Midwinter, 1991a). Goddard and Savage (1994: 1) report findings from the General Household Survey of 1991 which indicate that in 1991 'women constituted almost three fifths of those aged 65 and over, and among those aged 85 and over, there were more than twice as many women as men'. This feminization of old age is routinely ignored in writings on elder abuse, including very recent ones such as that by Biggs et al. (1995: 23) who maintain, for instance, that 'the link between gender and mistreatment in later life seems less strong' than in domestic violence scenarios. We would argue that, on the contrary, the link between gender and mistreatment in old age is very powerful, with women constituting by far the most victims but with a greater range of diversity as far as the abuser is concerned than we commonly associate with domestic violence situations where, within heterosexual contexts, most commonly the male partner abuses the woman (Johnson, 1995). Elder abuse comes in a variety of guises and as such can only in part be related to domestic abuse. It may occur in the domestic setting or it may happen within an institutional context. It may take the form of physical or sexual abuse but it can also involve financial or emotional abuse. It may occur between partners or across generations, between relatives and non-relatives. In all of these situations gender will play a role, as it is one of the main structuring devices in social interaction and hierarchization.

A number of questions specific to issues about elder abuse arise in the face of the data cited above. One is how the increasing proportion of women in the older population relates to the amount and types of abuse that occur. Are people more prone to being abused the older they are and if so, does this affect women and men in different ways? Secondly, does the type of abuse to which elders are exposed vary according to age group and, within that, according to gender? Thirdly, how do elders' experiences of abuse change with age, and is there a difference for women and men? Does who the abuser is change with elders' age, and is this different for women and men of diverse age groups? What role do socio-economic contexts play in the abuse of older women and men? Are there differences concerning the reporting of abuse of older women and men across different age ranges? What kinds of intervention are offered to women and men, and if there is a difference, how can this be accounted for? These are just some of the issues raised by the fact that there are proportionately more women in the general population the older the age range, but to date we have little by way of answers to these questions because gender has not been sufficiently factored into debates about elder abuse.

The Poverty of Older Women

Walker (1992: 176) writes that 'gender is one of the clearest lines along which the economic and social experience of old age is divided'. Older women are materially disadvantaged because of the gender inequalities which rule the labour market and women's access to resources prior to old age, because these inequalities inform the economic status of women in old age and because old age itself becomes a stage of discrimination and disadvantage through the allocation of resources at that time. Women's uneven participation in the labour market, with time taken out to raise children or to care for relatives and part-time and/or low-paid work, means that they cannot accumulate the pension rights men will collect during the same time period. Groves (1992: 193) demonstrates how occupational pension schemes based on the concept of salaried family wage earners systematically disadvantage women, whether married or single, with the effect that 'Elderly non-married women [are] substantially over-represented among the poorest. "Very elderly" women over 75 [are] among the poorest of all'. Walker maintains that 'the inequality between lone men and lone women is greatest among those aged 75 and over' (1992: 180).

Married women are constructed as financially dependent on their husbands because they frequently have to rely on their male partner's pension scheme (Walker, 1992: 182) and, upon death of the partner or upon divorce, are entitled only to a proportion of their partner's pension, which will amount to less than single women's pension. This situation is worse for working-class women who are likely not to have been part of an occupational pension scheme. Women's poverty in old age means that, if married, they are likely to be dependent on their partner for financial support and, if unmarried, they may need to rely on Income Support or other benefits. Financial dependence on a man or the state disadvantages women regarding the economically driven choices they can make. If they are abused by an older spouse, for instance, they may not feel able to move out or demand that their husband be removed because they have no resources, or may think that they do not have appropriate access to the household resources, to do so. Similarly, if they are abused in an institutional setting, they may not be able to react to this because they lack the financial power to do so and to go somewhere else. Lone women who are poor may be the victims of (self) neglect rather than abuse, choosing, for instance, to go hungry or without heat rather than to be unable to manage on an insufficient allowance. As Kappeler (1995) demonstrates, in a society based on exchange relationships those who have nothing or little to exchange are likely to be victimized.

Gender and Mortality Rate Differences among Older Women and Men

Women's ability to deal with abuse in old age is worsened by their likelihood to suffer from ill health and disability in old age, especially very old age. These require resources which are not available (Walker, 1992: 182–3). At present men die at an earlier age than women from ischaemic heart disease, strokes and some cancers (Medical Research Council, 1994: 24). They also have a higher death rate from accidents and suicide. Women, in contrast, suffer from a higher incidence of non-fatal disabling conditions such as rheumatoid arthritis, depression and osteoporosis. Their longer lifespan allows these chronic conditions to worsen (Medical Research Council, 1994: 25). In consequence many very old women will be frail and potentially prey to abuse, simply because they are not in a position to retaliate or react, and because their ill health with its attendant care needs can place great strain on their carers. These conditions have not been given much attention in the new British National Health Service funding structure. The White Paper *The Health of the Nation* (Department of Health, 1992) failed to identify any key priorities or targets for elders. Screening and hormone replacement therapy which are essential to dealing with osteoporosis, for example, should be made widely available. Yet they are not. In a recent letter to *The Times* (1995), Ian Fentiman, Deputy Director of the Imperial Cancer Research Fund, pointed out that 'Out of 30,000 women who develop breast cancer every year, half are over 65; yet this age group are not invited to come for screening as part of the national [UK] programme.' He called for a feasibility study 'to look at uptake [of screening for breast cancer] in women aged 65 or over', asking: 'how much longer will the health of older women be compromised?'

The refusal to address older women's health needs inherent in current UK government policies is not specific to the government or the health services. The health needs of older women have also been largely neglected by feminists – Germaine Greer, for example, has got no further than *The Change* (1991). Similarly, Wilkinson and Kitzinger's *Women and Health: Feminist Perspectives* (1994) moves from the menopause to coping with bereavement, with no recognition of the chronic diseases that affect many women in old age. The issues picked up by what one might describe as the women's health movement have tended to concentrate on concerns such as reproductive rights (where 'age' manifests itself only in the form of post-menopausal motherhood) and contraception. There has been little attempt to press for more research into dementia, for example, which is a significant problem for older women and their carers (Decalmer, 1993: 36–7). As Cynthia Rich writes in *Look Me in the Eye*: 'our society breeds ignorance and fear of both aging and death' (Macdonald and Rich, 1983: 12)

Dependency as Lived Reality and as Social Construct

Economic disadvantage and ill health both conduce to dependency. This is not to say that all old people are dependent but that there is a likelihood of greater degrees of dependence the older people get and that, given the gender distribution among the very old, women may be disproportionately affected by this. Dependence in old age is both a social construct and as such frequently presented as negative (e.g. Birmingham BASE, 1988), and a reality which needs to be faced and alleviated.

The national Census has tried to establish dependency in households but, through the very way in which that information is collected, it obscures gender-specific information and reproduces gender stereotypes in the kinds of question it asks. The needs forecasts for services done at a local level show that the complex shifts in household and socio-economic patterns raise questions about who lives with and/or looks after older people and may be in a position to exploit or abuse them. As Jack (1994: 78) states: 'the majority of old people are women. Similarly, the vast majority of formal (i.e. paid) carers for old people are women. The formal care of elderly people is therefore a markedly female environment, and any discussion of the nature of power, dependency and violation involving old people and their formal carers must recognize the importance of age and gender.' Gender issues, both perceptual and actual, play a central role in elder abuse. In consequence, the analysis of demographic trends which informs policy making needs to take into account gender differences in the older population as well as in those caring for older people. Dependence for support increases with age and is most marked amongst those aged seventy-five and over (Midwinter, 1991a: 6, 9). The General Household Survey did indicate that 'Except for washing and drying dishes, and washing clothing by hand – the tasks that people were least likely to have difficulty with

– the proportion of women unable to manage by themselves was, in general, about twice that of men' (Goddard and Savage, 1994: 5). This may be a function of women living longer and getting frailer than men, or of their being more prone to suffering from debilitating chronic illnesses. The implication is that women are more likely to be dependent than men in their old age. There is some evidence (Sadler, 1990; Laurance, 1994) to suggest that there is a correlation between the degree of dependence and the likelihood of abuse. In other words, those most likely to be abused are very old women.

Living Alone: A Fate Worse than Cohabitation?

Abuse, as opposed to self-abuse and self-neglect, involves an other who may be a cohabitee, a regular visitor or a stranger. In terms of service provision, here taken as an indication of (assumed) need but also associated with the possibility of (the discovery of) elder abuse, it is single pensioner households which tend to be targeted for service provision. According to the General Household Survey, 38 per cent of those aged sixty-five and over live alone, and because they are more likely to be widowed than men, more women live alone than men. Additionally, 'The proportion of elderly persons living alone increased steadily with age, from 26% of those aged 65–69 to 58% of those aged 85 and over' (Goddard and Savage, 1994: 1). Services for older people such as home help or meals-on-wheels are often concentrated on those living alone, although there is some research to suggest that this group is not in most need of health and social care resources (Taylor and Ford, 1983). Neither are they most at risk from elder abuse (Pillemer and Finkelhor, 1988), in part because living alone, they are not the objects of a cohabiting relationship which may lead to abuse. However, as we shall indicate in Chapter 5, significant numbers of abused people are abused by non-relatives and this needs to be borne in mind when considering the likelihood of people living on their own being the objects of abuse.

In our society it tends to be assumed that aloneness is a problem. In 1994 the *Independent* (2 December), under the headline 'More Will Die Alone', detailed the story of 'how a man lay dead for three and a half years in his council flat' before being found. An investigation into the case blamed ' "indifferently managed" home-help services' and 'a period of upheaval in the social services department' for this situation. The article concluded by citing the Director of Planning at Help the Aged, Wally Harbert, as saying: 'I think there will be more lonely deaths.' Being alone is supposed to make you vulnerable, especially if you are a woman, a child, or an older person. The notion of aloneness signalling vulnerability is constantly reinforced by the media, which report on the ways in which pensioners living by themselves fall prey to robbers and various kinds of intruders into their homes. This perception tends to foster anxiety. However, it has to be balanced by an understanding that older people overall are, in fact, less at risk of being victims of violent crime than young men (Mawby, 1983, 1988). A survey commissioned by the BBC in 1994 found that 'while 91 per cent of over-65s said they were very concerned about violence, Home Office statistics show they are one of the groups least likely to suffer assault' (Campbell, 1995: 5).

The picture painted above homogenizes older people both with regard to age and sex. However, as Pain (1995) has shown, if one disaggregates 'older people' into older women and men, a somewhat different situation concerning older people's fear and experience of crime emerges. Pain argues that if the gender composition of the older population is taken into account, not only is 'gender ... the strongest predictor of fear of crime in old age' (1995: 585) but also that the cumulative life experience of women's vulnerability within patriarchal society and particularly in the home means that 'elderly women's fears about violent crime and harassment present a reasonable reflection of risk' (ibid.: 596). Some research is needed to correlate actual experiences of abuse with the abused person's gender and age as well as with who the abuser is. Pain found that older women's fear of violence in a domestic setting was justified: 'When placed alongside marital violence, it is clear that the home is the location of greatest risk for elderly women in particular; and with regard to fear of crime, it follows that for those elderly people who are suffering or have suffered domestic abuse from partners and/or carers, there will be realistic concerns about danger in private space' (1995: 593). This does not, of course, apply in the same way to older women living alone.

One could argue that the insistence upon the problematic of aloneness is one way in which our society seeks to reinforce the idea of society as dependent on sociality, indeed on particular kinds of sociality in the form of specific social substructures such as *the family*. The family as a haven for women has of course come under sustained and justified attack, especially from women themselves (see Southall Black Sisters, 1994; Delphy and Leonard, 1992; Barrett and McIntosh, 1982). Barbara Macdonald and Cynthia Rich (1983) maintain: 'The power and promise of the present women's movement depend on our freedom to exist, however, precariously, outside of the system of familia' (1984: 102, 103). In *Backlash* (1992) Susan Faludi demonstrates how, as part of the backlash against the power of feminism to effect change in an androcentric world, various research studies have been (mis)represented to indicate that women suffer if they are outside the familial institution rather than within it. To counter this position, Faludi points to recent studies in the USA which show that 'married women report 20% more depression than single women and three times the rate of severe neurosis' (1992: 56). Other studies (e.g. Fineman and Mykitiuk, 1994) reveal the same picture in relation to women's physical health. These findings are in stark contrast to the idea of a generalized non-specific vulnerability attributed to women living alone. Kiernan in 1988 showed that the mortality rate is higher among single than among married women, and attributed this to health selection, commenting that a 'sizeable proportion of those women who remain single suffer from some physical or mental disability or illness' (cited in Pugh and Moser, 1990: 101). The issue of whether women who live alone suffer more from physical and mental problems than those cohabiting with a partner clearly represents a contested terrain with vested ideological interests on all sides. Women living alone defy ideas of the norm of the nuclear family and women's place within it. As the family has become the most debated micro unit in the Western society of the 1990s, withdrawal or removal from that unit, whether it is voluntary or not, becomes an issue.

Who Cares?

The average family size has reduced so there are fewer children to share the care. Marriages break up, with the effect that fewer daughters-in-law, one of the groups of women assumed to take on caring roles (Finch and Mason, 1993), are available to act as carers. More importantly, perhaps, complex remarriage relationships can affect the willingness of individuals and individual family units to accept responsibility for the care of older people. Who, for instance, should be responsible for those elders who have remarried on two or more occasions, possibly when their own as well as the children of the new partner had already left home? Perceptions about blood ties as a criterion for assuming care responsibilities for family members (Finch and Mason, 1993) become problematic in situations where serial partnerships are common in a large percentage of the population. Already a substantial number of older spouses care for each other (Arber and Gilbert, 1993). Changes in society at large mean that there will be an increasing reliance on the old caring for the old. This has direct implications for the abuse scenarios one is likely to encounter, which will be intra-generational, may constitute continuations of long-term domestic abuse, or may amount to neglect from those no longer physically and/or mentally able to care for each other.

Additionally, and on a different note, changes in employment patterns (Arber and Gilbert, 1992) mean that more women work, and while some will still combine this with a caring role, for others who may be sole providers either for themselves or for themselves and their dependants, caring for an older relative may not be possible. As regards men, in theory earlier retirement and redundancy as well as unemployment should mean that more men are available for caring roles. In practice, a gender difference in perceptions of caring roles (Finch and Mason, 1993) at present tends to prevent men's sustained involvement in caring except within particular parameters.

The 1991 Census began to identify households with dependants. Although this information divides young dependants from older ones, there is no way of telling the gender of the carer. Presumably, it is assumed that this will be a woman. Alternatively, who the carer is may still not be recognized as at all important in monitoring older people's life experiences, although this is clearly one instance where specific gender information would be useful. Despite small inroads into reframing the Census such as the one detailed above (i.e. identifying households' dependants by age), the validity of the information gathered through the Census needs to be questioned. The Census relies on the person who identifies herself or himself as the head of the household, in completing the questionnaire, making judgements about, for example, whether household members have 'any long-term illness, health problems or handicap which limits his/ her daily activities or the work he/she can do?' (OPCS 1991 Census). Among the questions that really need to be asked are 'Who is the head of the household?' and 'What are normal daily activities for a woman, and how do these differ from those of a man?' Without knowing what kind of gender role expectations and what sort of value judgements are made when these questions are answered by those who answer them, the information from the 1991 Census – that in Northamptonshire, for example, out of 224,144 households 27,487 included someone over pensionable age with a long-term illness – is in many ways quite meaningless.

In 1985 the OPCS conducted a sample General Household Survey which provided the first national data on informal carers. This exercise was repeated in 1990. In 1985 about 14 per cent of the adult population, roughly six million, described themselves as carers. Of these, 1.7 million were caring in their own homes. The rest supported people living separately from them. The gender difference revealed by this exercise was not as great as had initially been assumed: about 3.5 million carers were women and 2.5 million were men. The 'classic carer' – a single woman – accounted for only 11 per cent of the female caring population.

Carers were represented in all social groups and educational backgrounds as well as in all age groups. However: 'The proportion of men who provide personal and/or physical care to an adult with whom they live rises with age and is highest among men aged 75 years and over. The corresponding proportions for women are highest between the ages of 45 and 75 years' (Hancock et al., 1995: 1). The peak age for caring was between forty-five and sixty-four years. Within this age range, 50 per cent of the carers reported poor personal health themselves. This is significant because it can, of course, result in neglect due to incapacity on the part of the carer or to particular kinds of abuse related, for example, to increased general stress levels. By 1990 an additional 1 per cent of the population had taken on a caring role. Virtually all of this increase occurred in the middle years age group. This rise has to be seen in a context where predictions of demographic changes in Britain include a rise of 31 per cent in the number of older people in the eighty-five years plus range between 1991 and 2001 while the increase of people in the middle years population is anticipated to be only 12 per cent. This will leave a large care gap. Additionally, the caring population will be reduced by social and economic factors related to smaller and more mobile extended families, higher family break-up and divorce rates, and increasing employment activity by women.

Particular types and patterns of abuse will exist in contexts where older people cohabit and where informal care takes precedence over formal care. In heterosexual relationships between older people the man is likely to be older than the woman, therefore – by virtue of his age – potentially more in need of in/formal care than his female partner. Clearly, possibilities of women abusing men exist in such circumstances. However, due to the specificities of gender stereotypes in Western culture which, among other things, tend to assume that men abuse women rather than the other way around, little work has been done to investigate the particularities either of female abusers or of male victims, not just among elders (Macdonald, 1995; Dobash and Dobash, 1992). This may be because sexual abuse and domestic abuse centre on violence done to the body rather than other kinds of abuse such as emotional or financial abuse.

Caring for People (Department of Health, 1989) was the first piece of British legislation to state that service providers must make practical support for carers a high priority. Since then the Carers (Recognition and Services) Act 1995 has been established, which entitles carers to ask local authorities for a separate assessment of their 'ability to provide and to continue to provide care for the relevant person' when decisions are taken as to how an individual should be provided for. As no additional financial resources have been allocated to deal with such requests, local authorities may have difficulties complying with this Act if large numbers of potential or actual carers ask for such assessments.

Typically and predictably, when the dependent older person lives with the carer (a situation likely to lead to abuse; Biggs et al., 1995: 41–5) there is less likelihood of help being made available except in an emergency. Where informal care is a possibility, Social Services are likely to become involved only at times of acute need so that abuse going on in the privacy of a cohabiting home may not come to the attention of those outside. By contrast, older women living on their own may well be in receipt of formal services and thus be seen by Social Services workers. However, precisely because the women are living on their own, they are not as likely to be the objects of certain kinds of abuse.

The OPCS *Informal Carers Survey* (1985) looked at carers for the sick and disabled as well as elders and must be treated with some caution as its definition of caring was a very wide one. Thus Green (1988) states: 'The kinds of help that carers gave to their dependants covered a wide spectrum ranging, for example, from collecting library books to shopping once a week to almost continuous care' (1988: 6).

The problems arising from an analysis of the data gathered in the survey are very similar to the ones identified in relation to the Census in that account has to be taken of the definitions implied by the questions, and of the biases in response one is likely to get. A typical example of this sort of problem surfaces in a question such as: 'Some people have extra family responsibilities because they look after someone who is sick, handicapped or elderly ... is there anyone living with you who is sick, handicapped or elderly whom you look after or give special help to?' (Green, 1988: 6). Given the gender biases in the population as a whole concerning roles and responsibilities within the family as well as in care situations, this question could elicit different answers from different people. Arber and Ginn point out that 'A man might include shopping and cooking for his disabled wife as "extra family responsibilities", but this may not be the case for a woman caring for her disabled husband' (1990: 433). Women and men might regard a woman looking after another person as part of women's 'ordinary' role and duty, considering *extra* responsibilities to arise only where there are additional complications such as the older person being ill as well, or a chronically sick person having some additional acute problem. This survey is therefore likely to underestimate women's contribution to caring. Arber and Ginn

(1990) comment that the survey highlights the considerable contribution of older carers but they suggest that older people are likely to underestimate the amount of care they provide, especially for spouses. There are also no questions, for example, which would elicit information about the amount of care provided by older people for their grandchildren. The survey thus perpetuates the one-sided view of older people as dependent.

One drawback of using demographic information to examine the problems of elders which is, in fact, a problem of how the surveys examined here have been constructed, is that they confine discussions about older people, care and abuse to chronological age, which is not an accurate guide to functional ability or lifestyle. Sixty-five-year-olds may have few problems in common with ninety-year-olds and may, in fact, be caring for the latter. This recognition is still only paid lip service in some instances. Notably, Midwinter (1991a) for example, offers extended arguments for the use of 'stages' rather than 'ages' to classify older people; yet for the *British Gas Report on Attitudes to Ageing* (Midwinter, 1991a) he resorts to an age category ('over fifty-five') to denote elders.

Some commentators have attempted to divide older people into subgroups such as the young elderly, the elderly and the very elderly. When Northamptonshire Social Services started to think about drawing up guidelines on elder abuse, they found themselves confronted with precisely that sort of difficulty of classification. Initially, they focused on 'the old'. They were then advised to widen their brief to vulnerable adults in general. This category was meant to encompass younger people with physical and/or learning difficulties. However, it proved to be impossible to group all these people together as it would have involved the participation of too many representatives from diverse voluntary and statutory agencies, so the focus was returned to the consideration of elders who, in any event, were considered in some respects distinct from other groups of vulnerable adults. In a subsequent study, Penhale (1993c) found that many Social Services/ Social Work departments in the UK developed guidelines on elder and adult abuse but that 'no clear pattern emerged as to a distinct preference for either elder abuse or adult abuse. . . . A few respondents mentioned that they had commenced in one area of abuse . . . and were or would be looking to extend their work further. Other respondents indicated that they had commenced in one area of work and then changed to another (e.g. widening or narrowing the focus)' (1993c: 14). Such struggles around categorizing elders do not facilitate the recognition of elder abuse as a problem predominantly associated with women.

Older People from Diverse Ethnic Backgrounds

There has been a limited amount of research on elders from diverse ethnic backgrounds. This means that to date we know little about elder abuse in those communities. The most recent and most comprehensive analysis of Census data on people from the so-called 'ethnic minorities' in the UK is available from Warwick University's Centre for Research in Ethnic Relations, which has established a National Ethnic Minority Data Archive and, in 1993, published a series of papers on 'Ethnic Minorities in Great Britain'. Their analyses provide important pointers for trends in diverse ethnic minority populations which will impact on elder abuse and gender issues. Most specifically, and as evidenced in Ken Blakemore and Margaret Boneham's (1994) study, they indicate that to talk of 'black older' people without any further qualifications is entirely inappropriate, since age and gender structures, social and cultural norms, etc. vary substantially across different Asian, black and 'other' population groups.

Warwick's analyses found that 'the age structure of ethnic minority groups is very different from that of white people, and the overall average of 5.5 per cent of the population from minority ethnic groups varies considerably between age groups' (Owen, 1993b: 1). In general, the white population in the UK is considerably older on average than the populations from various ethnic minority groups, with black Caribbeans at present being 'the only ethnic minority group with a sizeable number of people of pensionable age' (ibid.: 12). The number of older people from diverse ethnic backgrounds living in the UK is relatively small at present, but should rise over the next decade or two as diverse ethnic groups 'age'. Demographic changes in these populations are, of course, related to British policies on immigration (Owen, 1993a), which have changed drastically during the post-World War II period, swinging from positive incentives for people from the West Indies to enter Britain in the 1950s to such a tightening of the immigration laws in the 1980s that it became all but impossible for immigrants from Commonwealth countries to enter Britain.

Immigration and settlement patterns of people from ethnic minorities interrelate with the very varied age and gender distributions in those groups. At present 'Black Caribbeans, Chinese, Indians and Other Asians tend to be oldest while Black-Others, Other-Others, Bangladeshis and Pakistanis are youngest' (Owen, 1993b: 12). Of these, 'the youngest ethnic minority group, Black-Others, has the largest percentage of its population born in the UK' (ibid.). This point is important, as one can expect that this group will eventually have a better knowledge of, and thus potential access to, services available to them in the UK, given that they were born here, than some of the current elders from ethnic minority backgrounds who, as several studies have demonstrated, tend both in the USA and in the UK to under-use the health and social services available to them (Blakemore, 1983; Moon and Williams, 1993; Mehta, 1993). This means that cases of abuse in these groups are less likely to come to any professionals' attention than they might for members of the white population. The difficulties older people, especially women who may not speak English, can have in seeking help in abusive situations are demonstrated by the case of Mrs Gandhi (Ford and Sinclair, 1987: 37–44) who eventually managed to separate from a violent husband through finding 'the community relations office and someone who spoke Hindi' (ibid.: 41). While such a situation can arise for any (Asian) woman caught in a context of domestic violence (Southall Black Sisters, 1994), it is particularly difficult for an older woman like Mrs Gandhi who has a history of being abused, silenced and marginalized in her family, little or no access to financial resources, with increasing age simply adding a further burden.

In considering possibilities of elder abuse in relation to people from ethnic minorities, age and gender structures need, *inter alia*, to be correlated with 'housing and family characteristics' (Owen, 1993c) because, as suggested above, diverse set-ups will foster different kinds of potentially abusive situations (Biggs et al., 1995: 60–76). Thus among black Caribbeans, the ethnic minority group with the highest number of older people in the UK, there are also 'high proportions of single-adult households, one-parent families and households with adult members of the same gender and dependent children' (Owen, 1993c: 13). This has implications for who the abuser(s) within a family may be. While elder abuse by spouses or partners may be less common among black Caribbeans, abuse by children may be as common as in other populations. Among Bangladeshis and Pakistanis who not only have the largest households (Owen, 1993c), the highest number of dependency ratios (children dependent on working adults) (Owen, 1993b) and 'relatively high levels of overcrowding in their accommodation' as well as 'relatively high levels of lack of housing amenities' (Owen, 1993c: 13), abuse by children may eventually be a more pronounced problem than in populations where the ratio of children per household is lower and where housing conditions are generally better.

The matter of older people from diverse ethnic backgrounds needs urgent attention. In 1988 Glendenning and Pearson pointed out that the variations between white older people with regard to sex and social class were just as real among black elders, and that if this was not taken into consideration they risked being stereotyped in unproductive ways. Prior to that, in 1985, Alison Norman conducted a study into the provision of services to older people from ethnic minority backgrounds. She called this study *Triple Jeopardy: Growing Old in a Second Homeland* because it referred to people who were at risk not only because of their age and because of the physical conditions and racist context in which they had to live, but also because of the inaccessibility of any services for them (see also Biggs et al., 1995, 72).

In Britain, as in the USA, there is still a lack of data on mortality and morbidity information relating to ethnic minority groups. There is some evidence that black people are more likely to have disabling conditions earlier in old age than white people. Poor housing and 'a lifetime of work in dangerous or unhealthy conditions can create chronic illness and disability' (Cameron et al., 1989: 231). The isolation of older Asian women who may not have learnt English and have little access to, or control over, financial resources, is highlighted in this same study from Birmingham.

Conclusions

The demographic information looked at in this chapter points to an ageing population, particularly in relation to the very old. Of these a high percentage are women, many of whom live on their own. In the 1990s British government policies have increasingly tended to be weighted towards older people being cared for in the community, with a reducing population being looked after in residential and nursing home care. The bulk of informal caring has fallen and will continue to fall on the middle-aged, with a higher percentage of carers from this group being women, many of whom will only just have relinquished caring for children and increasing numbers of whom will be in employment (Hancock et al., 1995). Some of these caring women will themselves be coming into the young-elderly age group. As such they may fall into the group of carers who are older people caring for their spouses. A study, *The Hidden Carers* (Hancock et al., 1995: 4), commissioned by the Princess Royal Trust for Carers, found that 'Few men under the age of 45 years provide personal or physical care for an adult with whom they live. Between the ages of 45 and 59 the proportion rises to about 3% and in the age group 60 to 64 to just under 4%. . . . Women are most likely to be co-resident carers between the ages of 45 and 74'. It is against this complex and shifting picture of changes in the population that elder abuse and its gendered dimensions have to be considered. In consequence there is a need to

- acknowledge that elder abuse predominantly affects women, especially among the very elderly;
- understand the impact of poverty and chronic illness among older women on the likelihood of their being abused;
- consider the impact of differential living arrangements, including the rising number of older women living alone, as part of patterns and kinds of abuse;
- revisit the changing pattern of caring relationships to understand shifts in elder abuse and neglect;
- investigate elder abuse in ethnic minority communities.

2

Gender Issues in the History of the Research on Elder Abuse

The old people were not taken care of. This is another thing which people like to think now, that grandfathers and grandmothers had an honoured place in the cottage. In fact, when they got old they were just neglected, pushed away into corners. I even found them in cupboards! Even in fairly clean and respectable houses you often found an old man or woman shoved out of sight in a dark niche. (Blythe, 1969: 231)

Worker Guilty. A Devon Social Worker has been convicted of duping an elderly care home resident out of £10,000. William O'Sullivan persuaded her to loan him the money and then laundered it through the account of another client. O'Sullivan, who will be sentenced later, was described as an exemplary social worker but was dismissed in 1991 over the fraud. (*Community Care*, 22 July 1993: 2)

The Background

It seems likely that elder abuse has always existed in most cultures. There are as many stories of older members of a society being pushed over a cliff or abandoned in some way when they become an economic burden as there are stories of revered old age. *King Lear* is one of the better known versions of the former variety. Fitzherbert (1992) relates a traditional Indian tale of an old man who has outlived his usefulness and is taking up room in the family home being taken to a cliff top by his son. ' "One day you too will be pushed off a cliff by your son", said the old man and down he fell.'

The relationship between cultural representation and social reality is of course not a straightforward one. However, the former can illuminate the latter by highlighting, for example, how and why we pay differential attention to diverse social phenomena. It is for this reason that we occasionally discuss cultural representations in relation to elder abuse in this volume.

What is interesting about both stories cited above (*King Lear* and the Indian tale) is that they present narratives of elder abuse which share certain characteristics:

● the abuser–abused relationship is very specifically gendered, involving two older males;

- it is inter-generational;
- it occurs within a family of – one assumes – blood relations;
- it involves the issue of succession;
- it involves physical violence.

While the characteristics of these still popular narratives play a role in *some* cases of elder abuse, they reflect cultural perceptions of the significance of patrilineal inheritance and succession rather than current social reality in which much more varied and complex patterns of elder abuse exist, with abused women constituting the majority of victims (see Social Services Inspectorate, 1992: i).

The two narratives do, however, point to key issues which need to be addressed when one tries to define elder abuse (see also McCreadie, 1991: 8). These are:

- the relative age of the abused and the abuser;
- the context as well as the setting in which abuse occurs (domestic, institutional, both);
- the relationship between the abused and the abuser;
- when an action or a failure to act can be termed abuse;
- the specificity of the abuse (physical, psychological, material, etc.);
- particular traits of the abused and the abuser (mental, physical, emotional);
- the issue of intentionality.

In this chapter we shall consider the history of research on elder abuse, highlighting how this research and the ways in which it has been conducted have both concealed the gender issues inherent in elder abuse *and* reproduced gender stereotypes prevalent in Western culture.

The history of how elder abuse has been tackled in the United States and in Britain during the last twenty years or so indicates the shifts in emphasis that have occurred in the research on and interventions regarding elder abuse during that time. However, the overwhelming conclusion still remains that 'Despite the growing attention in the British literature . . . and a welcome increase in the ability of professionals to admit to the existence of the problem, there has been little research on elder abuse in the UK' (Wilson, 1994: 681). This absence mirrors the relative silence which has existed concerning gender issues in elder abuse. As we shall indicate, many of the early studies on the subject revealed either a complete failure to deal with gender issues in elder abuse or a gendered agenda which, however, was not engaged with at a critical and self-reflective level by the researchers. The latter is particularly the case with the earliest reports of elder abuse which appeared in the British press.

From 'Granny Battering' to 'Elder Abuse'

Many writers on elder abuse (e.g. Decalmer and Glendenning, 1993; Ogg and Munn-Giddings, 1993) point out that baby battering was discovered in the 1960s, wife battering in the 1970s, and granny battering/bashing in the 1980s. The terminology around these phenomena has changed over time and bears some closer analysis. In the last few years it has shifted, become less sensational, e.g. 'battering' with its very specific connotations of physical violence has been replaced by 'abuse'. The latter term is an acknowledgement of the fact that abuse can be other than physical abuse. In the 1990s we talk of child abuse, domestic violence and elder abuse. What has been lost most obviously is the genderization of the terms. 'Granny' and 'wife' clearly index the gendered agenda referred to above. The degenderization of the terminology used to describe diverse abuse scenarios masks the fact that the vast majority of child abuse is still perpetrated by men on female children, and that, as the previous chapter indicates, the majority of the very old who are abused are women. It also disguises the fact that women abuse. At the same time these degenderized terms at least acknowledge that there may be male victims of abuse of various kinds (Dobash and Dobash, 1992: 258–84). Elderly men constitute one of the more vulnerable groups in our society whose vulnerability is, however, on the whole, unac-knowledged. This lack of acknowledgement is a function of power frequently being treated as unitary rather than as relative, with men in general being seen as more powerful than women. But while men may be more powerful than women in heteropatriarchal society, diverse groups of men will nonetheless have different degrees of power relative to other groups, both female and male. This needs to be recognized.

The recognition of elder abuse is a relatively recent occurrence (but see Thomas, 1977; Stearns, 1986) and as such it is still understood only to a limited extent. Significantly, Lynda Aitken found that most of the social workers she interviewed on the question of the significance of gender issues in elder abuse started with the stereotype of a male physical abuser. In other words, their most immediate view of the gender issues involved in elder abuse was that you would encounter a man abusing, not however, as the narratives cited at the beginning suggest, another man but a woman. This may not be entirely accurate, but it reflects very clearly one set of gendered perceptions that exists in Western culture concerning abuse:

men perpetrate (predominantly physical) abuse against women. While this is undoubtedly the case in many, if not most situations involving physical violence, it also masks the fact that women can be violent towards each other and towards men.

The gendered perceptions which inform stereotypical views of elder abuse were first reinforced (though little was done about it at the time) in articles on 'granny bashing' which appeared in Britain in the mid-1970s. Thus in August 1975 a much cited article entitled 'Granny Battering' was published in *Modern Geriatrics*. Written by a psychiatrist, this article discusses some cases of physical abuse of older people. The five cases presented are all, in fact, of frail, confused older women. The article repeatedly states that 'considerable damage can be done by third parties, such as doctors, to elderly patients' (Baker, 1975: 22) and it offers as examples of such damage inappropriate admission to hospitals and to residential care, and over-medication.

At about the same time that this article appeared G.R. Burston wrote a letter to the *British Medical Journal*, which was published under the heading 'Granny Battering'. Again fellow doctors were criticized, with the assertion that granny battering 'is just another manifestation of the inadequate care we as a profession give to elderly people' (Burston, 1975: 592). These two texts were both by doctors writing in professional medical journals predominantly for other doctors. Burston widened this circle somewhat by suggesting that community nurses, health visitors and social workers should have elder abuse drawn to their attention. On 7 August 1975 the *Observer* carried the headline 'Doctor Warns of Granny Bashing' but, apart from a few concerned individual health and social workers, the matter was not pursued in Britain for several more years.

Research and Action on Elder Abuse in the USA

The situation was very different in the USA, which led the field in research and action on elder abuse in the 1970s and 1980s. It may be that this was because money was made more readily available for medical and sociological research. Here the predominance of family violence theorists in the field of elder abuse served to construct elder abuse as a 'family' problem (Whittaker, 1995), thus keeping it within the domain of the family and privatized as opposed to encouraging debates about structural inequalities which might move elder abuse as an issue into the public domain. To put it crudely, it is cheaper to fund research on supposedly dysfunctional families and discover that they have a problem than it is to review pension schemes and care structures to provide adequately for older people, and specifically for older women.

The older lobby in America where groups like the Grey Panthers are more established than they are in the UK, also kept issues relating to older people on the political agenda. In 1978 testimony of 'the battering of parents' came before the Senate house sub-committee investigating family violence (Ogg and Bennett, 1992b). Unlike the early British texts on the subject cited above which set elder abuse in an institutional and medicalized context, the very phrase 'the battering of parents' brought elder abuse into the domestic arena of the family. This has remained the area most closely studied, partly because of the rise of interest among researchers and welfare agencies in intra-familial violence, an interest underwritten by funds and liberal agendas which divert attention from the structural inequalities that enable and sustain the conditions of elder abuse.

One of the first American pieces of research in the field was by Block and Sinnott (1979), who conducted an exploratory study of the battered elder syndrome. Although frequently cited, Block and Sinnott's research had a very poor response rate, of 17 per cent overall on a questionnaire they sent out. Only one agency out of twenty-four they contacted responded, and there was a similarly poor response rate from randomly selected professionals and elders in Maryland (Pedrick-Cornell and Gelles, 1982: 457). As a result any claims made on the basis of this research must be treated with caution. However, the figure they calculated for the prevalence of elder abuse, 4 per cent of the total older population, has been regularly used in Britain and in the USA.

One of the findings from their survey was that older people with mental or physical impairments are at greater risk from abuse than the unimpaired. A similar finding in child abuse studies (Friedrich and Boriskin, 1976, cited in Pedrick-Cornell and Gelles, 1982: 461) and, more recently, in relation to adults with learning difficulties (Craft, 1994), resulted in an image of the abused person as dependent, highly vulnerable and, typically, female (Brown, 1992: 15–17). It is of course very easy to blame the abused person's impairment as having promoted the abuse; victim blaming is a familiar strategy in desperate situations.

Categories of Abuse

Research of the 1970s and 1980s struggled with definitions of elder abuse which revolved around intention and acts of omission (neglect) versus acts of commission (abuse) (McCreadie, 1991: 11). The diversity of definitions discussed by McCreadie (1991: 5–15) offers a clear reflection of that struggle. The kinds of abuse described by McCreadie (ibid.: 11–13) include physical abuse, psychological abuse, financial abuse, sexual abuse, neglect, sociological abuse (referring to the social isolation or abandonment of older people) but also misuse of medication and the deprivation of food, heat, clothing and comfort. The difficulties concerning all these categories are that more than one type of abuse may be committed and, perhaps more pertinently here, that the kinds of abuse which occur do not necessarily fall neatly into just one or indeed any one category. Thus a grandson masturbating in front of his chair-bound grandmother may be regarded as committing sexual abuse and/or psychological abuse and/or emotional abuse. As a result of the difficulties associated with defining elder abuse, different researchers and agencies have used diverse categories, with all the attendant problems this causes in comparing research findings.

Block and Sinnott (1979), for instance, included physical, psychological, material and medical abuse in their study. The last two were increasingly neglected in subsequent research though they appeared in a small study done by Elizabeth Lau and Jordan Kosberg in 1979. In 'Abuse of the Elderly by Informal Care Providers' Lau and Kosberg looked at a sample of thirty-nine older people reported to the Cleveland Chronic Illness Centre which, Pedrick-Cornell and Gelles (1982: 460) maintain, is not representative of other agencies in Cleveland, Ohio or anywhere else. Lau and Kosberg's study highlights the difficulties of defining elder abuse; they included 'withholding physical care' in their definition of physical abuse whereas later researchers included this under emotional or psychological abuse or under neglect. They also included 'violation of human rights' as part of their definition of elder abuse and gave as an example being forced or tricked into giving up one's home to live with relatives or to go into residential care.

One of the social workers interviewed by Lynda Aitken described the opposite of the abuse cited by Lau and Kosberg: namely a son not allowing his mother to go into residential care because her house would then be sold to contribute to the fees and he would lose it as his inheritance. This issue has gained more prominence in Britain in 1994 since it is now the rule that older people needing care will not be eligible for financial support unless their overall assets – and that includes their house and their car – are worth less than £8,000. In Great Britain in the 1990s the reaction of the son detailed above is thus one possible pattern of abuse.

'Violation of human rights' has recurred as part of the definition of elder abuse in a number of diverse and more recent contexts (Lee, 1992). The *Guidelines* of the Royal College of Nursing, for example, refer to 'the ongoing inability of an informal carer to respond adequately to meet the needs of a dependent older person. This results in the violation or loss of that person's human rights' (1991: 1). In Sweden some professionals regard what might be described as a violation of human rights as a form of elder abuse. Saveman et al. (1993: 1396) report that district nurses regarded the 'overriding [of] the boundaries of a person's integrity/autonomy' as a central theme in 'what is meant by abuse of elderly people'. This study, like most of the others we looked at, says nothing about gender issues in elder abuse.

In *Inadequate Care of the Elderly* (1987) Fulmer and O'Malley suggest that describing abuse and neglect as inadequate care might get over the reluctance of the older person, their caregiver and professionals to call the problem 'abuse' or 'neglect'. However, the phrase 'inadequate care' is likely to cause many problems because of the difficulty of identifying what is and what is not inadequate care. Is the lack of provision of social activities for someone who is housebound, for instance, 'inadequate care'? Also, whereas the term 'elder abuse' leaves the specificity of the relationship between the abuser and the abused out of the definition and open to separate identification, 'inadequate care' presupposes that *the carer* is the abuser, thus naming the abuser for us, while at the same time widening the abusive act to cover subjectively just about anything which is short of perfect care. This is what Callahan (1988: 454) calls 'a code of human conduct exceeded only by the Sermon on the Mount'. But there is a big difference between an idea of 'perfect care', which is of course impossible to achieve, and deliberate abuse. The advantage of an approach which focuses on 'inadequate care' is that it might encourage professionals to identify the problem (Pillemer, 1994: 6). In Lynda Aitken's experience as a hospital-based social worker in Britain, doctors are often reluctant to invoke a reporting procedure on abuse because they do not want to make categorical statements to the police or Social Services by having to decide if bruises are accidental or non-accidental. This is in part because professionals often have a strong sense of sympathy and admiration for carers who are coping with someone who otherwise might fill an expensive long-stay bed.

Lau and Kosberg (1979) identified the typical abuser as a middle-aged daughter and the typical abused person as a very old woman, a view of the abuser challenged in later research (Pillemer and Finkelhor, 1989). Ogg and Bennett (1991b: 19) suggest that 'A more accurate description of the carer who may abuse in a family setting is that of a male (son or husband) who has a history of mental illness or psychological disturbance, and who abuses alcohol or other drugs.'

Here the debate about who abuses whom assumes a gendered dimension in which differential explanations – 'middle-aged and stressed' for the female abuser; 'illness or disorder and substance abuse' for the male abuser – are invoked. Such genderization is not, however, picked up and discussed by the researchers. Lau and Kosberg's study included a definition of self-abuse (commonly cited as one form of elder abuse in the USA; Ogg, 1993: 19), pointing to excessive use of alcohol or drugs, improper diet and refusal to accept medical care as typical examples. In contrast many other studies (see McCreadie, 1991: 9-10) consider self-neglect to be a different problem from abuse inflicted by others because it does not involve another person, and, in the UK, does not require new legislation to help the person neglecting her- or himself.

Two further studies followed Lau and Kosberg's in quick succession: O'Malley et al.'s in 1979 and Douglass et al.'s in 1980. Both studies were based on interviews with health and social care professionals, thus moving away from looking at the abused person and/ or the abuser. The professionals in both studies were asked about how they report, refer and treat abuse. O'Malley et al. found that professionals are not particularly well suited to spotting elder abuse: in 70 per cent of their reported cases third parties rather than the professionals had in the first instance identified the abuse and then notified relevant agencies. The cases of abuse that come to public attention, which may be only a small percentage of actual cases, may well represent a biased portion of the entire population of abused older people because they will be the ones that are labelled as abuse by professionals (see also Pillemer, 1994: 6). There is a need to separate out the reason for the labelling from the reasons for the abuse.

Both studies referred to above were very traditional, impersonal forms of medical and social research, concentrating on process issues and inflected by the professionals' own views of the subject. The researchers and workers in these contexts tend to come from a middle-class, higher educational background. In Britain they are also likely to be white and, particularly in terms of medical research, often male. This can, and frequently does, mean that not enough attention is paid to gender issues, cross-cultural differences, and economic/ class issues in research on elder abuse.

The limitations of the four American studies cited above (Block and Sinnott, 1979; O'Malley et al., 1979; Lau and Kosberg, 1979; Douglass et al., 1980) from the late 1970s and 1980 are ones of size of sample, their selective rather than non-random sampling techniques and their lack of a control group, which means that the researchers were unable to say if the factors present in cases of abuse were distinctive of abuse situations relative to the general population of older people.

Nevertheless, this research, whatever its limitations, promoted activity in the USA both at federal and at state level. The National Aging Resource Center on Elder Abuse was set up and funded by the Federal Government to co-ordinate research, information and policy development. A voluntary charity, the National Committee for the Prevention of Elder Abuse, was given the job of advocacy, research, public awareness raising and training. Mandatory reporting of all suspected cases to the state-funded Adult Protective Services began (Ogg, 1993: 20). By 1992, 'only three states [had] yet to enact mandatory reporting laws' (ibid.), and we understand that even those now have such laws in place. There is considerable doubt regarding the effectiveness of this in preventing abuse (ibid.: 21), and criticism that it infringes on the older person's right to choose whether or not they wish any action to be taken. The relevant legislation in the USA contrasts significantly with that in Great Britain in that the USA has opted for mandatory reporting and protective services as a means of intervening in abusive situations. However, as Malcolm Holt recently observed: 'A common concern about the US response to elder abuse has been that investigations by adult protective services may resemble police inquiries, hence the reluctance in the UK to follow the same route' (1995: 22–3). Holt counters this by suggesting that in the USA 'Case resolution is client-focused, individualized, and based on a social work model of problem solving. . . . The client participates in defining the problem and deciding the most appropriate plan of action' (ibid.: 23). But such an approach is clearly not possible for all clients and many of the issues raised by McCreadie (1991: 48–9) in relation to adult pro-tective services remain valid.

Researchers in America continued to struggle with methodological difficulties in working on elder abuse. These varied from considering only physical abuse to the setting up of three model projects at different geographical locations to provide a service, to intervene in abusive situations, to co-ordinate services and to raise public aware-ness (Wolf and Pillemer, 1989: 102). At the level of research, the Model Projects Study claimed to have overcome earlier criticism by using a control group, but although all members of the abused group had carers, fewer than half of the non-abused control group's members had. It was not a situation of comparing carers who abuse in a domestic situation with carers who do not. Wolf and Pillemer found that 71.2 per cent of the abusive carers were male, mostly husbands and sons, and although this high proportion has not been found in subsequent studies, it did begin to shift the focus from the abused person's dependency to considerations of abuse by an older spouse. Godkin et al. (1989) did not find that the abused elders in their study were more physically impaired than the members of the control group, but that the lives of the abused and the abuser had become interdependent. They concluded: 'Given the emotional and interpersonal problems of both parties, it is perhaps likely that a shared living arrangement becomes a "pressure cooker" situation that leads to abuse' (Godkin et al., 1989: 223). There was no comment on the significance of gender difference in this research.

The late 1980s and early 1990s saw a rise in studies looking at personality and behaviour traits of abusers as significant indicators of the possibility of abuse (e.g. Homer and Gilleard, 1990). Factors that were regarded as playing a role included the emotional and mental health of the abuser, and the presence of alcohol-related problems. These studies continued to explore elder abuse within a domestic and familial setting, individualizing it and ignoring other explanatory frameworks such as the promotion and exercise of power imbalances within heteropatriarchal society.

Pillemer and Finkelhor returned to the theme of the dependence of older people as a risk factor, as opposed to the sociopathic or psychopathic carer who abuses, in 'Causes of Elder Abuse: Caregiver Stress versus Problem Relatives' (1989). In this study they used a large-scale random sample survey, with a control group, in Boston. They found that 3.2 per cent of older people reported being victims of physical violence, verbal aggression or neglect. Males were the victims of abuse in 52 per cent of cases, women in 48 per cent, and 58 per cent of all abuse was inflicted by spouses. The researchers commented: 'The picture of maltreatment that emerged from the present study is . . . of relatively well-functioning elderly who have responsibility for, or at least are required to interact with, ill and socio-emotionally unstable relatives' (1989: 186).

Two of the situations that were described to Lynda Aitken by the social workers she interviewed fitted into this picture. In one instance an older woman was physically abused by her husband, who was fifteen years younger than her. Dependent on his wife financially and for accommodation, he was having an affair with her daughter from a first marriage. The other instance concerned a couple in their eighties who had only been married for a few years. He had been a loner who had not previously married; for her it was the second marriage. He abused his wife sexually and was then compulsorily sectioned to a psychiatric hospital. Pillemer and Finkelhor's (1989) research suggested that abuser characteristics are more powerful indicators of abuse than victim characteristics. While their research records incidents of violence, it does not, as James Nazroo (1995) puts it, explore the meaning of these violent acts. Nazroo's study on intra-marital violence suggests that 'although women may hit their partners more often than men do, if context and meaning is included in the assessment of violence, male violence is considerably more likely than female violence to be dangerous and threatening' (1995: 475). To what extent Nazroo's findings apply to older couples remains a matter of speculation. However, his point about the need for a more detailed analysis of the kinds and effects of violence perpetrated by women and men within the context of elder abuse is a valid one.

While it is important to remember the differences between the USA and Great Britain when applying American research findings to the British situation, there are significant similarities. Thus the underlying philosophy to maintain individuals in their own homes is the same. This led Kosberg to state that 'Less empirical work has been done on the abuse or maltreatment of the elderly by their families. It is the family that has been viewed as the "last line of defense" in the care of the elderly. The existence of children can keep the elderly out of institutional settings' (1983b: 263). Kosberg's use of gender-neutral plurals ('the elderly', 'children') obscures the fact that maintaining older people, in the over-seventy-four-year-old range predominantly women, in their homes results in 'the family', usually women, being the principal caregivers in a context where the structure of the family in both the USA and the UK has changed significantly, with more single parents, more women in employment, fewer children and so on. It has been suggested in the USA that elder care should be considered to be as important as child care, and that both should be subsidized and remunerated in the same way (Ogg and Bennett, 1992b: 22). Ogg and Bennett maintain that despite all the research and mandatory reporting statutes in the USA, there is a lack of political will to produce resources for the prevention of elder abuse and for education in this field. We would suggest that this is a function of the fact that the victims, older women, are a relatively disenfranchised group in society and of an underlying recognition that to make effective changes would require resources governments prefer to spend elsewhere.

Meanwhile Back in Britain

On the whole there has been both less research and less action concerning elder abuse in Great Britain. As recently as 1991 Virginia Bottomley, the then Minister of Health, said that abuse of elders is not a significant problem in Britain (*Dispatches*, Channel 4, 21 October 1992). The 1990s have seen more research and more conferences on the topic of elder abuse than the previous decade, and the journal *Community Care* completed an awareness-raising campaign aimed at social workers and their departments in 1993. The only significant interest in the issue in the media seems to have been the BBC2 programme *Forty Minutes* (17 February 1983) and the *Dispatches* programme nearly ten years later. The general public, not just in Britain, seems to remain unaware of the extent, indeed the existence, of elder abuse.

In 1980 Mervyn Eastman, a social worker in London with many years of experience of working with elders, decided that he could not be the only one encountering abusive situations in the context of his work. He started writing to social work and medical publications, and by 1983 he had received 500 letters from relatives of older people, telling of their personal experiences and knowledge of abuse. Through *Community Care* (26 January and 2 February 1984) he conducted a survey of social workers' attitudes to 'granny battering', and in the same year Age Concern published his book, *Old Age Abuse* (1984). This became a landmark text in the Social Services profession; it has been consistently referred to in subsequent writings on elder abuse by all professionals. The book contains much case material and although it has been criticized for being poorly conceptualized, Eastman did not claim to be a professional researcher and regarded his work as an introduction to the subject.

Eastman's research helped to set the care-centred agenda which has been prominent in debates about elder abuse. Working from experience, and pre-dating explanatory theoretical frameworks on elder abuse which might direct attention to issues of power, gender and resourcing, Eastman produced information which equated elder abuse with care. For professionals in social and health services, including one of the current authors, the issue of elder abuse within the context of care is still of primary importance, as it is within that context that elder abuse will come to these professionals' notice. But the equation of elder abuse with care itself has become increasingly problematized and needs revision.

One of the curious aspects of Eastman's 1984 study is that gender is not considered an issue. His focus, as was the case in the USA, is very much on the family and abuse within the family, and he cites extensive evidence which clearly indicates various forms of gender bias, for example that 'the majority [of battered elders] are female' (1984: 41). His own survey of social workers also shows that 53 per cent of abusers were women while 46 per cent were men (1984: 43). He compares this to 'American studies that have given percentage figures of 58 per cent for women [who abuse] and 44 per cent for men' (ibid.). In Eastman's view the overall picture suggests that 'daughters and daughters-in-law [are] by far the most likely to abuse' (ibid.). His discussion of the implications of these findings does not go beyond stating that 'These figures will not surprise us given that the care of the elderly falls in the main on the shoulders of a female relative' (ibid.: 44). Eastman works from a mechanistic model which suggests that in situations of care abuse will occur. Women care, therefore they abuse. There is no recognition that only *some* of the women who care abuse. Nor does Eastman consider the issue of *women* as abusers running counter to the stereotypes of femininity prevalent in Western culture, or the reinforcement of certain gender stereotypes implicit in the fact that women are expected to act as carers almost as a matter of course. Instead, he manifests surprise at the number of male abusers found in the studies he examines, asking: 'Does this suggest that the role of the carer is more stressful for the male than the female?' (ibid.). One might argue that this is a male social worker's explanation of the figures as it suggests that women are expected to carry out a caring role without being as affected by it as men are. In part this simply reproduces the stereotype of woman as carer. It also suggests that women might be expected to care without this resulting in abuse whereas for a man neither caring nor being non-abusive is part of their expected role. Yet Eastman also emphasizes the fact that the majority of abusers in his study were daughters and that this finding matches those of Elizabeth Hocking's unpublished study (Eastman, 1984: 121). While Eastman reports all these findings faithfully, he does not draw any gender-focused conclusions from his or others' work.

In 1994, ten years on from his first study, Eastman published the second edition of his book, now entitled *Old Age Abuse: A New Perspective* (Eastman, 1994a). This is an edited rather than an authored volume as the previous one was, bringing together many of the current British researchers eminent in the field of old age abuse. In his introduction, Eastman identifies two issues that have grown in importance for him since the publication of his first book in 1984. These are first, the question of whether ' "dependency" [is] a factor in abuse or simply a function of the sampling done by researchers?', and secondly, 'the matter of violence in the residential setting' (Eastman, 1994a: xv).

Eastman's concern with dependency has to be seen in the context of the changing politics of the 1980s and 1990s in Britain where the demise of the welfare state has signalled an accelerated stigmatization of the idea of dependency. If you are dependent you are not self-sustaining, and therefore a burden on the state or on other individuals. Dependency as an idea and a reality has increasingly become a problem in a society which favours self-sufficiency and relationships based on economistic models of exchange, value for money and mutual satisfaction of needs (Kappeler, 1995).

Eastman does not discuss what he means by dependency but for him it is 'a key factor' in abusive situations and he rightly identifies the interrelationship of dependency and power with its associated imbalance between abuser and abused as central to elder abuse. He does not, however, move beyond that recognition, stating only that the area of 'use and abuse of power in relationships . . . needs further work and will, perhaps, take several years' (1994a: xv). This is undoubtedly the case but we would argue that both at a theoretical and at a 'practical' level more is known about the issue of power than Eastman suggests and, most specifically, more is known about the specificities of certain power relationships than he makes out. Power does not randomly accrue to people or institutions; it is embedded in the structures of every society and affects particular people in particular ways. In our society men have more power than women, able-bodied people more power than disabled ones, middle-aged people more power than older ones. However, power, as feminism in its debates about differences between women (Milan Women's Bookstore Collective, 1990; hooks, 1984) has amply demonstrated, is relative. This relativity is person and situation specific. Being an older woman makes you less powerful than being an older man, but an older financially well off woman may have more power than an older impoverished male. Such a woman may not be able to defend herself physically against violence as well as an older man but she will have more power through her financial clout to decide how she is taken care of than a poor older man. Failing, in the instance of elder abuse, to interrogate power in differentiated ways means that the structural inequalities which allow the maintenance and propagation of power to the systematic advantage of some and the disadvantage of others are not addressed or named. It means that gender issues, complexly linked to issues of power, will not be surfaced. And, indeed, Eastman makes little of gender issues in his 1994 volume.

Only one chapter in Eastman's volume mentions 'gender' in its title. This chapter considers 'Dependence, Power and Violation: Gender Issues in Abuse of Elderly People by Formal Carers' and it links gender issues to the two concerns Eastman raised in his introduction: the relationship between dependency and abuse, and abuse in institutional settings. Eastman's 1984 edition was a product both of the kind of research he conducted and how he accessed the relevant information, and of the socio-political climate in which it was written which, since the end of World War II, has increasingly and paradoxically focused on the family and domestic settings as the site both of dysfunctionality and disturbance *and* of their resolution. This position has been reinforced through the emergence of 'care in the community' and Western governments' increasing need to review welfare provisions. The political climate of the 1990s is in this respect very much determined by the tensions arising out of the review of the role and structure of 'the family' (understood here as the nuclear heterosexual one with two parents, one of each of two sexes, and one or two children) in the light of the fiscally driven needs of the state to rely on private individuals to pay for or do jobs previously catered for by the public purse. As Ogg (1993: 19) puts it: 'there is a move in practically all industrialized countries towards community care, or what David Challis (1992) calls "downward substitution", i.e., the replacement of more intensive institutional environments by less intensive ones. This trend is in part ideological (stimulation of market forces) and in part financially driven (an escalation of health costs).'

These changes have been 'sold' to the general public through a rhetoric of 'choice' and supposedly enhanced possibilities for the individual to select what is most appropriate for her/him. As this rhetoric of 'choice' has entered the political arena, it has also raised the question of responsibility and of the criteria by which we choose, thus creating the necessity to investigate what we choose and how. Concretely, 'care in the community' has meant an increase in the number of ways in which elders are provided for and has resulted in, for example, larger numbers of residential homes for older people being established. However, such diversification has not enhanced the possibility of choice equally for all older people. Older women and many elders from ethnic minority communities, being financially on the whole worse off than men in comparable situations (Walker, 1992; Groves, 1992), are not necessarily able to choose where they go for their care or who cares for them. The increase in the range of care establishments available, especially in the private, less regulated sector, has also meant a rise in the range of contexts in which elder abuse will occur and the need to consider them is recognized by Eastman.

Eastman's 1994 volume offers overt recognition of the diversity of carers and circumstances under which care for elders occurs and in this way it picks up on research in this area that went on between 1984 and 1994, and on the earlier research conducted in the USA which was cited above. It includes the work of Pillemer and Finkel-hor (1989) already mentioned, which suggests that the pathology of the carer offers a more likely explanation of abusive behaviour than caregiver stress. Eastman ignores the statistical evidence of his 1984 study – that there is little numerical difference between males and females who abuse – but his analysis of this material is weighted against women, as he seems determined to profile the abuser as a daughter trapped by the 'unending burden of care' (1984: 45). The reason for this becomes clear when one takes into account that much of his case material was taken from letters he received from carers after an article on the subject was printed in the magazine *Woman* and following a feature in BBC Radio 4's *Woman's Hour* (11 January 1983). Assuming that caregivers would be women, Eastman targeted women for information, thus reproducing his view of who the caregivers might be. In making a point about the low self-esteem of many caregivers, his example of carers – as a result of their caring role – stopping 'gossiping with neighbours or getting dressed to go out' (1984: 47) could refer to *any woman* trapped in the home. The difference of female and male caring roles and caring relationships clearly needs further consideration.

In 1988 the British Geriatrics Society organized a multi-disciplinary conference in London on old age abuse. This event received very low-key publicity. A report was prepared, the title of which – *Abuse of Elderly People: An Unnecessary and Preventable Problem* (Tomlin, 1989) – should have goaded everyone into action. The society, along with a number of organizations (Age Concern, the British Association of Social Workers, the British Geriatric Society, the Carers National Association, Help the Aged and the Police Federation), produced *Guidelines for Action* (British Geriatrics Society, 1990) which offer definitions of abuse, indexes of 'medical and social factors which promote abuse' and of 'the family at risk', indicators of the occurrence of abuse and action plans for health workers. In 1990 Paul Kingston investigated how far district health authorities in England had 'developed policies and procedures for identifying and intervening in suspected or confirmed cases of elder abuse' (McCreadie, 1991: 18). All authorities were approached and 68 per cent responded. Of the latter, ten replies were inadequate to use (14.7 per cent) and only two authorities (just over 2 per cent) had a policy. The rest were at various stages of working on, considering, or being aware of the issue. This compares interestingly with Bridget Penhale's (1993c) survey of Social Services/Social Work departments' situation regarding guidelines for elder abuse conducted in July 1992. Out of 135 authorities approached, 101 (75 per cent) replied. Penhale found that 10 per cent had no procedures, no working parties and no plans for setting up either in the future; only 15 per cent of authorities had fully implemented and ratified guidelines; the rest were at various stages of working on or considering guidelines. Penhale notes that 'there appears to have been a distinct change in the attitudes of departments generally in this field over the past fifteen months' (1993c: 14). She concludes that 'This survey shows a rapidly increasing awareness of the problems of elder abuse and the abuse of vulnerable adults' (ibid.: 15). This is borne out by Lynda Aitken's experience of the drawing up and implementing of guidelines and related training concerning elder abuse in the county and authority for which she works.

In 1990 Homer and Gilleard reported on a survey carried out over a six-month period of all the older people referred to two London hospitals for respite care. Their carers were interviewed separately at home. Fifty-one carers and forty-three patients were interviewed. The patients suffered from various mental and physical health problems. As well as the twenty-one with dementia, twenty-four patients had had a stroke and twenty-four further patients had more than one additional problem such as Parkinson's disease or an amputation. The categories of abuse used were those presented by Pillemer and Finkelhor (1988), namely physical, and verbal abuse, and neglect. They did not include sexual or financial abuse. Several questionnaires were used to assess carers' mental health, the closeness of their relationship with the patient, and an indication of risk factors present that had been identified as indicative of possible abuse in other research, such as disturbed nights, whether the carer had had to give up work or not, and alcohol consumption. The carers were asked directly about abuse. Patients were interviewed on admission to hospital for respite care. They were physically examined, their mental state was assessed and if they had sufficient cognitive function they were asked about abuse.

Twenty-three carers (45 per cent) in this study admitted to one form of abuse, seven to two, and two to all three forms of abuse. Fifteen carers were male and forty-one female, with a mean age of sixty-six years. Most were spouses or children. All those abusing lived with the dependant. The factors most significantly associated with the abuse were alcohol consumption and abuse by the patient which often triggered physical violence by the carer. Physical abuse seemed to depend on the characteristics of the abuser rather than the abused. Verbal abuse and neglect were related to poor earlier relationships and were associated with depression and anxiety.

Homer and Gilleard did not distinguish between male and female abusers in the report beyond reporting the fact that they looked at fifteen male and forty-one female carers. When Aitken asked them about this they thought a larger study specifically addressing gender issues was needed. Aitken thinks (as did the social workers she interviewed) that physical abuse is more likely to be carried out by men, and verbal abuse and neglect by women. This, however, may simply reflect a particular kind of gender stereotype. Homer and

Gilleard found that many carers and patients had a longstanding mutually abusive relationship: 'among married couples they may be seen as the elderly graduates of domestic violence further stressed by the disabilities associated with aging' (1990: 1361). Homer and Gilleard mention that children who have been abused may in turn 'pay back' their parents or grandparents by abusing them. They found one instance of a male carer who admitted this in relation to his 'sadistic' father.

The important negative findings of this study were that physical signs of abuse and reports of abuse did not correlate. Neither did social isolation and lack of services, or abuse and a diagnosis of dementia. The presence of disruptive behaviour and the poor quality of early relationships were the most significant factors in predicting abuse (see also Biggs et al., 1995: 44–7). These findings challenged many professionals' views of the significance of dementia in abusive situations, and the solution often suggested by carers' organizations: the provision of more services. However, it is worth noting that while Homer and Gilleard found that 45 per cent of the carers they interviewed openly admitted to some form of abuse, few patients did. A similar finding is cited in the Social Services Inspectorate Report, *Confronting Elder Abuse* (1992: i). A commonly held view is that one of the reasons why elder abuse is a hidden problem is that neither the abuser nor the abused wants to admit to it for fear of shame, publicity and even legal action. Mutual dependency might mean that either abuser or abused or both could lose their home in consequence of action taken to deal with an abusive situation. Also, there is often a reluctance to admit the need for help. In the interviews Aitken conducted many of the social workers felt helpless because offers of respite care and additional help in the home were consistently refused by the carer.

The difficulties of researching elder abuse resulting from the sensitivity of the topic were highlighted by Bennett and Ogg (1993) in their report of a study which yielded zero returns regarding prevalence of elder abuse. This study was conducted by face-to-face interview. Subsequently, they, together with the Office of Population Censuses and Surveys Omnibus Team, devised a series of questions based on the work of Pillemer and Finkelhor (1988) in the USA. The Omnibus survey generated a nationally representative sample of 2,130 adults, 593 of whom were over sixty years old. Older people in residential care or the very frail (the ones most at risk of abuse) were not included. Adults over sixty were asked if they had been abused physically, verbally or financially during the previous year, and all adults were asked if they had physically or verbally abused a person above pension age. The results were that 5 per cent of elders reported verbal abuse by relatives, 2 per cent reported physical abuse and 2 per cent financial abuse. The study made passing reference to gender differences, stating, for instance, that sixty-six respondents who had been verbally abused in the year preceding the study were female. In the case of physical abuse, 'seven out of nine respondents were male' (Bennett and Ogg, 1993: 6). Bennett and Ogg drew no general inferences on gender issues in this study.

This work, and that of Homer and Gilleard, along with some case examples, was broadcast on TV in *Dispatches* on Channel 4 in October 1992. It was reported as a news item that day in the *Guardian* (21 October 1992) and two days later in the *Daily Telegraph* (Fitzherbert, 1992). That was the extent of the interest shown by the media in this phenomenon, and when the programme was repeated in 1993 in the run-up to the Community Care reforms, Tim Yeo, then a junior health minister, admitted that elder abuse was more of a problem than his boss, Virginia Bottomley, had thought. Both he and his successor, John Bowis, clearly did not want to upset the carers' lobby on whom community care depends. John Bowis said: 'The vast majority of families and other carers would never behave in this way' (*Community Care*, 17 June 1993: 2). The Social Services Inspectorate (SSI) of the Department of Health, on the other hand, thought the issue important enough to undertake a review on the way in which two London boroughs' Social Service departments responded to and managed elder abuse in domestic settings (Social Services Inspectorate [SSI], 1992). In this study managers were asked to identify staff who had worked in the context of elder abuse. They were then asked to select and talk about cases they had encountered. Sixty-four situations of abuse were considered. (This was the method also used by Aitken to select and interview social workers, relying on them to produce examples.) The SSI study differentiated between the sexes of both the abused and the abuser, indicating that '51 of the 64 abused people were females' and that 'over half the abused people (37) were aged 81 years or more' (1992: 5). As the older age group comprises mainly women, the SSI report's findings reinforce the notion of the vulnerability of very elderly women to abuse. The report also supports findings from the USA that 'abuse is likely to come from a close family member – usually an adult child – living with the abused person', with thirty-two of the abusers being men and twenty-seven women. Phillipson (1992) criticizes the SSI report for relying on professionals' ability to recall events over a five-year span and the distorting effect of memory on their reporting, the failure to provide staff with a definition of abuse, the possible consequent under-reporting of neglect as opposed to, for example, physical abuse and the restrictions of the types of abuse observed imposed by the non-randomness of the sample of staff who took part in the research. The concern is that such skewed information might form the basis of 'a guide for action' (1992: 2). Phillipson's critiques are, of course, perfectly valid. The SSI's findings indicate how the staff interviewed perceive elder abuse, which is useful because it indicates what further research is needed and what the parameters of the interviewees' perceptions are. If we assume that in the absence of other guidance staff in Social and Health Services will work from their experiences, then a knowledge of these experiences is important for understanding why elder abuse is profiled and treated as it is.

The samples in the SSI study are not large but it is noticeable that in the age ranges forty-one to sixty women outnumber men as abusers and there is a large number of female abusers compared to male abusers (nine to two) between the ages of forty-one and fifty. We shall return to this issue when we consider care in the family in Chapter 5. The survey concludes that abuse between spouses might be preceded by a history of marital violence (this was, indeed, so in six of the seventeen cases) but that in many cases the abuse did not start until old age had set in. This means that for some old women the experience of abuse will be new in old age and might explain some of the difficulties those women have in knowing how to deal with this experience. The survey states: 'It is also possible that in later life, due to sickness or disability, marital roles shift. This may lead to abuse where there was none previously or to a change in the direction of the abuse where, for example, after years of bullying behaviour, the "fallen tyrant" becomes the target of abuse' (SSI, 1992: 6). This of course replicates one of Homer and Gilleard's (1990) findings. As one of the boroughs studied had a large ethnic population (35 per cent of all residents living in households headed by people of new Commonwealth or Pakistani origin), and fifty-seven of the sixty-four cases were described as white English, four Irish, two Austrian/ Jewish and one Afro-Caribbean, the report concludes that 'it seems likely that the needs of ethnic elders in relation to elder abuse have not been recognized' (SSI, 1992: 5).

Elder Abuse in Ethnic Minority Communities

Attempts both in the USA and in Britain to investigate abuse in relation to elders from ethnic minorities have been limited, with little or no attention paid to gender issues in this context. Some researchers in the USA have suggested that there is no difference in patterns of abuse across different ethnic groups. In Britain the issue has either been ignored or the lack of numbers of elders from ethnic minority groups has been used as an excuse for not conducting the relevant research. The poor provision of adequate culturally sensitive services for black elders and their carers could be considered as inadequate care in Fulmer and O'Malley's terminology and therefore as a form of abuse in its own right. This is exacerbated by the fact that the group hardest hit by poor provision is that of older Asian women (Blakemore and Boneham, 1994; Mehta, 1993; Cameron et al., 1989), who may have little command of English and/or be illiterate both in English and in their first language. Significantly, there has been a history of maintaining that black and Asian elders (Donaldson, 1986) do not need services in the same ways as non-black and non-Asian older people do, due to the former's extended household arrangements. However, invoking cross-cultural differences has sometimes served as a means of masking inadequate information provision on services available. In 'Black Old Women, Disability and Health Carers' (1989: 235) Cameron et al. make the point that 'research which focuses on black people is in danger of reinforcing implicit or explicit racism or of being patronising' but fear of racism is an insufficient explanation for the virtual absence of research on elder abuse. The majority of Asian elders in Britain live with their families (see Chapter 5) but that should not lead us to assume as a matter of course that their needs are being adequately met. The elders most at risk of abuse in domestic settings, as Homer and Gilleard's study makes clear, are those living with their families.

One problem with research that focuses on black and Asian elders is that it tends to privilege ethnic origin as the most significant aspect in determining people's experiences. Moon and Williams's (1993) study of 'Perceptions of Elder Abuse and Help-seeking Patterns among African-American, Caucasian American, and Korean American Elderly Women' is a case in point. This very interesting project which asked the three groups of women who took part in the study to identify whether or not they regarded certain scenarios as abusive and whom they would seek help from should any of these situations arise, interpreted the Korean American women's significantly lower readiness to read a situation as abusive as a function of culture-specific norms, suggesting that 'their desire to maintain peace in the family at the expense of their suffering must be understood and respected in the context of their culture' (1993: 393). This interpretation ignored the fact that the Korean American women were also 'the least educated' with on average 'the lowest income', whereas the Caucasian American group, who were the most likely to identify certain situations as abusive and to seek help, were the most educated with the highest income. In other words, class as defined by income and education was edited out of the researchers' considerations though both play a significant role in determining people's knowledge of what help is available to them and in their sense of the appropriateness of seeking it.

Much research and writings on elder abuse in the USA and Great Britain from the 1970s and 1980s offered problematic generalizations about abuse and little by way of a clear gendered analysis on the data available. This is due to the lack of adequate definition of the phenomenon for data collection, the small samples, the absence of control groups, the problem of interviewing professionals and the narrow focus of some medical researchers. The variety of definitions of abuse used in the various studies makes comparing different kinds of research very difficult. Pedrick-Cornell and Gelles argued in 1982 that 'researchers must carefully construct precise, measurable and scientifically useful definitions of elder abuse' (1982: 463). In 1996 such definitions have still not fully been realized. 'Precise, measurable and scientifically useful definitions of elder abuse' may fulfil the quantifying needs of the scientific perspective typical of androcentric research but they do not offer the qualitative insights necessary for an understanding of the abused's experiences nor do they yield the explanatory theoretical framework which should inform public policy on elder abuse. Olive Stevenson (1989: 22) maintains: 'There seems little point in wasting research time on the incidence of old age abuse', arguing that what is needed is a raised level of awareness on the part of professionals and a willingness to entertain the possibility that it exists. Her perspective is echoed by Ogg and Munn-Giddings (1993: 395–6) who write: 'Whether further prevalence studies of elder abuse are needed is debatable.'

To date, most of the research on elder abuse has been conducted by doctors and sociologists, and it has been published in academic and professional journals as part of what David Morgan calls 'academic machismo' (in Roberts, 1981: 101). With few exceptions (e.g. Whittaker, 1995), where women have been the researchers, like women doctors in medicine, they have tended to accept the rules of conduct for research prescribed by the dominant male culture within their profession. Feminist research seems, on the whole and until very recently, to have passed older women by, other than in oral history terms, i.e. as first person accounts of the ageing process. Chapter 4 illustrates that feminists have tended to concentrate on women as carers while ignoring the disabled or older woman. As Lois Keith accurately points out: 'with only a few exceptions the "voice" of those researchers, the explanation and description of real lives, the development of concepts like oppression and dependency, has over-whelmingly focused on the disabled carer' (1992: 170). Clare Ungerson explains why the issue of caring is of personal significance to her: an only daughter, she thinks that 'my future contains the distinct possibility that I will sooner or later become a carer myself' (1987: 2). Ungerson fails to identify with the interests and experiences of older women, recognizing only *one* next step – that she might become a carer – while ignoring the more obvious other one – that she is possibly even more likely to become an older woman herself, maybe even someone who in her turn will need care. There is still a need within feminism for women to move beyond the specificity of their immediate situation to considering other possibilities and developments or changes in their lives which include the prospect and reality of ageing.

Gender Issues in the Context of Setting up Guidelines for Elder Abuse

The continuing gendered problems which inhere in research on elder abuse are demonstrated in the research that Aitken conducted, the results of which we shall discuss in Chapter 5. This work, and we shall just focus on the process here, began in July 1992 when Aitken in her capacity as a Social Services manager was asked to be part of a working party set up in Northamptonshire, with the brief 'to develop multi-agency guidelines for professional staff to enable them to function more effectively when confronted with the abuse of vulnerable adults'. The impetus for this working party came from a Social Services Inspectorate report, *Confronting Elder Abuse* (1992), which was followed by a recommendation from the Department of Health that local authorities in Britain produce guidelines relating to elder abuse for their staff. Northamptonshire's work on guidelines on adult abuse has to be seen in a context where one year on from the SSI report, in 1993, Jenkins reported that 'only 50 per cent of social services departments either had or were actively preparing policies on abuse; under 40 per cent had someone with a responsibility for implementing it; fewer than 30 per cent kept records of incidents. Four years ago (i.e. in 1989) only four health authorities had a policy on elder abuse' (Jenkins, 1993: 31).

The internal memorandum setting out the task of the Northamptonshire working party identified the following

Key Areas for Consideration

1. Definition of Abuse.
2. Methods of identifying vulnerable adults who are being abused and systematically recording this information and acting on it.
3. Development of policies and procedures for confronting adult abuse.
4. Development of a training package to equip staff to intervene effectively in identified cases. (This includes using existing legislation appropriately.)
5. Monitoring the effect of raising staff awareness in this area.

The memorandum also stated that

The guidelines should reflect the following values:

1. Privacy	The rights of individuals to be left alone or undisturbed and free from intrusion or public attention into their affairs.
2. Independence	Opportunities to act and think without reference to another person including a willingness to incur risk.
3. Choice	Opportunity to select independently from a range of options.
4. Rights	The maintenance of all entitlements associated with citizenship.
5. Fulfilment	The realization of personal aspirations and abilities in all aspects of daily life.

Our definition of abuse and our response to it will be closely related to the values we adopt and these therefore must be established very early in the process.

It is worth highlighting that in 1992, when a sizeable amount of research and knowledge on elder abuse was already available, the focus set for this working party was nonetheless 'adult' rather than 'elder' abuse (see also Penhale, 1993c), thus widening the brief considerably presumably to include those legally adult people who might be vulnerable to abuse (McCreadie, 1993: 44–6) rather than focusing on persons within a more specific age bracket. It indicates one of the many areas of problems of definition (and 'definition of abuse' was, significantly, first on this working party's agenda).

The working party was concerned with improving various professionals' ability to identify and intervene in cases of adult abuse. This was necessary because, as several studies (Saveman et al., 1993; Wilson, 1994) considering how professionals identify and intervene in cases of elder abuse have made clear, there is a considerable difference among diverse professional groups such as doctors, community nurses and social workers in their ability to identify and intervene in cases of abuse. Aitken, too, found this in her interviews with social workers, detailed in Chapter 5.

The working group of which Aitken was a part was a multi-agency one, consisting of representatives from Health Services, Social Services, the police, Northamptonshire County Council Legal Department and Age Concern. At the first meeting a decision was taken to split into two groups, one looking at elders, and one considering younger people with physical and learning disabilities. Aitken became part of the group working on elder abuse. The other group soon ceased to function (though more recently it has been reconstituted and is using the elder abuse guidelines developed by the remaining group as a framework for producing guidelines on vulnerable adults). The latter group's initial demise may in some respects have been associated with the fact that elder abuse, as opposed to abuse of vulnerable adults, has had more publicity within the health, nursing and social services professions in recent years. Additionally, it may be that elders are regarded as a single category by virtue of their age and it seems easier to establish guidelines for them than for other vulnerable adults who may be regarded as falling into more diverse categories. Finally, the focus of work on elder abuse has been very different from that of abuse of younger adults. The latter tends to concentrate on abuse within institutions, while work on elder abuse has tended to focus on intra-familial abuse. Abuse within institutions was not part of Aitken's working party's original remit.

There was also a clear gender issue involved in the lifecycle of this working party. The initial working party consisted of a mixture of female and male participants, from gendered professional bases such as nursing and social work which have a very high proportion of female staff, and from the police, which has a very high proportion of male staff. After the first two or three meetings the working party on elder abuse turned into an all-female group. The drop-outs were the male legal representative from the County Council Legal Department, the male police inspector and the male training manager from Social Services, all occupying fairly high-status positions in their organizations. This left the female community psychiatric nurse, a female health visitor, a female ward sister and two female social workers. The men ceased to attend, thus implying that issues related to older people were of little importance to them or, possibly, that they considered elder abuse an issue for/about women. This in itself raises many concerns, a major one of which must be that elder abuse is difficult to confront unless (a) it is systematically and comprehensively addressed by all concerned with its occurrence and, (b) gendered attitudes to this issue are confronted and changed.

Conclusions

A number of key issues emerge in the history of research on elder abuse which help to explain the absence of gender as a central issue in the analyses of elder abuse. They include:

- the degenderization of elder abuse through changes in terminology which mask the gendered specificities of such abuse;
- the homogenization of older people within research contexts which do not distinguish between sixty-five- and eighty-five-year-olds, for example, with the effect that the proportional preponderance of women over men in older age is lost;

- the failure to construct research so that gender is factored in as an identifiable and therefore analysable phenomenon;
- gender blindness on the part of the researchers at the point of data analysis despite the fact that they construct gendered conclusions (e.g. Ogg and Bennett, 1991b; Eastman, 1984; Lau and Kosberg, 1979) – i.e. the failure of researchers to interrogate gender as a significant dimension in elder abuse;
- absence of a sustained feminist engagement with elder abuse which would privilege gender as an issue;
- the relatively recent emergence of debates about dependency and power in the context of elder abuse which can act as a stepping stone to recognizing gender issues as significant;
- a preoccupation with the quantification of elder abuse (prevalence) as opposed to qualitative information, commonly associated with ethnographic and feminist research methods;
- the prevalence of research centring on professionals associated with intervening in cases of elder abuse over research involving those abused;
- an associated absence of qualitative research on the meaning of diverse acts of abuse for abusers/abused and how they are experienced by abusers/abused;
- the tendency to locate the causes of elder abuse in individualized (abused/abuser traits) and privatized (domestic/family) contexts which deflect from the structural inequalities which promote abuse and which affect women disproportionately;
- the absence of studies which correlate the specificities of the abused with detailed analyses of the abuse to illuminate, for example, what type of abuse is committed by whom at what point in their lifecycle;
- the difficulty within the research of accepting explanations as partial, thus constructing either/or scenarios when both/and might be the more appropriate way of thinking about elder abuse (i.e. both inter- and intra-generational abuse can exist; some, but not all, carers abuse; both women and men can abuse);
- the reproduction of gender stereotypes in the framing and analysis of research on elder abuse;
- the reluctance of some male professionals to become involved in debates about elder abuse.

3

Ageism and Sexism – Discrimination in/of Old Age

The Insidiousness of Ageism

> Ageism is the notion that people cease to be people, cease to be the same people or become people of a distinct and inferior kind, by virtue of having lived a specified number of years. (Comfort, 1977: 35)

In this chapter we shall consider ageism and sexism and their effects on women and on people from diverse ethnic backgrounds. Ageism and sexism are the positions which inform elder abuse – after all, elder abuse affects older women disproportionately. The feminization of old age would not matter in the same way if we did not live in an ageist and a sexist society. However, the number of years a person has lived plays a significant and ambivalent role in Western cultural perception, significant in that age is tied to multiple structures of regulation (economic, legal, political and social), ambivalent because the passing of time associated with ageing is constructed simultaneously as a cause for celebration and a cause for mourning. The most obvious index of this paradox, a function possibly of ageing signifying both life and death, are those birthday cards saying 'What??? 29 Again???' which one is supposed to send to people over that age. Ageism, expressive of the notion of progressive decline, starts early in every person's life, for example when people in their early twenties are supposed to be losing physical and mental abilities, such as being brilliant at maths which they possessed until then.

Legally, economically and politically age functions as an indicator of the parameters within which the individual is 'allowed' to operate. Certain forms of punishment rather than others are meted out for specific crimes if the offender is considered to be legally 'under age'. In the past few years, for example, both in the United States and in Britain, the use of so-called minors, ten- and twelve-year-olds, to commit certain kinds of crime, including killings, for which they cannot be given life sentences due to their age, have hit the headlines. Until you are a specific age, your parents, older than you of course, are legally responsible for you. Leaving children below the age of fourteen by themselves at home is illegal in Britain, and in 1993–4 there were a number of cases in the UK where mothers leaving their under-age children at home while they went out at night or went away on holiday attracted media, Social Services and police attention. This so-called 'home alone' issue, named after the hugely successful film of the same name, surfaced in the UK in the wake of the Conservatives' 1993 back-to-basics campaign, which was intended to reassert supposedly traditional values such as the primacy of the nuclear family. According to a Gallup poll, among the basics ministers did not feel it necessary to get back to were good-quality health care, an adequate pension, a roof over one's head and equality of the sexes, all of which, as we suggested in Chapter 1, have direct bearings on elders and on elder abuse (*Daily Telegraph*, 13 December 1993: 7).

While mythically the idea of old age shading into a notion of immortality as encapsulated in the figure of Methuselah has been cautiously celebrated, in reality there is an inverted-U relationship – otherwise known as ageism – between age and status. Ageism, one of the most insidious forms of discrimination in Western society, is associated with the ways in which power is expressed and enacted in our culture. To the extent that paid employment, financial independence and physical and mental fitness are considered expressive of 'having power', the loss of these attributes entails the loss of power and hence status. Advertisements commonly circulated in British magazines for alarms for elders demonstrate the loss of power associated with old age by visually constructing the older person as a victim: the accompanying picture for such ads usually presents a woman, dressed in the 'housewife uniform' of an apron to signal her domestic(ated) and non-income-earning status; she is lying (thus in a prone defenceless position, rather than being erect), often at the bottom of some stairs (a mark and symbol of her fall and decline), alone of course (for why else would she need the alarm?), and dependent on that gadget for the help she is unable to give to herself.

This image corresponds to the kinds of headlines of lone older women being victimized and attacked which can be found in newspapers every day. As we write, the papers in Britain are reporting the case of a teenager who systematically attacked and killed older women, with headlines such as 'Life for Teenage Killer Who Preyed on Elderly' (*Independent*, 28 September 1994: 3) and 'Gran's Ordeal: My Night of Terror at Hands of Killer' (*Daily Mirror*, 28 September 1994: 5). This particular case is interesting because the history of the young man who committed the crimes and who was described in the *Independent* as having a low IQ, apparently involves the repeated loss of female carers: 'When Casey was 12 his mother died. His grandmother, who took over caring for him, died a year later. An older sister to whom he was close was drowned' (*Independent*, 28 September 1994: 3). A not dissimilar story can be found in Christopher Hope's novel *Serenity House*, nominated for the Booker Prize in 1993. The relation of individuals to their female carers at different stages in their lives is clearly one issue that needs to be looked at in the context of elder abuse. When editorials such as the following one in *Community Care* maintain that 'Elder abuse is the most frightening and dangerous manifestation of our society's marginalization and institutionalized oppression of older people' (6 May 1994: 13), they ignore gender issues involved in that oppression in favour of ageism. Yet, as the evidence above suggests, gender issues clearly play a role in that abuse.

Ageism is widely accepted and rarely challenged. One measure of this is the degree to which ageism has been internalized and is expressed by older people themselves who experience their sense of age-induced disempowerment radically and overwhelmingly. As Rich points out in *Look Me in the Eye*, and despite the recent books by ageing feminists on issues of ageing, on the whole feminism has distanced itself from older women: 'our literature, our music, our visual images, our political analyses and organizing, tell us less about old women than about how thoroughly we younger women have absorbed male society's avoidance (masking the underlying terror and hatred) of our ageing selves' (Macdonald and Rich, 1983: 54). Here is Betty Friedan's reaction to ageing:

> When my friends threw a surprise party on my sixtieth birthday, I could have killed them all. Their toasts seemed hostile, insisting as they did that I publicly acknowledge reaching sixty, pushing me out of life, as it seemed, out of the race. Professionally, politically, personally, sexually. Distancing me from their fifty-, forty-, thirty-year-old selves ... I was depressed for weeks after that birthday party ... I could not face being sixty. (1993: xiii)

Friedan's reaction is, of course, not a personal idiosyncrasy but indicative of the socio-cultural construction of ageing to which she has been exposed. This construction often obscures issues of gender by the use of inclusive language with phrases such as 'the elderly' or 'the old' or, more patronizingly, 'oldies' and 'wrinklies' which conjure up images of decay and degeneration. Where a possibly well-intentioned effort to avoid sexist language is made, frequently a genderless, classless, raceless older person emerges, obscuring the effects of structured gender inequalities in Western society. However, as Beth Hess remarks: 'the life experience of older women is not the same as older men, nor is that of persons of colour the same as for whites, regardless of gender or age' (1992: 22). Because every individual's life course is played out within various interrelated systems of stratification, sex, race and class distinctions remain crucial to understanding the process of ageing and elder abuse in any society.

Within the context of how elders are linguistically presented, the language used to describe old women such as 'crone', 'witch', 'old bag', 'hag', and 'battle-axe' is particularly demeaning. The following description from a documentary novel by Pat Barker illustrates this. In this extract the central character is looking into a mirror:

> She looked to herself like a mad woman. The kind of person who gets put away. Her hands came up. She hid herself from the mirror. For years she had avoided looking into it: the hag it showed bore no relation to the person she thought she was. (1982: 255)

In many societies old men are considered to be repositories of wisdom and knowledge (Bytheway, 1995: 45–8). To the extent that old women, on the other hand, are considered or presented as powerful, their power often takes the form of 'sinister wisdom' or 'secret knowledge', both of which tend to be regarded as somehow malevolent rather than benevolent. This supposed malevolence, associated with the image of the witch, is often used as a way of justifying attacks on older women. Arber and Ginn (1991) describe the images of older women in mythology and discuss the way goddesses of ancient civilizations were portrayed in myth. They claim that goddesses who could not be assimilated for the purpose of sustaining male-centred society were transmuted by the Greeks and Romans into witches (1991: 37–8). So, although older women often dispensed herbs and wise advice, instead of being venerated for their wisdom, they became objects of fear and derision in line with patriarchal mythology in which power is used to dominate rather than nurture. Men projected their fear of emasculation on to witches, as women possessing powers outside men's control.

Whatever the material reality of older women, the language used to describe them is intended to convey either states of disempowerment expressed through contempt for them, or a malevolent power which needs to be contained. This is part of the way in which women's definition through language serves to control and dominate them (Mills, 1991: xiv–xv, xvii–iii). Feminist linguists such as Casey Miller and Kate Swift (1981) have suggested that sexist language is symptomatic of cultural attitudes towards women which may well be unconscious. Others like Dale Spender (1980) have maintained that language actually causes women's oppression, a perception which has led to radical feminist attempts to reclaim and change the language used to describe women (Daly, 1978; Daly and Caputi, 1988; Kramarae and Treichler, 1992).

The need for such revisionism becomes clear when one considers how older women are presented in fairy tales, which are part of a shared Western cultural heritage. Here older women often feature as the bad witch, as in 'Snow White' or 'Hansel and Gretel', or as the wicked stepmother, as in 'Cinderella' or 'Rapunzel', threatening to harm, kill, banish or otherwise destroy children. Even nice old granny in 'Little Red Riding Hood' is quickly gobbled up by the wolf. From there it is a very short step to the modern mother-in-law jokes. Calling someone of either sex 'an old woman' is clearly an insult.

American writer Aletta Olin Hill (1986) provides a graphic description of how terms of endearment – as opposed to outright expressions of contempt – can be used to put women in their place. Her eighty-five-year-old mother was admitted to 'one of America's best hospitals' where staff obviously assumed that anyone of that age must be senile. They took away her comb, her teeth and her glasses, lost her nightdress and dressing gown. Hill's mother was German and, due to how German as a language encodes different types of relationships she was used to being called 'Anne' by her family and closest friends only. However, the young nurses called her 'Annie', 'Doll' and 'Grannie' which she hated and protested against. She lapsed into her native tongue and the neurologist, who had no knowledge of German, assumed that she had become psychotic. She died terrified, two days after her admission for a minor problem (Hill, 1986: 92). We shall discuss forms of abuse such as those described here, which are common in institutional settings, further in Chapter 4. It is worth noting, however, that culturally we are conditioned to see older women in a negative light.

The institutionalization and imbrication of ageism in Western society through the legal, political, economic and other systems mean that ageism has in many and diverse ways become 'naturalized', thus hard to detect and counteract. A seemingly well-meaning attitude can easily become paternalistic, with references to old age as a second childhood. In an odd and interesting article Hardy Diessenbacher (1989) suggests that caring for elders can be like caring for infants, but with one crucial difference: elders are expected to die within the foreseeable future while babies are expected to live. Diessenbacher writes: 'Baby care and the care of the elderly become convergent phenomena, except for one difference: that a baby is felt to be the bearer of hope, whereas an elderly person . . . is seen as a destroyer of hope . . . The carer will search an old person's face in vain for the charm of that of a child, which summons up a caring impulse almost by reflex . . . it is more likely to be marked by grief deriving from a consciousness of mortality' (1989: 65–6). One very serious point made in this article is that the impending death of elders acts as an incentive to abuse and neglect. This might be a function of regarding an older person as not much of a loss to society or it may be an expression of Western societies' unease around death or near death.

Another concrete and very typical example of the equation of older people with children is the way in which both children and old people are often given what is termed 'pocket money'. In the instance of the old person this may occur when an individual or a nursing or residential home draws the old person's pension on her or his behalf and retains some of the money to cover various expenses. When we, even unconsciously, categorize elders alongside children, it is inevitable that their right to self-determination will be compromised as we seek to make decisions for them.

Ageism in the Media

Ageist attitudes are fuelled by the media which – if they show elders at all – tend to present images of old people which are caricatures of real life, ranging from the sweet silver-haired granny to the doddery old fool and the dirty old man. Relative to their numbers in the population at large, older people are under-represented in the media. Betty Friedan writes of 'the *non-existence* of images that [are] not "young" ' (1993: 5), providing a range of diverse evidence from different media to highlight older people's, but specifically older women's, under-representation. If there was proportional representation of all age groups on television, every fourth person we see would be retired. Friedan points to the British Broadcasting Corporation's assertion that women and ethnic minorities are better represented than older people (ibid.: 4). However, it is clear that this assertion refers to younger rather than older women; as Ann Jones's (1993) research on women newsreaders showed, increasing age may be an advantage, or at least no detriment, to the male broadcaster but women newsreaders tend not to last beyond their forties before they are replaced with 'a younger model'.

In 'When a Woman Reads the News' Patricia Holland (1987) points out the extent to which female newsreaders' sexuality is commented on relative to that of men. Women newsreaders are, of course, not the only ones to be the objects of such comment. All women are assessed in terms of their sexuality in public and in private contexts. As women age, that preoccupation does not lessen but takes on a different perspective. When Brigitte Bardot celebrated her sixtieth birthday in 1994, the media were full of comments which focused on her sexuality. The *Guardian* (28 September 1994: 9) ran the headline, 'Mellow Bardot Drops her Pout As She Turns 60'.

Bardot was, of course, a sex symbol and press reports on her are informed by perceptions of her past; it is unlikely that Mother Teresa would draw a similar headline. But this is not just because of her specific past – it is also associated with the fact that older women are expected to negate their body and any physical desire, and are not meant to be thought of in physical terms that focus on their sexuality. Part of why sexual attacks on older women are sensationalized in the news is because the assumed desire for that person's body which is supposed to inform the attacker's act is considered shocking and transgressive as only a particular kind of young body is culturally endorsed and reinforced as desirable.

This type of ageist taboo around the older woman's body was also evident in the cases of post-menopausal motherhood which hit the headlines in 1993–4 (Bytheway, 1995: 78–80). The women in question were largely condemned by the media for their desire to become mothers late in life. Yet how many people react in that way to older men such as Jack Nicholson, Clint Eastwood, Charlie Chaplin or Pablo Picasso becoming elderly fathers?

Taboos about the older female body have been internalized by feminist writers as much as by the media. In *Sister Gin* (1979), June Arnold describes one of her older women characters as follows:

> Mamie Carter looked forty at forty. Among women of her class in America, she seemed old while everyone else looked even younger by comparison. But . . . [she] looked forty at fifty and at sixty, growing in effect younger each year while her companions inevitably aged. Now, at seventy-seven, she looked an *old* forty . . . (1979: 11–12)

The point about this description is that it precedes a love affair between Mamie and a much younger woman – the author thinks it necessary for Mamie to be presented as youngish-looking in order for her to be a plausible (and this is a realist novel) object of desire.

Advertising reinforces the image of youth and beauty as the prerequisite for desire by using predominantly young glamorous women to sell to both sexes products which may be used at any age – cars, washing powder, ice cream, shower gel. The man going through hell and high water to deliver the chocolates is not giving them to his granny. Granny sweeps the yard and looks on approvingly as young men set off to meet the girl (and drink) of their dreams in a downtown dive. The products aimed at the old such as Saga Holidays in the UK, stairlifts, financial services and personal alarms tend to be promoted by well-groomed sixty-year-olds who have been given the once-over by make-up girls and hairdressers. Female role models presented to the over-sixties are stars such as Joan Collins and Elizabeth Taylor whose wrinkles and double chins are skilfully airbrushed in magazines and, in any event, kept at bay by the constant attention to the body beautiful which money can provide. In *The Beauty Myth* Naomi Wolf appropriately comments that on the basis of magazines alone, women would have no idea what an average sixty-year-old looks like (Wolf, 1990: 62–3).

Where older women are portrayed as frail and dependent, or dotty like Beattie in the British Telecom advertisement, men are presented as wise. An older man in a white coat (presumably a doctor) sells wrinkle cream and John Stalker (a retired and in the UK very well known police chief) sells us security windows. It is clear that older women suffer from a complex mixture of ageism and sexism, and are considered inferior to men in general and to younger women because they are seen as less attractive and as less desirable than the latter, having apparently outlived their usefulness as wives, mothers and carers. If a man (whatever his age) finds an older woman attractive in any way, this is met with incredulity. Take, for instance, Joanna Trollope's novel *The Men and the Girls* (1992) in which a younger woman, Kate, living with a much older man, James, is deeply distressed when he develops an interest in an older spinster. Here Kate is arguing with another older man about this:

> 'Thing is,' Leonard said, . . . 'she's nothing to be alarmed by. Nothing. Old stick of a thing. Old schoolmarm.'
> 'I know.' . . .
> 'Then what in the devil's name is there to get worked up about in James being kind to a funny old woman?'
> Kate looked at him.
> 'Exactly that,' she said. (1992: 101)

This is, of course, a novel rather than 'real life' but the equivalent of Kate's incredulity can be found every week in women's magazines where articles about women having relationships with younger men regularly appear, suggesting precisely the same attitude as manifested by Kate here. It is also evident in the belittling tone often adopted when older couples get married. And this attitude is not confined to heterosexual relationships. Barbara Macdonald and Cynthia Rich (1983) offer a vivid account of the same phenomenon within their cross-generational lesbian relationship as responded to by the outside world with questions being 'stated or implied: Am I looking for a mother? Is she looking for some security in her old age? Is lesbian love, then, really, asexual?' (1983: 11). Overall then, society constantly reinforces ageist and sexist attitudes towards older women, and advertising is just one of the many contexts in which this is highlighted. While advertising ignores or invalidates the ageing process beyond a certain point, the old remain invisible and the media silent on what in Britain has been called 'the nation's most dramatic realignment since the industrial revolution' (Midwinter, 1991a: 19).

Double Jeopardy: Ageism and Sexism

Ageist attitudes isolate elders from the rest of society, portraying them as a social problem or as parasitic on the younger generation. This hinders the recognition of inequalities amongst elders, of differences among them. These may be economic or health-related or a function of cultural diversity, but they are also to do with being female or male. Arber and Ginn (1991: 178) suggest that older women are doubly devalued through a combined ageism and sexism. They have outlived their status as sex objects and their usefulness as childbearers, and are to some extent freer from direct male control than younger women in whom males still have vested interests. One might argue that the patronizing attitudes frequently displayed towards older women are one means of social control of these women's behaviour, exerted because they have this greater degree of freedom.

Ageist attitudes can arise from changes in the physical appearance and the functioning of the human body. As one woman put it: 'Women have so few role models of older bodies, the cult of youth is so pervasive. We have been conditioned to look at our own bodies through the lens of the advertiser's camera' (Hen Co-op, 1993: 149). Apart from being an obvious and visible way of identifying old age, changes in the body of an older person can provide a disconcerting link with the changes workers and carers see in themselves. Fear and anxiety about ageing and our own future older selves is probably common to us all. We cannot deny that the prevalence of disability increases with old age, or that women suffer this disproportionately. The loss of control over bodily and mental functions is dreaded and often hidden. As Anne put it in *Growing Old Disgracefully* (1993): 'My memory already plays tricks on me, and I fear senility. Will I become unable to make decisions for myself, or become child-like in a world of my own – making phone calls to relatives in the middle of the night, wandering the streets without aim like a lost soul? The thought of losing control terrifies me' (Hen Co-op, 1993: 195). Old people may well lose their memory. But if they also become incontinent they may find themselves stigmatized and excluded from day centres and activities even though modern continence appliances can greatly assist with the problem. However, the strain on carers in persistently providing this level of personal care can result in their treatment of the older person as a less than competent adult. From there it is a short step to neglect and abuse. Changes in the human body may be a crucial agent in creating conditions for abuse and neglect.

'Age stereotypes and sex stereotypes work together in constructing the oppression of women' (Itzin, 1984: 176). They provide an 'education' for women about their place in the social structures, teaching subordination to women and dominance to males. Stereotypes function to (re)produce fear, division and hatred. The title of Erica Jong's *Fear of Fifty* in itself illustrates how this manifests itself in women growing older. Another, much more pernicious version of the same syndrome can be found in David Plante's (1984) description of his relationship with the writer Jean Rhys in which his ageism and sexism are blatantly revealed through the misogyny which informs his dealings with Rhys.

We live in a culture which over-values the young female body as the source of women's positive or negative self-identity. This is evidenced by the innumerable women's magazines designed to offer self-help solutions or cosmetic surgery to women who have sagging skin, breasts, buttocks. Women, endlessly constructed as lack and lacking in a capitalist culture which incites them to regulate and control their bodies through the consumption of appropriate self-reducing products, find their bodies in conflict with the dominant image of the desirable woman as they age. In *Look Me in the Eye* Barbara Macdonald – although proud to be old – movingly describes her feelings when looking at her ageing body:

> Standing before the mirror in the morning, I feel that my scalp is tight. I see that the skin hangs beneath my jaw, beneath my arm; my breasts are pulled low against my body; loose skin hangs from my hips, and below my stomach a new horizontal crease is forming over which the skin will hang like the hem of a skirt turned under. A hem not to be 'let down,' as once my skirts were, because I was 'shooting up,' but a widening hem to 'take up' on an old garment that has been stretched. (Macdonald and Rich, 1983: 23)

Macdonald's allusion to the skirts that were let down to cover parts not to be exposed by the growing girl link the changes she sees occurring in her body directly to her history (and that of most women) of making adjustments not just to accommodate changes in shape but to the implications of the sexual self revealed/concealed through those adjustments. Itzin (1984: 177) maintains that the combined message of ageism and sexism is simple and devastating: 'Women have two functions, sexual and domestic. Each involves children; the first child bearing and the second child rearing. Each involves availability and services to men, sexual and domestic'. Conventional heterosexist views of women's lifecycles suggest that each begins at the point of marriage and continues until a woman is in her mid-forties. With the menopause comes 'retirement' from these tasks and a consequent sense of loss (or freedom, as the case might be). Perhaps the most famous representation of this in Christian mythology is the story of Sarah in Genesis who bears a male (of course) child of her own at the age of ninety. When Sarah first overhears God telling Abraham that they (the ambiguity of who 'they' are is deliberate here) will have a child, she cannot believe her ears:

> Now Abraham and Sarah were old and well stricken in age; and it ceased to be with Sarah after the manner of women.
> Therefore Sarah laughed within herself, saying, After I am waxed old shall I have pleasure, my lord being old also?
> And the LORD said unto Abraham, Wherefore did Sarah laugh, saying, Shall I of a surety bear a child, which am old?
> Is any thing too hard for the LORD? (Genesis, 18: 11–14)

On one level this can be read as a story about female sexual redundancy beyond women's procreational term. On another it is about male power in the face of female disbelief and over the female. It is very reminiscent of the reports on post-menopausal motherhood which appeared in the press in early 1994 and caused much controversy. But it also represents the idea of woman being controlled by men (well into her old age) through and because of her childbearing function. The correlation between ageism, sexism and childbearing indicated in Sarah's story has its contemporary equivalent in a newspaper report headed 'Age Blow to Childless Seeking IVF' (*Guardian*, 18 October 1994: 2) in which the plight of a woman who was denied infertility treatment on the National Health Service because 'she was deemed too old at 36' was raised. As the woman in question said: 'We have heard of sex discrimination and race discrimination – now what we face is age discrimination.'

In *The Change* (1991) Germaine Greer devotes Chapter 4 to a discussion of the stereotypes which have historically informed depictions of menopausal women who, once past their mid-forties, may decline into melancholy, malevolent, masculinized, lecherous individuals in need of restraint. While men are considered to be in their prime, women begin the second half of their lives with little status and value. In discussing the ways in which representations of women reflect and/or produce the values of society, Itzin suggests that the effect is not dissimilar to the propaganda disseminated in George Orwell's *Animal Farm* (1945) after the animals take over where 'four legs good, two legs bad' has become 'young legs good, old legs bad' (Itzin, 1984: 182). The consequence for many women is that although they may disapprove of, indeed resent that position, it is difficult to resist it when everybody else appears to act as if they subscribe to it – eventually you give in and join the exercise class or sign up for the facelift.

Ageist Attitudes of Health Professionals to Elders

Discrimination in health care can be the result of doctors', nurses', and other health professionals' attitudes towards elders. Typically, for example, there may be an attribution of ill health to old age despite the fact that an Age Concern survey in 1987 showed that 75 per cent of elders lead independent lives. Simultaneously, there is evidence of under-diagnosis and failure to recognize certain medical conditions and disorders, many of which are common in older women such as depression, dementia, incontinence, alcoholism and physical abuse. There can be a reluctance to refer old people for medical investigation; it is not uncommon for old people to be told that they have to 'expect it' at their age, whatever 'it' is. Inappropriate prescribing which can lead to automatic repeat prescriptions over long periods of time also occurs. Over-medication can of course in itself cause many physical and mental health problems. The readiness to sedate older patients (discussed in the British media in March 1996) is one problem, with doctors colluding with carers to keep the older person quiet. If communication between doctor and older patient is poor, inadequate information may be passed on to the patient or the carer about disability aids, benefits and entitlements. Add to this the older generation's reverence for the medical profession, the fact that most consultants are male and most older patients female, as well as the over-representation of doctors whose first language is not English in the less popular medical specialisms of geriatrics and psycho-geriatrics, and an alarming mix of sexism, racism and ageism can emerge.

An editorial by A.J. Tulloch in the *British Journal of General Practice* (1991) points out that the training of medical students in geriatric medicine is centred on hospital in-patients, while in fact 95 per cent of the care of elders happens in the community. In-patients are, on the whole, very frail and disabled, which means that students leave medical school with a distorted image of disease, disability and dependency among elders. Medical students will have had little, if any, contact with carers and although GPs in Britain now have a responsibility to monitor the over seventy-five-year-olds, the problem of carers and their concerns is not an area of investigation specifically included in the terms of the current GP contracts. The responsibility for monitoring over seventy-five-year-olds caused some panic amongst doctors, who felt they should be given additional resources to cope with this demand (Perkins, 1991: 382). As they were not provided with additional resources, many devolved their responsibilities, in time-honoured fashion, to their district nurses. One implication of this appears to be that the older population, largely female, can be served by the nursing profession, also predominantly female, and that older women do not warrant the attention, even on the basis of an annual check, of the doctor.

Research studies quoted by Elizabeth Perkins (1991) suggest that patients over seventy-five who do not consult their doctors are in fact healthy. One might therefore argue that to assume that the general public suddenly becomes unable to decide sensibly whether or not they should consult a doctor when they reach the age of seventy-five is ageist. However, Perkins also points to one study covering all age groups which found that middle-aged women are at greater risk of self-neglect than others. Perkins suggests that 'older middle class women may constitute an important and barely recognized low resource and potential risk group, lacking social support as they enter old age and losing their health advantage when over 70 years of age' (1991: 383). If these women – who are also often carers – have unrecognized health problems in addition to the strain of caring, the risk of elder abuse must be increased, as shown by Pillemer and Finkelhor (1989).

The issue of the relationship between elders and the health services provided for them was addressed in 1991 in a letter to the *British Medical Journal* by J. Grimley Evans who holds the Chair of Geriatric Medicine at Oxford University. In this letter he pointed out in the first instance that 'senescence commences at the age of 12 or 13 years and there is no biological basis for separating the elderly from the rest of the human race' (1991: 869). Further, he argued against geriatrics as a specialism within medicine, maintaining that 'age as a variable tells us only something about the average perform-ance of a group, and to determine the care given to an individual person on that basis is unscientific and inequitable' (ibid.). He suggested that age as a variable is used in the manner it is because we are still largely ignorant of the physiological variables we should be measuring when considering the physiological conditions of older people. 'We get away with it because, outside middle class America, older people are unsophisticated consumers of medical care and rarely ask awkward questions' (ibid.). Grimley Evans maintains that older people are disadvantaged in their health care by the changes that have occurred in the National Health Service as they risk being identified as a 'politically supine group who can be segregated into cheap geriatric services with limited access to medical technologies' (ibid.). He argues for an assessment of individual needs, wishes and likelihood of benefit, based on physiology rather than on age, and although this would give the National Health Service accountants high blood pressure, the cost of adequately assessing elders would be

offset by 'some younger people being spared the heroic but predictably futile intervention currently lavished on them simply because
they are younger' (1991: 870). It is important to note that the
National Health Service, simply by the way(s) in which it organizes
its services to elders, discriminates against them. This inadequate
care is a form of abuse of long-stay patients and can result in a failure
to identify abuse in the domestic situation.

As Ann Oakley suggests: 'a classist, sexist and racist medical
system simply does not and cannot attend to the voices and needs of
those who are perceived to be on the margins' (in Morris, 1993: 30).
Attitudes of health professionals towards elders are largely paternalistic and have changed little in the last sixty years. This is evidenced
in a chapter from a nursing textbook on 'Health Visiting and the
Elderly' which, though written in 1986, could have come from a text
produced in the 1920s when that profession was in its infancy. The
1986 text states: 'Clearly health visitors have a role to play in the care
of elderly people. Uninvited visits allow the health visitor to carry out
regular surveillance, anticipating future needs while advising old
people about diet, hypothermia, financial entitlements and so on'
(White, 1986: 460).

Triple Jeopardy: Ageism, Sexism and Racism

Ageism can affect black older people in many ways. In the Health
and Social Services it can mean non-provision of services relevant to
the needs of black elders. Lynda Aitken has come across a number of
social workers who say they have no black clients. Yet they often do
not ask themselves why that might be so. Are meals-on-wheels, for
example, suitable for the dietary needs of people from other cultural
backgrounds? What do Asian elders feel about English home helps
coming into their homes? How are the particular hair and skin needs
of black women and men in residential homes provided for? Do black
elders enjoy the same kinds of leisure activities as white people in
day care? Is there access to a good interpretation and translation
service for people whose first language is not English when they are
admitted to hospitals, rather than relying, often very inappropriately,
on family members? All these questions need attention by the
planners of our services and are timely, since in Britain in 1996 we
are operating under the market-led philosophy of the Patient's and
Citizen's Charters which, ironically, state that 'You have the **right** to
receive health care on the basis of your clinical needs, not on your
ability to pay, your lifestyle or any other factor' (Department of
Health, 1995: 4). Ageism and sexism interrelate, and for older black
women this is compounded by racism. In *Waiting in the Twilight*

(1987) Joan Riley provides a vivid fictionalized account of the experience of this triple jeopardy through the portrayal of her central character, Adella, a fifty-eight-year-old Caribbean woman living in Britain.

For black elders, one thing ageism can mean is vulnerability to (the effects of) racist attacks. It can also mean low self-esteem after years of experiencing a devaluation of themselves as black people living in a racist culture. This is compounded by the fact that the proportion of older people from an ethnic minority background in Britain, and in some counties such as Northamptonshire is still small (see Wright, 1993: 2.5–2.8). An analysis of the 1991 Census information by the Warwick University Centre for Research in Ethnic Relations (1993; Paper No. 4) indicates some of the long-term cultural differences between Asian and white households in Britain. It confirms that more Asian householders (meaning: families from India, Pakistan and Bangladesh) live as traditional family units (two or more adults of different genders and a number of dependent children) (83 per cent) compared with white households (65 per cent). Mohammed Qamar, Secretary of the Moslem Liaison Committee in Birmingham, UK, commented on the Warwick University study in the *Daily Mail* (5 June 1993): 'As far as the care of the elderly is concerned, we believe it is the duty of the family to give them care.' Unfortunately, this position is often used by professionals and policy makers as an excuse for not providing (appropriate) services to this group of older people and their carers. It also means that elder abuse in ethnic minority groups is less likely to come to professionals' attention and that there are fewer avenues of help for those who are abused. More recently, there have been attempts to combat this problem by identifying and seeking to remedy the conditions in Social Services that lead to an absence of culturally sensitive services (Wright, 1993; Woolham, 1994).

Aitken came across a case involving one of the social workers of her team where an Asian couple who had no children lived together in Northampton while their extended family lived in London. When the husband had a stroke, it was assumed that his wife would cope. This assumption was based on the racial stereotype that Asian families look after each other, on the Western relational stereotype that in a marriage one partner will look after the other, and on the sexual stereotype that it is the woman's role to look after those in need of care. In this instance it became clear that the wife had great difficulty in understanding what her husband's needs would be on his return home from hospital. It was assumed that this was because of language difficulties, so an interpreter was brought in. This interpreter deduced that the woman had learning difficulties because of her problems in understanding what would be required of her. Additionally, an assumption was made that she would provide personal care for her husband, i.e. wash him, help him to the toilet etc., but it transpired that the woman's difficulties arose not only because she had learning difficulties but also because doing such tasks was against this couple's cultural mores. It was then suggested that his brothers fulfil this role. But how were they supposed to do this, living in London? The man in question had become very physically disabled by his stroke but his religious beliefs and customs made frequent washing important. He needed male help with this . . . and so it went on. Basically, complex racist, sexist and ageist assumptions had been all utilized to excuse the provision of culturally sensitive services.

The demographic trend can be predicted: we know that there will be a sharp increase in the number of the very old in populations from ethnic minority backgrounds over the next two decades. In *Triple Jeopardy: Growing Old in a Second Homeland* (1985: i) Alison Norman pointed out that younger people from Asian and black communities in Britain already suffer from disabilities and disadvantages more commonly associated with ageing in the white population. In 1991 Gill Hek, a district nurse, undertook a survey of the uptake of the district nursing service by black elders in an inner city area of Bristol in the UK, focusing particularly on Asian elders. She found a very low take-up of services compared to what one might have expected on the basis of the population distribution as evidenced in the 1981 Census. This low take-up figure did not even take into account the poor living conditions, poverty and ill health of black elders described as their triple jeopardy by Norman (1985). Some of the nurses Hek interviewed thought that the low uptake was the patients' problem. They made comments such as 'perhaps they don't want to be looked after by someone who's white' (Hek, 1991: 14), and held stereotypical and prejudiced views, evidenced in statements like 'I think we're always cautious when we take blood from Asians' and 'the older Asian ladies tend to take to their beds' (ibid.). Most professionals seem to take for granted that (potential) clients are aware of their role and the service they offer. The white elders in Hek's study all knew about the district nursing service but only two of the ten Asian elders had heard about it but did not know what kinds of service it provided. Such lack of knowledge has been highlighted elsewhere (Mehta, 1993; Cameron et al., 1989) and suggests that caution should be applied in emphasizing cross-cultural differences as the reason for a low uptake of services (Blakemore and Boneham, 1994: 115).

The implications of Hek's study are considerable in terms of training of professionals as regards the needs of people from different cultures, in terms of recruitment of black and Asian district nurses, and as regards a general commitment to providing an equal service for all. In Britain it is acknowledged that 'the lack of case material relating to minority ethnic groups suggests that the voice of black elders is not being heard' (Social Services Inspectorate, 1992: i). But research studies which rely *only* on professionals for their information will not be able to adequately address the problems of black elders, unless those professionals are in close contact with the relevant communities.

The Warwick University study found that relatively few black elders live alone (1993: 5–6). This is significant because research into elder abuse such as that done by Wolf and Pillemer (1989: 34) shows that 75 per cent of abusers live with their victims and that people who live in families are more at risk from diverse kinds of abuse. However, in the longer term the migration patterns of these elders which we discussed in Chapter 2 may mean changes in the household structures elders from diverse ethnic backgrounds inhabit. They therefore need particular attention. As the (assumed) veneration of old age in some groups may change as a consequence of living in a multi-racial society with diverse attitudes to elders, it seems likely that abuse of ethnic elders may take place, but this has not been adequately researched to date (Ogg and Munn-Giddings, 1993: 397). Indeed, as Blakemore and Boneham highlight, the idea of 'unconditional reverence for old age in pre-industrial or traditional societies' is a myth (1994: 28–30).

Many services such as home helps, meals-on-wheels and day centres are under-used by ethnic minority communities, unless these are set up to cater specifically for their needs. At the same time, the criticism has been voiced that people from ethnic minorities over-consult their GPs (Gillam et al., 1989; Donaldson, 1986: 1081). *If* this is the case, it would be interesting to know whether this is a function of the GP, who is usually male, being accorded a status within the community which encourages people to consult him on all family problems. In contrast, Roy Carr-Hill and Kai Rudat (1995) report that recent consulting rates show that nearly twice as many females and males from Indian, Pakistani and Bangladeshi communities in Britain in the over-thirty-five-year-old age ranges go to see their GP compared with the rest of the UK population. They conclude that 'the Bangladeshi community [show] the worst health profile' (1995: 29). Two complementary articles in the *British Medical Journal* in 1989 (Gillam et al., and Balarajan et al.) pointed out that people from ethnic minority groups in Britain *do* suffer from poorer health than their white counterparts. Rather than having 'exotic' complaints associated with their country of origin, however, problems such as diabetes tended to occur (which in turn can contribute to ischaemic heart disease and strokes) as well as asthma, TB, anaemia and osteomalacia in Asian women (Greenhalgh, 1995; Mehta, 1993: 18). If people from some ethnic minorities suffer poorer health than the rest of the UK population and they under-use services intended to support those with chronic health and other problems, this means that such people are presumably dependent on others in their community to help them. As suggested in the previous chapter, this dependence can become the seed bed for elder abuse and neglect. Women will be disproportionately affected by this as their status is lower in all patriarchal societies than men's.

Vulnerability to anxiety, depression and dementia is common amongst very elderly people of any background, but those from immigrant ethnic groups may be especially at risk (Blakemore and Boneham, 1994: 106–8). In Britain many immigrants, especially first-generation ones, intended to return to their homeland but do not do so. They see their children grow up in Britain and adopt Western styles and values, and as old people they are faced with an accumulation of losses: loss of their homeland, their social role and status, of a familiar and safe environment, of easy verbal communication, sometimes within their own families, and possibly of a partner. Past persecution and maltreatment, for instance amongst the Jewish community who survived the Holocaust, may increase the older person's sense of vulnerability and may generate a vicious circle of fear and hostility. Those suffering from dementia are most vulnerable of all because of the loss of short-term memory which can result in utter bewilderment in relation to present surroundings. Social workers and others in related professions working with elders and providing day care for older people with mental health problems sometimes use reminiscence therapy. This is very difficult when young white women, for instance, work with black older women whose homeland is on another continent and to whose cultural background they have very limited access. Again, this has very clear implications for the recruitment of appropriate members of staff into the groups of professionals working with elders. Many factors contribute to the individual experiences of elders from diverse ethnic backgrounds. If they suffer the lack of an extended social network, have lifelong experiences of discrimination, are in declining mental and physical health, are confronted with inadequate services and insufficient information about services, this will obscure occurrences of elder abuse in these groups, including the gender specificities inherent in such abuse.

The vast majority of old people occupy a relatively low position in the social structure, with poverty, inadequate housing and social isolation often exacerbated by poor health. Old women are affected more by these problems than old men as they live longer, are frailer and have lower incomes. Black old women are the worst off in these respects as their average incomes are even beneath that of the average white older woman. Black older women also frequently live in deprived inner city areas which have more than their share of social problems. Norman (1985: 45) points out that 'Afro-Caribbeans and Asians in council properties tend to be put in high-rise flats on unpopular estates, and those who have bought their own houses have been forced by availability and cost to take on old property in poor condition'. They are more likely to be isolated by disability and language, having come to this country late in life or having remained within the home with few opportunities to learn English. In Cameron et al.'s (1989) study in Birmingham, 'Black Old Women, Disability and Health Carers', none of the thirty-eight older Asian women spoke fluent English and only fifteen of the forty-six Asian men did.

A specific and distressing hardship in old age involves those who came to Britain since 1980 and whose relatives declared 'that he [*sic*] will maintain and accommodate his dependants without recourse to public funds, in accommodation of his own or which he occupies himself' (Norman, 1985: 41). Norman argues that this clause of the Immigration Act has the effect of creating a group of older people who are 'utterly without statutory rights to housing or financial benefits, and if they ask for such help they can jeopardize their sponsor who will have broken his oath and thus commit a legal offence which can render him and his dependants liable to deportation' (Home Office, 1984 in Norman, 1985: 10). Apart from this being a scandalous condition to impose on anyone, intolerable in a country suffering from a recession, it is significant for elder abuse because there is research (Ogg and Munn-Giddings, 1993: 399) to suggest that a high level of co-dependency of whatever kind between abuser and abused predisposes to an abusive situation.

It is important to ensure that we do not fall prey to cultural stereotyping. We need to differentiate between the needs of different groups. Norman, for instance, draws attention to Jewish, Cypriot, Irish and Chinese immigrants as well as the Asians and Afro-Caribbeans who all have their own culturally specific needs. According to Barker (in Stevenson, 1989: 113) there are four main groups of black and Asian elders in Britain. The first are men from Asia who came to Britain in the 1930s and 1940s; the second are 'the early migrants, men from one part of India and women from the West Indies, now in their 60s and 70s' (ibid.). A third group are the parents and wives of the early migrants. These often have no pension entitlement and are completely dependent on their children who managed for years without them. The last group are the refugee Asians from East Africa of the 1960s and 1970s, often professional and managerial workers. It is obvious that the needs of these groups in old age will be very diverse. How they are catered for requires urgent consideration.

As part of the empowerent of older people, there needs to be a recognition that they can and should have a say in how they are provided for and in the running of residential homes and other facilities provided for them. In Britain a Black Community Care Charter is currently being produced by the National Association of Race Equality Advisors to ensure that the needs of the black community become integral to the operation of community care legislation, and to bring to life policies devised to secure the needs of black and ethnic minority communities (Johnson, 1991: 318).

Structured Ageism and Dependency

Structural ageism (re)produces individual ageist attitudes. As Pillemer and Finkelhor (1989: 186) comment in the light of their work: 'the view that the elderly cause their own abuse by becoming frail and dependent should be discarded. It lacks empirical support and appears to be based on anecdote and opinion, rather than on a true assessment of the causes of elder maltreatment'. The Marxist view of capitalist values being determined by productivity has important implications in British society where a compulsory retirement age is common, and people are judged by their productive worth. Those who stop 'producing' feel they are 'on the scrap heap' and are considered a burden. One woman describes the effects as follows:

> There are some Sundays when I am at home and the phone never rings. No-one knocks on my door. When I was working full-time such a day would have been a relief, a welcome break from the rushed, hectic week. Now that I am retired . . . it is the other way around and I miss the contact with those who themselves are still in need of that weekend respite. (Hen Co-op, 1993: 198)

There are no anti-ageist laws in employment which would outlaw discriminatory practices in advertising and the filling of job vacancies. Yet firms that have a policy of recruiting older workers report less sickness and a more responsible attitude to work in their older employees. The theory of disengagement and withdrawal from social life as part of ageing leads people to believe that these are normal aspects of ageing and not a product of enforced retirement, low income, low status and, perhaps, widowhood. One need only remember the unspeakable suggestion that old people who suffer from hypothermia do not need adequate pensions or help with heating bills but woolly hats. It is a typical excuse by politicians and policy makers that old age is the problem, not inadequate pensions and services, forcing people into positions of vulnerability. Economic and political forces contribute to feelings of powerlessness amongst older people and their carers, preventing an understanding of structural dependency as a social construct rather than as a biological or individual issue.

Structural neglect of older people reaches its peak when they become frail or dependent and vulnerable to abuse. This is because caring for older people is a low-priority job in Health and Social Services. One of the social workers Lynda Aitken interviewed shared her shame that Northamptonshire Social Services Department had considered introducing a ruling whereby unqualified social workers could not be appointed to a permanent social work job except for work with elders. What does this suggest about the importance of elders and their problems for these Social Services?

Combating Ageism and Sexism

In order to deal with ageism it is necessary to understand how it works. Barbara Macdonald (Macdonald and Rich, 1983: 61) asserts that ageism 'is a point of convergence for many other repressive forces, such as the violence of men against women, and their lifelong poor economic and social status'. Understanding this means that as part of a strategy for change it is necessary to campaign for better pensions and services. More has to be done, too, to attempt to change the image of elders portrayed in the media.

The impetus to raise awareness will in part have to come from older people themselves. Unfortunately the Grey Panther movement has not crossed the Atlantic to Britain yet, and the pensioner movement in the UK is growing only very slowly and often appears unrepresentative of the older population. What is more, its organiza-tional leadership is predominantly male. Greater wealth through occupational and private pensions has divided the 'haves' from the 'have nots', and the idea of abandoning a universal state pension in Britain is in 1996 being considered in all political quarters, including the Labour party.

Macdonald and Rich (1983: 104) point out that the women's movement betrayed older women: 'Ageism was branded onto the women's movement with the word "Sisterhood".' The point they make is that that term implies same-generation women rather than being inclusive of women from different age groups. While one might argue that the term also has a symbolic significance which is ignored by Macdonald and Rich, suggesting sameness among all women (in itself, of course, a highly problematized position in the 1990s), it is also the case that the women's movement has all but silenced older women and that their concerns are only now, in the 1990s, being raised as leading feminists themselves enter the third and fourth age. This is in contrast to the early part of the twentieth century when many of the politically active feminists were older women, for example Susan B. Anthony and Emmeline Pankhurst. Pankhurst was fifty-nine years old when she was arrested at King's Gate. MacDonald and Rich point out that 'the second wave [of feminism] has come from a different time in patriarchal history, from a patriarchally supported white middle class *youth* culture' (1983: 37).

Against this grain, there are some encouraging signs of older women beginning to celebrate ageing. The now only intermittently operational Hen House, a centre for women in Britain, has run courses for older women on ageing, and six women aged between sixty and seventy-five who met there have written a book entitled *Growing Old Disgracefully* (Hen Co-op, 1993) which challenges conventional views of ageing. These are of course micro moves towards change which do not necessarily influence the structural inequalities that promote ageism. However, as Ruth Raymond Thone suggests in *Women and Aging: Celebrating Ourselves*: 'aging gracefully may mean simply not causing any trouble' (1992: 16). Thone encourages women to be advocates for each other and to 'refuse to accept our culture's lie that old age is ugly' (ibid.: 2).

There is a need for older women to assert themselves politically. The issues pertinent to them such as care-giving, which is undertaken disproportionately by women, many of whom are old themselves, and the need for care could bring older women into the political arena. As Robert Hudson and Judith Gonyea (1992: 136) suggest: 'The continuing absence of an older women's political presence will reinforce demeaning and inappropriate stereotypes of dependency and failure to organize will contribute to the further reification of old women as passive and helpless.'

Conclusions

We live in a society in which older women are demeaned because of the prevalence of attitudes of ageism and sexism. These attitudes are promoted by

- women's impoverishment through the economic disadvantages they experience prior to and in old age;
- the decline of physical and mental health in old age;
- the cessation of their labour as childbearers, mothers and wives, around which female roles are traditionally structured in patriarchal cultures;
- the absence of representations of older women in the media and the negative stereotyping of older women in cultural representation;
- the sense of older people as close to death and thus redundant.

The consequences of these attitudes are that

- age and sex are used as regulatory mechanisms in society;
- older people, especially women and people from diverse ethnic backgrounds who have been subject to lifelong discrimination, may internalize the ageism and sexism with which they are daily confronted;
- public resources are not made available either sufficiently or appropriately to cater for older women and people from diverse backgrounds, thus effecting active forms of disempowerment of these elders;
- in the stagnating economies of the West the emphasis is increasingly on self-help rather than on the implementation of structural changes.

As Caroline Ramazanoglu puts it: 'male violence towards women would be absent or limited only where women have effective economic and political power of their own, are not dependent on men, and have means of redress in the public sphere' (1989: 66). At present and not only in this society women certainly do not have effective economic power of their own (Hugman, 1994: 83–4). They may have political power in that they are able to vote but they are not organized effectively to utilize that power to their advantage. Women as much as people from diverse ethnic communities remain dependent on men, if not in the private sphere (though this is the case for many both financially and otherwise), then publicly through the dominance of men in decision-making positions in politics, the judiciary, medicine, etc. Women and people from diverse ethnic groups may well have – theoretically – means of public redress if they are abused or discriminated against but access to such means is limited by

- their restricted financial circumstances;
- their knowledge of and the accessibility of appropriate services to support them in seeking public redress;

- institutional ageism, sexism and racism;
- their declining physical and mental health;
- cross-cultural and inter-gender differences which inhibit them from seeking redress.

In the face of such formidable odds, it is not surprising that elder abuse remains a largely 'hidden' problem, even in 1996.

4

Paid to Care – Gender Issues in Elder Abuse in Institutional Settings

Being a nurse or social worker does not in itself create an immunity against being an abuser, neither does it prevent the possibility that, as we become older and perhaps dependent on our own adult children, we too may become victims. (Eastman, 1988: 16)

She was actually frightened of the old and the frail. Ever since childhood, while talking to the very old, she had been frightened by visions of herself attacking them, hitting them, assaulting them . . . These visions would appear, unsummoned, while she sipped cups of strong tea in clients' bedsitters. (Evelyn, a social worker, in Margaret Drabble's novel *The Middle Ground*, 1981: 63)

Institutional Abuse vs Domestic Abuse

Abuse of older people in institutional care, either in residential or nursing homes or in hospital, is usually regarded as a form of abuse which is distinct from abuse within the home. However, with the growth of shared and respite care, some older people may be abused in both settings. One difference between institutional abuse and domestic abuse is that in the former case the abuser is usually a paid, female employee, although in one of Aitken's interviews a social worker talked of a son who sexually abused his mother while she was in residential care. The home, suspecting the situation, should of course have investigated it but it may be one of the effects of that institution's ethos that staff were reluctant to do so. Wardhaugh and Wilding (1993) indicate 'particular models of work organization that promote inward-looking and narrowed models of internal reporting; attention is drawn to the stifling of self-criticism and complaint, professional isolation, routinization and undue hierarchy' (in Biggs et al., 1995: 84) as institutional modes which deter staff from confronting abusive situations.

The distinction between formal, that is *paid*, and informal, *unpaid*, care reflects the economically driven ideology which informs care of elders. But common to elder abuse, whether it occurs in an institutional or in a domestic setting, is that it involves an act of violation (of whatever kind) perpetrated by the abuser against the abused. Such acts may be differentially motivated in diverse situations but they are fed by what Susanne Kappeler (1995) describes as a culture which endorses violence through its 'primary identification with the subjects of violence and our lack of solidarity with the victims. It is itself an act of violence: the exercise of ideological violence, of the power of the discourse which legitimates violence, stigmatizes the victims, and treats people not as agents of their own actions but as material for ('our') social policy' (1995: 7). In other words, those who act violently are 'excused' by pointing to conditions which may promote violence and which need changing rather than by considering their responsibility as individuals for their actions. This position is evident in some feminists' (ourselves included) and others' tendency to identify with the plight of the carer and to see themselves as potential carers, that is subjects in control of the action, rather than acknowledging the possibility that they might need care, become the objects of care-giving. Further, both the individual's actions in committing abuse against an older person *and* the circumstances which contribute to this need to be considered (see also Kelman, 1973). Kappeler maintains that the structures of thought and argumentation which legitimize violence in Western culture and inform our actions are so 'deeply rooted in our everyday thinking' that they inform all our behaviour. More significantly,

> What is remarkable is that this everyday behaviour, in so far as it does not fall within the competence of criminal law, is hardly the subject of a serious theoretical discussion. Neither does it attract explicit legitimation; rather, the violence of everyday behaviour draws its legitimacy from the ubiquity of such behaviour in our society and the social consensus about its relative 'harmlessness' compared with other, that is recognized forms of violence. (Kappeler, 1995: 7)

A good example of this was the acceptance by the social workers Aitken interviewed of financial abuse (see Chapter 5). Elder abuse in both institutional and domestic settings is informed by the same attitude of legitimation of violence through the primary identification with the perpetrators (subjects) rather than the victims (objects) of violence.

Aronson (1990: 62) maintains, 'It is estimated that . . . "informal care" of the elderly constitutes 90% of the total care provided in society, the remaining 10% being supplied by the formal health and social services.' While these figures are likely to shift to some extent, they nonetheless suggest that institutional abuse may not be as extensive a problem as domestic abuse simply because fewer elders are in institutions than at home. This may in part account for the lack of research in this area. Another reason for the absence of such research may be the low level of status attached to working with elders

(Treharne, 1990: 777), which in turn is partially determined by the fact that those working with older people, and older people themselves, especially in the post-seventy-four-year-old age range (see Chapter 1 in this volume), are women. As Aronson (1990: 69) points out in relation to the older women dealing with service providers: 'many were acutely attuned to their devalued status as old women'.

Discussions of institutional care and abuse tend to mask the gender specificities pertinent to them, either completely ignoring it by employing a gender-neutral discourse or by failing to remark on the gendered specificities which emerge in the findings. Hilary Brown and Helen Smith (1993) have commented on the ways in which the 1990s rhetoric of care has invisibilized its gendered implications. The 'reality' of elder abuse occurring in institutions devoted to the care of older people is that we have a situation where a predominantly female workforce abuses a predominantly female client group (Jack, 1994: 78). But there is little willingness to acknowledge this. Women abusing women constitutes a problem because it violates socio-cultural expectations of role distributions and behaviours for women and men which construct women as non-violent and men as violent. If, for the moment, we reduce the notion of elder abuse to violence, we are faced with the problem that female aggression is poorly understood and rarely discussed in Western culture – it has the aura of a taboo and in consequence is vested with little knowledge and much mystique. Typically, female violence is regarded as the expression of someone who is either 'mad' or 'bad'. The issue has as yet not entered mainstream debates on role definitions of women and men because for it to do so would require major rethinking of our conceptions of 'femininity' and 'masculinity'. Where female violence has become an issue within dominant culture, this violence has frequently been read in the light of inter-sexual relations, i.e. the woman is violent because she is enthralled to a 'bad' man (what one might call the Myra Hindley syndrome) or she is acting out revenge for being spurned by a man (as presented in the film *Fatal Attraction*), or she is simply in and of herself dysfunctional, i.e. 'mad' (the explanation in the Beverly Allitt case, in which a nurse, found guilty of killing several babies, was described as having Münchhausen's Disease). In these instances, the focus of enquiry tends to be on the individual woman who is presented as an exception to the norm; structural inequalities which might contribute to her behaviour are ignored in order to establish her deviance as 'not the norm' as far as women are concerned. The maintenance of the status quo as regards gender stereotyping takes precedence over an investigation of gender roles which might reveal the inadequacies of the norms so extensively taken for granted in explanations of female behaviour.

In this context it is not surprising that the greatest inroads in considering gender role stereotyping and how it relates to violence enacted by women on other women has been made by women who themselves have only a limited, if any, investment in the gender stereotyping which dominates mainstream thinking. Lesbians have been at the forefront of discussing violence and abuse between women and seeking to review women's roles and behaviours from a less obviously gendered perspective (Hollows, 1996; Lobel, 1986). This is not to say that violence and abuse between women is specific to the lesbian community. On the contrary, violence between women can and does occur across a range of settings but we are not culturally accustomed to thinking about women as violent and abusive towards each other (or towards men), except, perhaps, in the context of 'cat fights' over men.

However, the statistics clearly indicate that the vast majority of over seventy-four-year-olds are women and the majority of carers are women. The question of elder abuse in a single-sex context still awaits sustained investigation and analysis. At the same time the issue of violence among women should not obscure the fact that elder abuse occurs in a range of gendered settings and in diverse ways.

In this chapter we shall explore some of the factors which contribute to the occurrence of abuse in institutional settings, in terms of both the abusers and the abused. We wish to highlight that such abuse is predominantly abuse between women, that it does not merely entail physical forms of aggression but extends to other areas of abuse and that this whole area of elder abuse still needs extensive investigation which takes into account both the social and economic realities of women abusing and of those abused.

Dependency, Power and Control in Institutional Abuse

One effect of current policies of promoting care within the community by informal female carers, supplemented with care packages delivered by female staff, and reducing residency in hospitals and homes, is that women and men enter institutional care as a last resort as opposed to a first choice. At the point when informal female carers can no longer cope with the needs of the older woman, that person usually has become dependent on care to get through the business of daily living, with the degree of dependency on intensive and sustained levels of care often being crucial in the transition from domestic care to institutional care (Ross et al., 1993: 1533).

In contemporary Western culture, dependency is negatively constructed as the opposite of autonomy, not dissimilar to the opposition between victim and agent or object and subject. As Martha Mahoney

(1994: 60) puts it: 'Agency – acting for oneself – is generally seen as an individual matter, the functioning of an atomistic, mobile individual.' An older woman in need of extended caring can – within these terms – clearly not be regarded as possessing agency and the assumption, on entry into a caring institution (note the irony of the phrase), tends to be that of the older woman having relinquished agency, often and to a considerable extent prior to entering the institution. But physical infirmity should not be confused with mental decline; older women's health problems do not necessarily mean that they should be infantilized or have all their choices made for them.

The reduction of older women's agency once they enter a home is reinforced by the territorial issues, or by who determines the parameters of the interactions which come into play when someone enters an institution and which are enacted through daily routines and regimes, many of which are, or verge on the, abusive. These are imposed on older people regarding even the most basic of their functions, from when they are 'allowed' to eat or drink, to when they are toileted, whom they can share a room with or have in their room, what personal possessions they can bring, etc. Such regimes are standard both in state-run and in privately owned homes, reinforcing the idea that on entering the caring institution the older woman loses her individuality and decision-making powers in favour of becoming an institutional unit. As Blank et al. (1993: 279) put it:

> An institution is generally a bad place for elderly persons to exert or desire direct, overt control . . . because the institutions run most smoothly when elderly are passive recipients of care from the staff; that is, when the distribution of control activity is almost totally in the direction of the staff and staff are in control of the allocation of control by the nature of the setting. In such situations, a strong desire for control will go unquenched; actual control attempts will be met with resistance.

A very clear example of this is provided by Catherine Bennett (1994) who describes visiting various nursing homes for elders. At one point, 'In one corridor a woman was poised between a chair and a Zimmer frame, struggling to heave herself upright. As we passed her, the manager placed her hand on the woman's shoulders and without comment, forced her back into the chair' (1994: 12). Here impairment and institutionalization contribute to the objectification and victimization of the older woman who is acted upon without explanation or recourse to redress. Ageism and sexism converge in this situation of dependency to result in the objectification of that woman and in the 'freedom' – even in front of an 'outsider' – to abuse her.

The very fact of the abuse, of course, reinforces the power differential between the older woman and the abusing matron and thus serves to perpetuate it.

Much of the writing on problems about control, power and institutions assumes that those institutionalized are in a position to act on their own behalf in situations of abuse. However, high degrees of dependency which may be the result of both physical and/or mental decline are not necessarily conducive to putting up a fight. Quite apart from the anxiety about who would care for one if one were to accuse the institution and caring individuals within it of abuse, there is the difficulty of whom to turn to and what to say – provided the older person is in a state to make such claims. Francis (1993b) describes this problematic vividly. It is exacerbated by the inadequate inspection system which prevails, especially in the private sector.

Where the possibility of victimization of patients or clients is, in a sense, inherent in institutional set-ups, there is a less obvious but equally important 'victimization' of staff which contributes to the way in which they act towards the women in their care. The female workforce employed in these institutions is gathered at the lower and often unskilled end of the working spectrum (Brown and Smith, 1993), reflecting the low status of work with elders on the one hand, and the economically driven, increasing de-skilling of the workforce in general on the other. The women working as care assistants or home helps, for example, work not in order to do some 'labour of love' but because they need to survive on the money they get. The assumption that women care because they are nurturant, implicitly encoded in many contemporary care proposals (Brown and Smith, 1993), is in direct conflict with the fact that for many women caring is 'just a job'. As Kappeler (1995: 27) puts it: 'so-called selflessness can become rational self-interest, namely the means by which to realize the advantages (however meagre) which patriarchal society offers to women'. In her view, 'the deprivation of women in patriarchy consists not in the loss of self through self-sacrifice, but in the lack of political rights and material opportunities to survive and exist other than through the labour of "love" and care, that is, other than as dependants and primary carers of men' (ibid.). The effect of such a strategic revaluing of caring work is evident in the words of one matron of a nursing home: 'You've got to distance yourself, got to. To be honest, sometimes I get home and I'm fed up with the lot of them, I'm fed up with hearing [here she puts on a mewling voice] "mummee, mummee", and "Oh, nurse, nurse", and "matron, matron", and it's hard for the staff, they get fed up with it too' (Bennett, 1994: 14). While dependent older people may cast paid female carers in the (unwanted?) role of mother, 'Nurses who work with elderly people often see their patients as children and, as previously suggested, there is a visible power struggle which the patients usually lose, leaving them dependent on nurses for their physical caring tasks' (Helen Jones, 1993: 59).

Nurses as much as unskilled women working in caring are on low incomes. Paid carers' relationship to their 'charges' is an overtly economic one. As one woman nursing home manager said: 'Staff-wise you get some that are not so good – it shouldn't be like that, but you're talking economics' (Bennett, 1994: 14). In other words, residential and nursing homes employ women in response to the institution's economic 'needs' rather than to ensure best possible care for their clients. In *The Will to Violence: The Politics of Personal Behaviour* (1995), Kappeler discusses the prevalence of economistic terminology in current descriptions of all kinds of different relationships, suggesting that with this vocabulary comes an attitude which focuses on 'value for money', 'exchange value', etc. She maintains, rightly in our view, that the use of economic metaphors serves to transform relations of potential equality into ones of domination and submission when the exchange is seen to be unequal. In the case of service providers such as carers on low pay, the question of what these women get out of doing their work is an important one. In a climate in which equivalence of return is the dominant expectation, being asked to do a physically, and potentially emotionally, demanding job without a sense that an equivalent return (possibly, but not inevitably, in pecuniary form) is offered, will lead – at least in some people – to a need to seek other kinds of recompense. These can include the pleasure of power over others, exercised through not responding to their needs, for example. Residential and nursing homes, while needing their clients to exist, are nonetheless sites of inequality where the dependence of the clients on the staff's support is matched only by the staff's need to earn a living but where the living earned is small compared with the work required. Such disequilibrium in an economically driven ideological climate provides a seed bed for abuse.

Institutional Abuse: The Client's Perspective

Institutional abuse is affected by the culture and nature of institutions and their effects on both staff and vulnerable people. As Hugman (1994: 130–2) notes, theorists such as Goffman (1968) and Foucault (1977, 1989) have developed models to analyse the effects of being institutionalized on their constituent communities. The removal of decision-making powers, the lack of privacy and the infantilization experienced in institutions all contribute to this. A graphic picture of these effects was created in Valerie Windsor's 1986 play *Effie's Burning* which arose from publicity in Britain in the early 1980s about women who had been long-term hospitalized in mental institutions for 'moral turpitude', meaning for getting pregnant out of wedlock. These forgotten women suddenly came to the public's attention as part of the Conservative government's drive towards care in the community. In Windsor's play Effie is a sixty-four-year-old woman who has been in a large mental hospital since she was sexually abused and became pregnant when she was a teenager. When she is separated from her long-term female friend within the institution and moved to a community home, sleeping by herself and in her own room for the first time, she is unable to deal with this 'freedom' and sets fire to herself in an effort to effect a return to the institution in which she was before and which is closing. It is important to note here that the play presents a woman who is multiply abused: sexually at first, then by her family who reject her and have her sectioned for a 'crime' – being sexually abused – she did not commit, and lastly, by the institution which refuses to see her as an individual with needs and rights.

An in some respects similar 'real life' case was recently (Blackhurst, 1995) reported in the *Independent on Sunday* under the heading 'Long-stay Patients Ejected by Hospital "Lost Will to Live" '. The article detailed the story of three older women who had spent forty-seven, fifty-six and sixty years respectively in a long-stay hospital and, at the ages of eighty-one, seventy-five and sixty-seven had been forced to move out of that hospital because it was phased out, 'tipped out, to people they did not know'. One of the women apparently 'pleaded not to be sent away'. All three women died within two weeks to eight months following discharge and 'their former nurses believe their deaths were due to the trauma of the move'. According to the article, this view was – not surprisingly – contested by the relevant health authority's public health director but support for such a position comes from a study by Dugan and Kivett (1994: 341) which states that 'Older adults, especially the very old, are vulnerable to shifts in residence because of changing . . . circumstances'. 'Instability of residence' was, in the instance related above, compounded by loss of friends and a familiar environment – all of which can and do contribute to decline in older people (Dugan and Kivett, 1994). The article from the *Independent on Sunday* states that 'Staff were not allowed to accompany the women to help them over the shock of leaving.'

Both *Effie's Burning* and the article just cited deal with older women in institutions for the mentally ill. While institutional abuse of the mentally ill tends to be fairly well publicized and has been one reason contributing to the closure of mental hospitals in Britain, older people with mental illness have been in the same situation as older people with a physical illness. As they do not tend to commit dramatic and media-worthy acts such as climbing into lions' cages or murdering someone when they are released into the community, their needs go unrecognized and many simply transfer to smaller residential or nursing homes, having exchanged a large institution for a smaller one.

In the 1960s Peter Townsend's *The Last Refuge* (1962) and Barbara Robb's *Sans Everything* (1967) exposed institutional abuse. Townsend's text, which pre-dates the gender consciousness of the late 1960s and therefore unselfconsciously reproduces gender stereotypes, concerned the residents' 'loss of occupation, isolation from family, friends and community, difficulty in forming more than tenuous relationships with members of the staff or other residents, loneliness, loss of privacy and identity and collapse of powers of self-determination' (1962: 226) and recommended the closing of old people's homes. He also suggested an increase in sheltered housing (which has happened) and an extension of the hospital system (which has, in fact, declined).

Townsend was clearly not thinking of promoting the hospitals visited by Barbara Robb (1967). Florence Nightingale's dictum that the very first requirement of a hospital is that it should do the sick no harm was constantly violated by the geriatric wards which Robb encountered both in general and in psychiatric hospitals where patients were 'housed in the hospital merely because they [were] old, [had] all their personal possessions removed, including spectacles, deaf-aids and dentures. They [were] given nothing to do and [could] not even read or sew' (1967: 146). Such depersonalization, indeed dehumanization is, according to Hugman, a function of how the care of older people within institutions has come about:

> First, institutional care is provided for those who cannot make other arrangements. It is culturally and socially constructed as a 'last resort', of final choice or of no choice, at all. Second, institutions are focused on the common connection between the residents (their need for care) and not on degrees of individuality which may distinguish them. People are there because they are old. (1994: 128)

Hugman's position is vividly illustrated by a woman living in a nursing home interviewed by Ford and Sinclair (1987) who said: 'I came here about four years ago but I wish I hadn't done so . . . [My son and his wife] said I'd be better looked after, so when it was decided I'd move for good I said I'd come here but I wish I hadn't done' (1987: 33). Catherine Bennett (1994) cites a report by Counsel and Care which states that 'only 36 per cent of older people in residential homes claimed to have made a choice themselves, and 60 per cent had not visited any other home before admission. For nearly two thirds, the choice of a home – the home that is no home – had been taken for them' (1994: 18). Such disempowerment, even prior to admission into a nursing or care home, sets the tone which then dominates the older person's remaining time.

Accounts such as the ones above have been influential in the last twenty-five years in improving the basic living conditions of elders in institutions and much of the outright cruelty has probably gone, but as the situation at Nye Bevan Lodge which came to light in 1987 showed, institutional abuse still occurs. In 'What is Elder Abuse and Neglect?' Glendenning (1993) maintains that about 5 per cent of older people both in Britain and in the USA live in institutional care. He views these people as more at risk of abuse than the 95 per cent living in the community. He offers no references to back up this claim and we found no research into the numbers of older people suffering abuse in residential settings. However, first-person accounts of people living in residential homes and a recent cover story by Catherine Bennett (1994) in *Guardian Weekend* are indicative of the constant infringement of older persons' rights to privacy and dignity which are part of the abusive patterns visible in institutions. Bennett describes visiting several nursing homes for elders and observing what were obviously routine violations of the 1984 'code of practice called Home Life ... published by the DHSS' which 'remains the principal source of guidance on the residential care of the elderly' (Bennett, 1994: 12). These include entering residents' rooms without their permission, giving them no lockable storage space, lack of choice in activity or with whom rooms are to be shared. Ford and Sinclair (1987) report interviewing a ninety-year-old woman about her life in an old people's home. The woman's story typifies the 'batch' treatment meted out to people in institutions. She stated that as part of her everyday routine 'they come and give you a tablet. It's a water tablet [she whispered, and grinned at me and laughed]. I don't need it but you have to take it from them so then I put mine down the sink' (1987: 34). As Helen Jones (1993: 58) puts it: 'Older people, as patients, clients or customers, are considered incapable of making decisions regarding their own health and/or social care, reinforcing a structured dependence. What is more, the range of options for care and/or treatment is dramatically reduced when a person's age is taken into account.' Later during Ford and Sinclair's interview, '[There was a knock at the door and an attendant came in without waiting for a reply. He did not seem to have come in for any particular reason and looked around and went out again.] You see, that's the trouble with this place [she whispered]. Often they don't even knock. I told them not to come in today' (Ford and Sinclair, 1987: 35). The old woman's whispering can be read as an index of her internalization of institutional requirements and her own disempowerment. She clearly did not feel able to protest openly.

In 1993, 855 women and 300 men were in local authority homes in Northamptonshire. Many more than these will live in privately run homes or occupy hospital beds, but no figures are available on this. The gender difference indicated here is consistent throughout all types of residential care. Given that there are nearly three times as many women in residential care as men, older women are likely to be the objects of abuse in such settings. Since 1 April 1993 there has been a decline in the number of people who need public funding entering residential care in the UK because of the new assessment and funding system, undertaken by Social Services departments as part of the community care policies. This is likely to continue until a levelling off occurs when those placed in residential care prior to 1 April 1993 without assessment of their need for such care die. People privately financed will still be able to move into residential care whenever they want to, whether they need it or not. Some homes will close and the end result is likely to be a two-tier system of high-cost private care and cheaper, mixed-economy care paid for by state funding.

In advance of these changes, many hospitals closed long-term geriatric and psycho-geriatric beds. Some decanted whole wards of patients into private homes, many run by former National Health Service staff, as Aitken observed within her county, though as a practice it is not specific to that region. Some existing hospital employees, both doctors and nurses, own or have an interest in privately run residential homes. The National Health Service appears to see nothing unethical in this. The staff, of course, take their institutional attitudes with them to the homes. Writing in the *Nursing Times* in 1986, Liz Day maintained that 'it is very easy for nurses caring for older people, especially in hospitals, to develop a rather jaundiced view of ageing. Exposed to elderly people who are in a state of acute or chronic physical illness, mental incapacity and increasing dependence, it is not surprising that nurses believe all elderly people experience the same decline' (1986: 67).

It is worth pointing out here that while there has been a growing body of research on nurses and their attitudes and experiences of working with elders – presumably because they are 'easily accessible' within institutions – no such research has been carried out on home helps and other semi- or unskilled carers, the vast majority of whom are women. As Northamptonshire was establishing training on elder abuse for home helps in 1995, we considered doing research to find out home helps' knowledge and position on elder abuse. They, after all, are one of the groups likely to detect such abuse. However, it became clear that the research would be difficult to carry out as the home helps were paid on an hourly rate to attend the training sessions, and funding to ask them to stay on and to employ alternative helps to do their job while they were being interviewed was not available. Such economically driven decisions not only reflect the contradictions inherent in the phrase 'paid to care' but also highlight the ways in which women in insecure, hourly paid employment are marginalized.

Hospital Care and Elder Abuse

In the UK in 1989 there were still 73,000 patients over sixty-five years of age in long-stay hospital beds (Tomlin, 1989: 8). This figure had fallen to 59,600 by March 1993 (Waterhouse, 1994: 5). Some argue that there is a need for a small number of beds for these older people whose long-term health needs are such that they have to be met within a hospital. Peter Horrocks, a consultant geriatrician and former Director of the Health Advisory Service (HAS), questions this. At the British Geriatrics Society conference in 1988 he analysed reports on long-stay wards made to the HAS in 1987 which indicated 'passive abuse on a massive scale' (Tomlin, 1989: 11). 'Nursing care,' for instance, 'was provided in "batch" form: patients being fed, washed, toileted, taken to bed and got up in groups, according to the needs of staff' (ibid.: 12). Here we have the enactment of power and control in an institutional setting where the former is an expression of the latter and the two reinforce each other.

The changes in the British National Health Service, which has devolved budget managing from central to local bodies such as hospital trusts and individual GP fund-holders, have meant that care of elders in hospitals is no longer a cost-effective proposition. Hospitals have been quick to realize that fast throughput is one of the most important ways of controlling their budgets. Care of elders is also a strain on GP budgets because of the increased home and surgery visits associated with such care and the higher drug bills elders incur. Economically induced ageism is thus rife in the National Health Service and is structurally underwritten by the ways in which fund-holders are encouraged to manage their budgets. Professor Grimley Evans, Vice-President of the Royal College of Physicians, is reported as saying that 'The NHS was bound up in a culture of ageism that dated back before 1948 to the days of charity hospitals and workhouse sick wards' ('NHS Suffering from "Ageism" ', 1994: 13). As evidence for the ageism inherent in the NHS he cited 'the 40 per cent of coronary care units which imposed an upper age limit on the use of clot-busting drugs – even though trials had demonstrated that more lives were saved by their use among older people'. He further 'blamed "half-baked health economics" for spreading the ethical premise that it was the health service's view, not the customer's, that mattered'. The pervasive ageism which informs the NHS means that wards caring for older people often have fewer qualified and poorly motivated nurses with fewer promotion prospects because geriatrics is not considered an exciting, high-tech area of medicine. This produces a disincentive to work to the best of the patients' interests or the staff's ability. Additionally, hospitals can increase older patients' dependence through the ways in which they infantilize such people both structurally and in their treatment by staff (Hugman, 1994: 125-51).

Abusive Regimes

Passive abuse occurs not only on long-term wards. Luker and Waters (1993) found similar problems in a rehabilitation unit for older people. The unit, as is the case in Northampton, was sited in a former workhouse, an 'appropriate' location, given the history of the emergence of institutions to care for older people (Hugman, 1994: 127–9). This must conjure up awful fears, particularly for older women who in the past were more likely than men to end up in workhouses. In the rehabilitation unit the 'getting-up' process for women began at 6 a.m. at the top end of the ward. Those at the other end, the male patients, were woken an hour later. Did someone make the assumption that women were used to getting up earlier than men after a lifetime of lighting the fire, cooking the breakfast and seeing the children off to school? As well as having to rise too early, other causes of complaint were having to wash in a bowl by the bedside instead of being allowed to go to the bathroom, and being told to sit at the table half an hour before the meal arrived. The researchers made the important point that old people have preconceptions about institutional care. They are easily pleased when they recognize that the workhouse no longer exists. Additionally, old people are less likely to complain, especially about hospitals and doctors, for whom they can have an unhealthy reverence.

The differential power relationship between patients and GPs is magnified in the paternalistic institution of the hospital. And yet, Roberts suggests, 'The power and control aspects of going to see the doctor are rarely recognized as such by either party' (quoted in Sidell, 1992: 90). It is the 'he can call you Jane, but you can't call him Fred' syndrome. Wallen looked at the effect doctors' sexism had on the information process (cited in Sidell, 1992: 180). Women, it appears, ask more questions than men but are given brief and perfunctory answers, while men are more likely to be given a technical answer. When Sidell (1992) conducted a number of life-history interviews, she found that many older women wanted to talk about their experiences of health care. While one woman complained, 'A few weeks ago I went to the Northern and had this here chest X-ray but the doctor don't tell you anything. They should tell you what was written down there, shouldn't they, there was plenty written there' (Sidell, 1992: 183), another felt completely erased by the situation: 'I ain't a person to say anything to doctors.' A man who had been an out-patient in a hospital described the following incident: ' "Mabel", intoned the loudspeaker, twice and then three times. Finally an elderly lady got up looking frightened. She was already worried and her concern was multiplied by the fact that she had never been called "Mabel Robinson" by a stranger for fifty years.' He goes on: 'I felt it was only a short distance to the querulous, demanding and frightened old lady on the ward, provoking irritation in her carers' (Julian-Allen, 1993: 35). While one might be inclined to agree with the implicit critique of how the National Health Service deals with patients, the writer is reinforcing the negative image of older women with his use of an adjective like 'querulous'.

One way of avoiding or delaying the hospitalization or institutionalization of older people which is usually a function of physical and/or mental decline is through preventive care and monitoring. Boult et al. (1993) carried out a study in the USA to assess elders for risk of admission to hospital. Their research was disarmingly frankly motivated by economic considerations: 'The major part of the Medicare's program's expenses for the hospital care of elderly people is incurred by a chronically ill minority (15%–20%) of the elderly population. In the United States, 5% of elderly Medicare enrollees account for 55% of the group's hospital days and for 62% of its hospital expenses' (1993: 811). The study sought to 'find screening criteria that could be used to identify groups of frail elders that, without intervention, would experience frequent health-related crises and consume a disproportionately high level of hospital resources' (ibid.: 815). Among the various interesting findings of this study were that the hospitalization records of females tended to be less likely to be available than those of men (ibid.). Women, it seems, get lost in the system. The factors Boult et al. identified as risk factors for repeated admission were: 'older age, male sex, poor self-rated health, availability of an informal caregiver, having ever had coronary artery disease, and having had, during the previous year, a hospital admission, more than six doctor visits, or diabetes.' This research confirms the relationship between acute health crises in older age and being male.

Well-woman or women's health clinics might have a role to play in health care for older women but in Britain it seems that few have begun to provide a service specifically targeted at older women. In December 1994 we sent out a brief questionnaire asking about health care provision for older women to thirty health and care centres (gleaned from a health promotion directory) who professed to have a direct interest in women's health. Of nine replies, three stated that they had no specific provision for older women while five said they did (one did not fill in the questionnaire but sent an information leaflet). Where specific services for older women existed, these included 'referral knowledge' (i.e. information dissemination on request) but also, interestingly, 'peer health counsellors using retired women' (direct quotation from returned questionnaire) and continence clinics. Concern was expressed by all about the lack of support services for carers and, in one case, concern was expressed about the inappropriateness of available services for Asian women. We did not follow up unanswered questionnaires and therefore cannot say whether the low return rate (30 per cent) reflects the absence of services for older women we suspect, or whether non-response was due to other factors.

Hospitals as institutions are hierarchical and paternalistic. The changes in the National Health Service have done nothing to alter this. They have in the main simply shifted some power from the predominantly male consultants to the predominantly male managers. The gulf between doctor and nurse is as great as ever, and gender plays a significant part in this. Male doctors are in charge, make decisions, give orders and the mostly female nursing staff, although their jobs have become more technical, take the orders and tend to the needs of the patients, performing a traditional female caring role. Most of the other female staff are auxiliaries, the ward maids and the cleaners. In large inner city hospitals (even if cleaning has been contracted out) they are often poorly paid immigrant workers. In *The Diaries of Jane Somers* (1984) Doris Lessing's narrator notices the difference between these women and the porters. The women are tired and frightened 'because their poverty allows them no margin and because they support others. In the wards it is they who slip purses out from handbags, help themselves to a pound here, a few pence there' (1984: 248). She goes on: 'they are kind, too, putting into the hands of some crazed old one a bright red flower'. No one notices them, abused women who also abuse.

Nursing Homes and Residential Homes

Insufficient staff, inadequate equipment, lethal electrical wiring and, finally, media exposure closed a nursing home in Sussex in the early 1990s. Tying old people into bed at night with sheets and putting them in chairs with tables on the front so that they were trapped in them were among the reasons why a private residential home in Northamptonshire was closed. These kinds of occurrences are things that inspectors should check on and relatives rarely discover. Verbal abuse, over-medication, leaving old people for long hours with nothing to do, rough handling, pushing and shoving with bruises that can be explained away are even less easy to observe (although Catherine Bennett, 1994, vividly describes some such incidents which she observed). In a culture where violence and violation are recognized by their visibility, the absence of such visibility prevents engagement with abusive situations. However, even where marks are apparent, these may not necessarily lead to action. Esther Oxford describes the case of an eighty-two-year-old woman, obviously mistreated and possibly sexually abused (indexed by repeated vaginal infections and 'unexplained bruises on her upper legs') by a younger man. Both home helps and social workers were aware of the situation but 'Helpers look on, frustrated and afraid for her. There is little they can do' (Oxford, 1995: 21). The difficulty is that 'There is no coherent legal framework designed to protect old people' (ibid.). Additionally, solutions may not always be straightforward. This may be compounded by the ' "learned helplessness" among the helping professions as a phenomenon which occurs when a systematic lack of resources gives rise to the inability of professionals to meet the needs of [abused] women, resulting in the erosion of hope and initiative among professionals' (Mahoney, 1994: 64).

In Britain there are no overall national guidelines for the inspection of nursing homes (Bennett, 1994: 18). They are registered and inspected by the health authority. Residential homes are inspected by Social Services. Staff in homes are usually poorly paid, untrained women and there is a high turnover. Many genuinely care but there is little incentive to provide a high-quality service. Relatives and staff members rarely report bad practice. Relatives may feel guilty about not doing the caring themselves, especially if, as Finch and Mason (1993: 105) suggest, they take the view that 'relationships between parents and children *are* founded on a sense of obligation'. Relatives may also have nothing to judge standards by. Staff are not prepared to whistle-blow because they need their jobs and stand to lose them if homes are closed down as the result of a complaint. Insecurity of employment can breed silence. When a private home in Northampton had its registration withdrawn, Social Services were amazed at the wide discrepancy of comments from relatives concerning the care their older relations had received. This is less likely to be the result of different treatment of individual residents than of diverse expectations regarding standards of treatment and lack of knowledge of what constitutes good care among the relatives (Bennett, 1994: 14, 18).

In a letter to *Care of the Elderly* (September 1991), Ruth Chambers, a GP, detailed a typical example of neglect which had gone unreported. A female resident in a nursing home was left alone with a hot drink in a cup and saucer rather than being supervised with a feeder cup. The drink was spilt on her leg. Left untreated, an ulcer developed. This was then left covered for three days without treatment and became infected. The GP was called and left a prescription which was not collected until the following day. Septicaemia and gangrene developed and the resident died. Inadequate care by untrained, overstretched staff went unreported by the GP and by relatives.

The problem of abuse is not confined to the private sector. One of the worst scandals in recent years occurred at a local authority home, the Nye Bevan Lodge in Southwark. The report (Gibbs et al., 1987) spoke of care that was abysmal and in some instances amounted to cruelty, with vindictive and punitive measures taken against the incontinent. Staff refused to talk to residents because 'if you talk to them, you'll get mad like them'. This is an interesting comment as it points to the fear of identification with the abused (object) which was discussed earlier in this chapter. Some residents believed they had to pay for services like bathing (Tomlin, 1989: 11). A sub-culture within the care profession was identified which was characterized by unacceptable behaviour by staff having become the norm. Various factors had contributed to this. One of these was the staff–resident ratio; in a home where there are too few staff – particularly in a large one, and Nye Bevan Lodge had ninety residents – staff may establish unacceptable and fixed routines in order to get jobs done. Additionally, poor line management can prevent problems from coming to light. The ultimate victims were the residents.

In 1988 the Wagner report reviewed residential care in England and Wales, and recommended improved training and status for staff. It suggested an automatic right to privacy for residents, involvement in decision making, financial autonomy and overall independent inspections of homes. Many of these recommendations were implemented, so why does abuse still occur?

There is a lack of control over the activities of the independent sector (Carrington, 1993), and many local authorities in Britain were enabled to transfer their own homes to independent trusts by the NHS and Community Care Act 1989. This could be seen as a callous disregard of the rights and wishes of older people and an example of institutional abuse. The inspection units of both the health authority and Social Service departments are often overstretched, and although they can close a home, the action taken by courts and professional bodies against workers found guilty of abuse is indicative of the low regard accorded older people. For instance Dumfries and Galloway Social Services Department managers were found to be complacent and inept in failing to identify and rectify the brutal regime of a matron at a residential home over a twenty-year period. She was found unfit to plead at her trial on thirty-one charges of cruelty. Despite the recommendations of the enquiry, the home was not closed by the local authorities ('S.W.D. Found Guilty',1993: 2).

A local newspaper in Northampton reported in June 1992 that a nurse manager who ran a private home 'roughly dragged a senile seventy year old woman, yanking off her underwear, calling her a "filthy pig" and slapped her' ('Bully Nurse Escapes Ban', 1992: 4). Similarly, when 'an eighty year old man with heart disease collapsed in a lift, she dragged and kicked him to his room'. This story did not hit the national newspapers. It transpired that previously (in 1987) the nurse had been convicted of common assault but it then took five years before her case came before the Nurses Professional Conduct Committee. The nurse was found guilty of misconduct but her name was not struck off the nurses' register (Anon., *Northampton Chronicle and Echo*, 6 June 1992).

Here the identification with the perpetrator of violence enabled the repetition of that behaviour to occur and failed to protect future victims. The nurse's solicitor argued that 'she suffered extreme duress from her violent and tortuous marriage'; again, the story of the abused abusing. The old man in the case was also reported to be 'difficult and cantankerous'. The nurse's victimization by her husband was used in this instance to explain her abuse of others. On one level, this (reassuringly) reduced her behaviour to the level of the unfortunate individual who reacts in response to her own violation. She is thus cast, as women often are, as a 'victim', an object, who did not intentionally commit abuse but responded to being abused. This affirms dominant stereotypes of femininity, thus retrieving the status quo of gender roles threatened by her behaviour. The containment of her having been abused within the domestic sphere, i.e. her marriage, suggests not only an 'accepted' pattern of inter-gender violence but also indicates the boundaries of the abusive scenario: someone else's home.

This case clearly raises the issue of two-sided violence which is frequently voiced by professional associations as an issue for their staff. Peter Giancola and Amos Zeichner's critical review of 'Aggressive Behavior in the Elderly' (1993) sought to provide an overview of rates (apparently ranging from 7 to 91 per cent) and definitions of aggressive behaviour, and modes of intervention because as 'many nursing homes and similar institutions will have to absorb an increasing number of elderly patients . . . the implications of caring for large numbers of aggressive elderly individuals are cause for additional concern' (1993: 3–4). The varieties of aggressive behaviours which these authors list include agitated behaviour such as 'talking too loud, refusing to eat or take medication, refusing to follow directions, urinating where inappropriate' as well as 'screaming, spitting, purposeful falling, cursing etc.' (ibid.: 4–5). It is very difficult to know what to make of these categories, many of which can be read as offering resistance to being regimented within an institution and many of which in fact seem to reflect the institutional desire to regiment. The authors rightly say that 'these types of behaviors may be the only manner in which many older individuals can express their anger, frustration, or hostility' (ibid.). At the same time the authors of the article focus extensively on neurophysiological causes of aggression and, having extendedly discussed drug use (much of which amounts to sedation) in containing aggression among older people, they detail a behaviour modification programme which had good results (and no chemically induced side effects) but conclude:

> At the moment, pharmacotherapy is the most frequently employed form of treatment for the aggressive elderly. Although nonpharmacological treatments have been found to be quite effective, considering the projected increase in the elderly population, the use of such treatments may become extremely laborious. (Giancola and Zeichner, 1993: 17)

The last phrase is, of course, a euphemism for 'not cost effective'.

The Royal College of Nursing Annual Conference of 1992 considered issuing advice on circumstances in which a nurse can refuse to treat a patient who may be offensive or violent; at present they do not have that right other than in relation to previously registered conscientious objections to matters such as abortion or the administration of electro-convulsive therapy. However, the *Patient's Charter* allows the patient the right to choose not to be treated by a particular nurse (Brindle, 1992: 2). Violence in patients may be a problem for nurses (Biggs et al., 1995: 87), particularly with patients suffering from Alzheimer's disease, and violent acts from an older person can incite violence in the abuser.

At present, residential homes tend to be more concerned about caring for the resident with dementia who may wander off rather than about coping with potential violence. Allowing older people to take risks without endangering their safety is a recurrent issue in residential care. Staff can easily resort to a defensive form of practice which regards locking residents into chairs with an incontinence pad inside every pair of pants as safer than encouraging them to move about, take initiatives and risk accidents. Balanced decision-making is hampered by the paternalistic ethos that pervades residential care. Staff, especially managers, feel accidents are to be avoided at all costs, as is adverse publicity, for fear of litigation for negligence and the coroner's court. When a unit has residents with varying needs and abilities, a policy which protects the most vulnerable will restrict the most able. Locked doors, chairs that residents cannot get out of without help, sedation, observation by video camera and monitors are all now considered abusive. Staff are encouraged to allow older people to take risks but some elders have chosen residential care because of fear for their safety if they live alone. However, residential homes are, of course, not always safe from violation from outside; every so often there are reports that an older woman has been murdered by an intruder or that, as happened in a home in Northampton, care staff were tied up while intruders ransacked rooms. Offering residents a dull, contained existence can often seem the safest option.

The reality of residents' rights and the right to take risks were described in a report by the charity Counsel and Care entitled *What If They Hurt Themselves?* (Smith, 1992). The report made clear that while physical restraints are being phased out, electronic tagging is sometimes used. The association of this practice with criminals and with animals makes its use for older people very demeaning, and tagging without consent could be considered 'tantamount to assault or illegal imprisonment' (Counsel and Care, 1993: 2). One attraction of this practice for residential home owners lies in the possibility of economies of scale in staff numbers.

Policing or Protection? Sexuality among Elders

All residents in Northamptonshire local authority homes have keys to lock the doors to their rooms in recognition of their right to privacy. This is not invariably the case elsewhere (Bennett, 1994). One arena in which privacy is an issue is that of sexuality. In Western society sexual activity of elders is recognized only in the instance of an older man having a sexual relationship with a younger woman. Intra-generational sex between older people is taboo, and there is relatively little knowledge of older people's sexuality. Typically, sexual activity is rarely raised as an issue in the case of elders. If it is considered at all, it is thought amusing or touching; and staff may make comments such as 'well, we only have two male residents'. In other words, sexual activity among elders is either belittled or dismissed. Staff and relatives are often horrified at the thought of relationships developing among older people, whether heterosexual or homosexual, and Lynda Aitken has had some difficulty in trying to get her colleagues to consider HIV/AIDS as an issue for elders.

In 'No Sex Please, We Live in an Old People's Home' (1992) Helen Frank describes an older couple's experience of developing a relationship in a residential home where there was nowhere for them to be alone. They were found in the hall, away from other residents, with his hand inside her dress. There was uproar: the staff were blamed for not 'protecting' the woman, who was called 'common'; the man was called 'a dirty old man' and quite enjoyed his 'enhanced reputation'. The couple were treated like naughty children. The woman never had the courage to go into the lounge and sit with the other residents again. In this case an immediate assumption was made by the staff about a gendered power structure operating between the couple which cast the male as subject and perpetrator and the woman as object and victim of abuse. While this may well reflect a common situation in sexual abuse scenarios, it does not allow for the possibility of consensual sexual activity between the couple. The notion that we live in a culture which systematically privileges those who act over victims was reinforced in this instance by the woman's response to the couple's being discovered – she bore a sense of shame, having become the outsider because of how she had supposedly allowed herself to be treated. This is very familiar from rape scenarios where the victim, whether it be a man or a woman – and more usually it is a woman – is ostracized and feels shame as the result of having been the victim of violation.

Aitken has been asked about the issue of sexual activity between residents where one is confused, and whether or not we are then dealing with a case of abuse because 'she cannot possibly know what is going on'. The first thing to note is, once again, the reproduction of gender stereotypes in this example: it is assumed that the woman will be the victim of a situation where *she* rather than he is confused. In Aitken's view this kind of question frequently masks the staff's anxiety about sex, which prevents them from acknowledging the needs of older people.

There appears to be little written in English about abuse in residential settings in other countries (though see Hugman, 1994). One exception is the account of a set of horrifying murders which occurred in Germany in the second half of the 1980s. The murders were explained in terms of the needs of the carers to be loved and feared, combined with elders taking over the symbolic function of parents, who are then punished for having rejected the 'children' in childhood (Diessenbacher, 1989: 66). This reinforces an idea gleaned from psychoanalysis, that adult relationships constitute a replay of parent–child relationships, a view attacked by Kappeler (1995) because it assumes an inevitability about such interactions, which reduces individuals' responsibility for their behaviour and casts adults endlessly in the position of victims of their past.

The kinds of 'punishment' meted out by abusers to their victims can take a variety of forms, one of which may ultimately be euthanasia. A survey in Holland in 1987 showed that 63 per cent of residents in old people's homes feared that their lives would be taken without their consent (Stammers, 1992). As 1,030 cases of non-voluntary euthanasia were reported in Holland in 1991, their fears may in some respects be justified (Stammers, 1992: 290). However, a recent report in the *Guardian* (Brindle, 1994: 3) stated that 'more than 90 p[er] c[ent] of pensioners in [a] poll back voluntary euthanasia'. The poll was 'carried out by *Yours*, a pensioners' magazine, among 2,500 readers with an average age of 69' (ibid.). Interestingly, 'Eighty-nine per cent [of respondents] believe[d] mercy killing already goes on unofficially' (ibid.). This should be considered in a context where a man like Jacques Attali, President of the European Bank for Reconstruction and Development, has been quoted as saying: 'As soon as he goes beyond 60–65 years of age, man lives longer than his capacity to produce, and he then costs society a lot of money. Euthanasia will become one of the essential instruments of our future societies' (Twycross, 1992: 25). Euthanasia as a capitalist form of population control is an outrageous proposition, but the rather more complex issue of its use in cases where people's quality of life is severely diminished due to incurable, progressive illness is another matter and is the subject of continued debate both in the UK and elsewhere.

The British policy of community care means that more elders living at home will have to rely on domiciliary care. Council-employed home helps' work has changed from providing a cleaning job to doing personal care tasks. These jobs are usually low paid and part-time, and as in nursing and residential homes, the workforce is almost entirely female. Older male clients cannot be given a choice of the gender of their carer, for example. As the same applies to staff in residential homes there is no easy way of changing gendered caring roles. While local authorities take up references and carry out police checks on their employees, private domiciliary care agencies in Britain do not have to do so. Indeed, the British government has recently refused a request from the Association of Directors of Social

Services (ADSS) and the UK Home Care Association for the compulsory registration and inspection of all private home care agencies (Cervi, 1993: 2). Thus a reputable private agency recruited Claire Bastow, who is now serving life for murdering a disabled woman (Francis, 1993c). Bastow provided references and had no criminal record so a police check would have revealed none. The fact that she was on bail at the time she committed the murder would not have shown up on the kind of check done by the police for local authorities. Reputable agencies are planning to adhere to guidelines set up on a voluntary basis, but cowboy firms keen to make a quick profit from older people will ignore them.

The National Health Service and local authorities consistently fail to identify abuse. In 1993 the *Health Service Journal* reported that among 533 people placed in private residential and nursing homes by a 'homefinder service' at Charing Cross Hospital, no abuse had been found. This was asserted although 3.4 per cent of the patients had moved, and at least one elderly man was 'unkempt and scruffy and unhappy' (Miskelly, 1993: 30). The writers had reached their conclusions by monitoring the reports of the people who had made the placements, without seeking independent verification or, indeed, asking the views of those who had been placed in these homes.

Older people in residential care, who are mostly women, must be empowered to reflect on their experience and if necessary be helped to complain rather than accept what is meted out to them. Advocacy and mediation by a third party could be an important tool for both residents and staff, but this would not work without a basic culture shift in many homes to empower residents to set the agenda. Case management in the context of providing enhanced home care has been one means by which services have sought to improve and safeguard the interests of older people (Challis et al., 1993; Dant and Gearing, 1993). Such management seems to have proved quite effective in improving elders' living conditions and support structures. One advantage of such provision for institutional contexts would be the possibility of an older woman suffering from abuse having a third, independent party to report it to. Case managers might also keep a supportive eye on staff in institutional settings. What is clearly needed is a review of how issues of gender inform elder abuse in institutional environments. The tendency to reduce reported instances of abuse to individual cases, complete with explanations which reinforce the idea of the uniqueness of the occurrence and its intelligibility within dominant discourses of gender and power, has resulted in an unwillingness to address gender issues in institutional settings critically and constructively.

Conclusions

We live in a culture which endorses violence as everyday behaviour to such an extent that everyday violence becomes invisible. We also live in a society which promotes agency rather than dependence, with the consequence that those who act as subjects – the perpetrators of abuse – are identified with rather than their victims, the objects of such abuse. The extent of the expectation of such an identification was made clear in Bennett's (1994) report detailed above in which one matron obviously did not feel in the least compromised by how she was treating an older woman in her care in front of a third person who supposedly was contemplating putting one of her older relations into that home. In consequence, little is done when elder abuse in institutional settings occurs. This inaction is associated with the fact that both workers and clients in institutions for elders suffer from low social and economic status which 'legitimizes' the neglect of both groups. We have yet to acknowledge properly that

- the vast majority of workers and clients in institutions for elders are women;
- institutionally based elder abuse is predominantly of women by women;
- these women are socially and economically disempowered;
- there are power differences between female workers and female clients by virtue of their respective intra-institutional in/ability to determine their daily lives;
- institutions for elders foster abuse through a variety of direct and indirect means, including the regimes and hierarchization which exist within them;
- an uneasy relation exists between the policing and the protection of elders, with a tendency to emphasize the former at the expense of the latter, with the former often itself being abusive;
- a sustained investigation of the kinds of abuse that occur under these conditions needs to be instigated which moves beyond the consideration of physical abuse alone;
- workers may not know how to identify abuse or deal with it when they encounter it;
- the government has little incentive to investigate elder abuse in institutional settings as it relies on these settings to implement its funds-starved policies.

Who Cares? A Gendered View of Care and Elder Abuse in Domestic Settings

I haven't been away for years. I once let him go to Woodlands but not again. My sons said it wasn't doing their dad any good being there. (Family Policy Studies Centre, 1984: 9)

You see neighbours shy away because of this incontinence. They're frightened. No-one will sit with grandma. Never. (Kohner, 1988: 44)

All my life I've been close to my dad and I've been able to say anything to him, and now suddenly I don't know what to say any more and it's like the illness has got between us. I can't be 'normal' with him and sometimes I know I treat him like a baby and it's wrong. (Kohner, 1988: 106)

Who Cares?

It has frequently been suggested that elder abuse tends to happen within the context of a caring relationship (though see Pillemer, 1994 and the conclusion to this volume). Any consideration of elder abuse therefore needs to take account of the caring context in which it occurs. While the previous chapter explored this phenomenon in an institutional setting where the carers are in a professional, formal, remunerated relationship with the older person, this chapter will focus on the significance of gender in elder abuse as it manifests itself in an informal caring relationship within domestic settings.

The term 'carer' has come into regular and popular use only in the last decade. It has become part of the language which inhabits political arenas, arising from the Thatcherite notion of a return to old-fashioned values, with the family (for 'family' read 'female') having responsibility for its members. This is considered politically neces-sary in the face of the rapid growth of residential care, the ageing population, and the budget deficit which governments are seeking to control through cuts in spending. The term, like the phrase 'elder abuse', masks the gender specificity which informs informal care situations and, indeed, elder abuse occurring in a domestic context.

The quotations at the head of this chapter are indicative of how a very large proportion of the literature on domestic elder abuse deals with that issue, namely by focusing on the problems encountered by the carer in care-giving situations. We still have very little sense of the victim's or survivor's view or position, though some research on this is currently being conducted by Hazel Morbey in Bristol. Those abused tend to be treated as secondary. This in part reflects the point we argued in the previous chapter: that we live in a society which encourages identification with the subject rather than the object of violence, the perpetrator rather than the victim. It is also a function of the desire to establish causes for abusive behaviour in the hope that understanding what motivates such behaviour may enable its identification, prevention and/or intervention/treatment. The idea is, most commonly, to help the carer, with the expectation that the cared-for will derive secondary benefits, i.e. that the abuse will stop.

In this context, Grafstrom et al.'s (1993) follow-up study of 'caregivers [of demented older people] who had previously reported abuse' in domestic settings is of interest. The study was conducted two years after abuse had been reported. It is not clear what intervention had taken place since that time, nor is it possible from the study to establish the nature of the original abuse. But: 'Age of demented persons ranged from 79 to 91 years (median = 84) and age of the family members ranged from 36 to 91 (median = 74). Relatives consisted of two husbands and five wives, one son, four daughters and one grandchild' (1993: 1748). While it is impossible to ascertain the gender of the abused, at least 69 per cent of the former abusers (five wives, four daughters) were women. The study does not comment on this fact. It focuses instead on its finding that no further abuse was reported and suggests that the period of the onset of dementia is the most difficult time for caring relatives and therefore the phase when they need most support to prevent abuse from occurring. We shall return to the issue of dementia and abuse but for the moment, we want to re-emphasize the point that work on elder abuse tends to focus predominantly on the carers as the subjects of abuse and what needs to be done for them rather than on elders as victims of abuse. In the current economic and political climate, carers – because they constitute a resource, a 'positive asset' – are more important than the cared for. As Jill Pitkeathley, Director of the Carers' National Association, put it: 'Professionals like community nurses need to remember that the carers themselves are our most important resource' (Sadler, 1990: 21). The resource issue is crucial here. We 'invest' in what we expect to derive 'benefits' from and carers are regarded as being of greater benefit to society than the elders they care for. This of course obscures the fact that many carers are themselves older (Steinmetz, 1983). Further, the term 'carer' obscures the gender specificity of that role both in terms of expectations raised of *who* will care and in terms of *what* that person is expected to do.

Dealing with elder abuse in domestic settings is still a relatively new phenomenon. In consequence, research that is done in this area works from comparisons with other kinds of abusive situations such as, for example, child abuse (Penhale, 1993a). The problem with this kind of approach is, of course, that it can encourage reproduction of the stereotypes and particularities which inform those other abusive situations and, while there will be common denominators, there are also major differences. Importantly, for the context of this study, there is a need to move beyond the silence which informs the gender issues involved in domestic elder abuse on the one hand, and the gender stereotyping which implicitly and explicitly characterizes discussions of that abuse on the other. In a society where only what is visible and nameable is recognized, making gender issues visible and nameable is crucial to dealing with domestic elder abuse.

Informal carers do not form a homogeneous group. They can be of any age, either sex, related by blood and/or legal relationships, close friends or neighbours. Many people who clearly are carers do not regard themselves as such because they care within the context of 'for better or worse, richer or poorer' or as parents or children. This is significant because it reinforces the idea of a division between a private and a public practice, the former 'contracted' through the specificity of a socio-affective relationship which places it outside the idea of a necessary external intervention, the latter established through statutory regulation, a seemingly 'artificial' relationship where the first is constructed as part of the 'natural' ties, obligations and duties among people related to each other (Finch and Mason, 1993).

Caring Daughters

Much of the early work on elder abuse (e.g. Eastman, 1984; Steinmetz, 1983) focused on a specific group of carers – middle-aged daughters. We have already discussed how the way in which Eastman collected his data skewed the image of the carer derived from it and thus constructed a picture of an abuser of older people as a harassed married woman in her thirties or forties at home, with family commitments, losing her restraint under trying circumstances: 'When I am busy Dad always wants something from the shops, you cannot reason with him that an hour won't make any difference, he gets his jacket and says if you cant be bothered I'll go by myself. How can you let someone of 83 do that, the roads are busy, I end up with tears streaming down my face going bananas and thinking maybe if I let him go someone will run him and his wheelchair over' (Eastman, 1984: 55). This woman offered a sustained narrative of continuous power struggles with her older father, resulting in recurrent fantasies of harming or killing him. The implication of the text as a whole was that (a) this woman was severely provoked by her father's trying behaviour; (b) such provocation could, justifiably, result in fantasies of violation; (c) it would probably not be a very large step from thinking about harming the old man to doing it; and (d) if this happened it would hardly be surprising. In other words, the woman was implicitly exonerated by the conditions under which she was expected to care and, more importantly here, by the truculence and difficulty of the father for whom she cared. There was also something interesting about Eastman's reproduction of this and other narratives by caring women, apparently verbatim. This specific letter to him is full of colloquialisms and grammatical infelicities, representing a written version of an oral narrative, the effort of someone who is articulate but not very highly educated. It has little punctuation so that the overall effect is one of a verbally uncontrolled effusion, reinforcing the idea of the slightly hysterical, 'on-the-edge' woman producing a stream-of-consciousness narrative with the breathlessness one might associate with someone at the end of their tether.

While Eastman's research produced middle-aged married women, often caring for older fathers, Steinmetz found that in her sample 'the overwhelming majority of caregivers (90%) were women. Likewise, they comprised the overwhelming majority of vulnerable elders (more than 82%)' (1983: 141). Additionally, and in contrast to Eastman, in Steinmetz's sample 'the caregivers are often elderly themselves (by the standard definition of 60 or older)' (ibid.). This latter finding has been confirmed by Hancock et al.'s (1995) *Hidden Carers* report. The implication that in many cases of domestic elder abuse we are dealing with women abusing women, indeed possibly older women abusing older women, has, however, not been overtly acknowledged or investigated as a gendered phenomenon. It is as if the gender of the people involved were invisible.

Rethinking Who Cares: The Northamptonshire Study

Since the 1970s and early 1980s there has been more research into domestic elder abuse which has changed the picture of the potential abuser as detailed above. According to Hancock and Jarvis (1994: 3), 'Analysis of large-scale survey data has identified three groups of people heavily involved in the care of elderly people – married women under retirement age, single adult children, and elderly spouse carers.' Only the first of these three groups identifies a gendered constituency. We would suggest that this is a hangover from the early days on elder abuse when that group was pinpointed as the one most likely to abuse.

Although numerous attempts at defining elder abuse have been undertaken (e.g. McCreadie, 1994; Bennett and Kingston, 1993; Glendenning, 1993) and we now have a number of categories such as physical, sexual, emotional, psychological and material abuse to delineate the kinds of mistreatment to which elders may be exposed, few attempts have been made to look at the relationship between the kinds of abuse indulged in, the gender of the abused and the gender of the abuser. One of the relatively rare studies of this kind is a hitherto unpublished one conducted by a multi-agency group working on guidelines to deal with cases of elder abuse in Northamptonshire in 1991–2, which we referred to in Chapter 2. For this study responses were solicited from a variety of professionals including district nurses, community psychiatric nurses, day centre workers and managers of social work staff who were asked to report on cases of abuse already known or suspected in their caseloads between November 1991 and October 1992. Ninety-one cases were reported on. Asked to identify other professionals who had been involved in their cases, the participants almost all identified social workers. In order to avoid over-reporting it was decided to focus on the social workers' reports for this study.

The study did not involve gathering information from elders themselves and might therefore, *inter alia*, be criticized on the grounds that it was a survey of professionals (Pillemer, 1994; Phillipson, 1992) but it has to be seen in its historical context: in the early 1990s when this study was conducted awareness of elder abuse among professionals and the general public was relatively low in the UK. Part of the justification for the need to establish guidelines in relation to elder abuse was the presentation of data which indicated prevalence of such abuse. That was one of the purposes which this study served. Additionally, it was intended to raise awareness among professionals about elder abuse.

Correlating Abuser, Abuse and Abused: The Plight of Men

Northamptonshire's study produced a detailed analysis of who abused whom and in what ways. The findings also distinguish between abused males and abused females. Regarding the former the study found men to be physically abused, as detailed in Table 5.1.

In three out of four cases where the wife abused her husband, he was suffering from severe dementia. (We return to this issue on

Table 5.1   *Men who were physically abused*

Age			
70s	80s	90s	
2	4	1	
Abuser			
Wife	Son	Daughter	Other (1 neighbour; 1
4	1	0	stepson)
Suffering from dementia			
None	Mild	Moderate	Severe
3	1	0	3

Source: Unpublished report on elder abuse, Northamptonshire County Council Social Services Department, 1992

pp. 123–5.) In the case where the son was the abuser the man also suffered from mild dementia. Dementia featured less prominently in the cases of men being psychologically abused (Table 5.2) but, again, female relatives outnumbered male relatives as abusers, with wives constituting the majority of abusers.

Where men were neglected (Table 5.3), this seems to have been self-inflicted except in the case of the man in his fifties who was suffering from dementia and was neglected by his wife.

Financial abuse of men (Table 5.4) seemed to involve non-relatives not living with the abused to a considerable degree (50 per cent).

Overall in this study, twenty-five men were abused, fourteen of whom suffered from dementia. In twelve cases the wife was the abuser and in eight the men were abused by someone who was not a close family member. Nothing can be said about the gender of those persons as this was not identifiable from the questionnaires. Eleven of the men who were abused were in their seventies and ten in their

Table 5.2   *Men who were psychologically abused*

Age			
70s	80s	90s	
7	4	0	
Abuser			
Wife	Son	Daughter	Other
5	2	0	(1 no relative; 2 granddaughters; 1 sister)
Suffering from dementia			
None	Mild	Moderate	Severe
6	3	0	2

Source: As Table 5.1

Table 5.3   *Men who were neglected*

Age				
50s	60s	70s	80s	90s
1	0	1	1	0
Abuser				
Wife	Son	Daughter		Other
1	0	0		0
Suffering from dementia				
None	Mild	Moderate		Severe
1	1	1		0

Source: As Table 5.1

eighties. In comparison to the abused women in this study men were generally slightly younger than women who experienced similar abuse. At the same time vulnerability clearly increased with age, with men more likely to become the objects of abuse once they reach their seventies and eighties.

It is interesting to note that no sexual abuse of men was reported, perhaps because of the taboo that informs sexuality in general. As Joy Francis (1993b: 19) put it: 'Many elderly people are still strongly influenced by the values of their youth when sex was not discussed openly.' Disclosure may also 'be at odds with abused people's instinct to protect their families' and, according to Sile Burns, a Sheffield social worker, 'elderly people are more reluctant to disclose than children because they do not want to be placed in residential care' (ibid.). It is certainly the case that older men are occasionally the objects of sexual abuse. Neate quotes Jacki Pritchard of Sheffield Social Services Department as saying: 'I'm aware there are a lot of gay men who are abused by young men financially, and I think they

Table 5.4   *Men who were financially abused*

Age			
70s	80s	90s	
1	1	2	
Abuser			
Son	Daughter	No relative	
1	1	2	
Suffering from dementia			
None	Mild	Moderate	Severe
1	2	0	1

Source: As Table 5.1

may be raped as well' (Neate, 1993: 19). Sexual abuse of older men must not be regarded as specific to homosexual circles, though. Recent reports of rapes of males suggest that these are frequently committed by heterosexual men who see raping a man as a specific form of humiliation.

Correlating Abuser, Abuse and Abused: The Plight of Women

As regards the physical abuse of women detailed in the North-amptonshire study (see Table 5.5), thirty-four women in total suffered this kind of abuse. Twenty-four of these (70 per cent) suffered from dementia. Sons were the most frequent abusers, followed by husbands. In eight of the eleven cases where sons abused and in eight of the nine cases where husbands abused, the mothers/wives suffered from dementia. In four out of seven reported cases of daughters abusing mothers, the latter suffered from dementia. The majority of abused women were in their eighties and in twenty-eight cases abuser and abused lived together. Physical abuse by men of women accounted for at least twenty-two out of thirty-four cases (65 per cent of reported cases), with no possibility of finding out the gender of three of the four non-relatives who abused.

The number of reported cases of psychological abuse of women (Table 5.6) was smaller than that of physical abuse, possibly suggesting the greater difficulty of detecting abuse which may leave no obvious marks.

As in the case of physical abuse of women, the most likely abuser was a son but dementia appeared to be less of a feature. In only five

Table 5.5 *Women who were physically abused*

Age				
60s	70s	80s	90s	Unknown
1	13	16	3	1
Abuser				
Husband	Son	Daughter	Other	Unknown
9	11	7	(2 granddaughter; 1 nephew; 4 no relative)	1
Suffering from dementia				
None	Mild	Moderate		Severe
10	10	9		5

Source: As Table 5.1

Table 5.6 *Women who were psychologically abused*

Age				
60s	70s	80s	90s	Unknown
2	5	6	0	0

Abuser			
Husband	Son	Daughter	Other
2	5	2	(2 sister; 1 son-in-law; 1 no relative)

Suffering from dementia			
None	Mild	Moderate	Severe
7	2	2	2

Source: As Table 5.1

out of thirteen cases did the abused and abuser live together. This suggests that cohabitation is more likely to foster physical violence than some of the other forms of abuse.

Men were more likely to abuse women financially than women (Table 5.7). As with men who were financially abused, non-relatives featured more prominently than in physical abuse, for example. Of the fifteen women who were financially abused, nine had dementia and one was reported as suffering from mental illness. Women in their eighties appeared to be most prone to this kind of abuse.

The two cases of neglected women which were reported (Table 5.8) concerned women in their eighties who were neglected by their husbands. Both women suffered from moderate dementia.

Overall, women were reported as suffering more from physical than any other kind of abuse (Table 5.9). This may be a result of the easier detectability of physical abuse. The women in this sample were

Table 5.7 *Women who were financially abused*

Age			
70s	80s	90s	Unknown
5	8	1	1

Abuser		
Son	Daughter	Other
4	2	(1 sister; 1 nephew; 1 grandson; 6 no relatives)

Suffering from dementia				
None	Mild	Moderate	Severe	Mental illness
5	4	4	1	1

Source: As Table 5.1

Table 5.8   *Women who were neglected*

Age	Abuser	Suffering from dementia
80s	Husband	Moderate
2	2	2

Source: As Table 5.1

Table 5.9   *Total number of abused women and their abusers*

Type of abuse/r	Husband	Son	Daughter	Other	Total
Physical	9	11	7	7	34
Psychological	2	5	2	4	13
Financial	0	4	2	9	15
Neglect	2	0	0	0	2
Sexual	0	1	0	0	1
Total	13	21	11	20	65

Source: As Table 5.1

abused more by their sons than by any other relatives, and most women who were thus abused lived with their sons at the time of the abuse. This includes the woman who was sexually abused by her son and who also suffered from moderate dementia.

These findings correlate with those of Arber and Ginn (1990) who found that a marked gender difference exists between care for older people living in the same household *with* the carer and care when the carer lives elsewhere. Twice as many women as men care for people living outside their household (Arber and Ginn, 1990: 449). Men care for their spouses, and probably have little choice while sharing the same household, but tend not to take on responsibility for people living elsewhere. While the reference here is to spouses, it can be extended to sons. An interesting, and contrasting, picture can be found in Pat Barker's novel *The Century's Daughter* (1986) in which a male social worker's care for an older woman living by herself is contrasted with his relationship with his older parents whom he has difficulty in going to see.

Issues of Multiple Abuse in Domestic Settings

The Northamptonshire study made clear that, contrary to the impression one might get from the data analyses above, many of the people who were abused suffered multiple forms of abuse. Table 5.10 shows the types of abuse reported by the social workers. This table indicates that in many cases abuse across at least two categories occurred. While it has to be remembered that it can be difficult to place abuse

Table 5.10   *Multiple abuse – Northamptonshire study*

Physical abuse only	6
Physical abuse with other types of abuse	16
Total number of cases where physical abuse featured	42
Psychological abuse only	20
Psychological abuse with physical abuse	11
Psychological abuse with other types of abuse	3
Total number of cases where psychological abuse featured	28
Financial abuse only	18
Financial abuse with physical abuse	4
Financial abuse with other types of abuse	6
Total number of cases where financial abuse featured	28
Neglect only	5
Neglect with physical abuse	4
Neglect with other types of abuse	3
Total number of cases where neglect featured	12
Abuse of medication with other types of abuse	2
Sexual abuse	1
Multiple abuse over more than three categories	5
Total number of reported cases	91

Source: As Table 5.1

in one particular category, it is also obvious that one type of abuse, especially physical abuse, may go together with others, possibly because once the inhibitions to abuse *per se* have been lost, it may seem less heinous to the perpetrator to commit multiple types of abuse. It may also be that certain kinds of abuse situations which involve, for instance, physical abuse may be part of a whole complex of interactions whereby the abused person is, for example, shouted at and pushed to make her compliant, and then has money taken from her, or medication given, or she is sent to bed as part of a more generalized pattern of interaction designed to maximize control over her.

Conclusions from the Northamptonshire Study

The six general conclusions on ninety-one cases of abuse in the Northamptonshire study were:

1. Most of the abused were female and in their eighties (see Tables 5.11 and 5.12).
2. The abuser was most frequently male, with sons being reported most often.
3. At the time of the abuse the abused and abuser lived together.
4. Physical abuse was most commonly reported.

Table 5.11   *Gender of people abused*

Females	Males	Unknown
65	25	1

Source: As Table 5.1

Table 5.12   *Age of people abused*

50s	60s	70s	80s	90s	Unknown
1	3	34	44	6	3

Source: As Table 5.1

Table 5.13   *Number of people reported as suffering from dementia*

Mild	Moderate	Severe
23	19	14

Source: As Table 5.1

5. Two-thirds of the cases featured dementia (see Table 5.13).
6. Social Services were reported as being involved in almost all cases identified by professionals in other agencies (e.g. health professionals).

It is interesting to note that in this study most abusers were male, indeed sons. This confirms findings of another research project by Malcolm Holt, specifically on sexual abuse of elders, where 'The ratio of female to male victims [was] six to one' (Neate, 1993: 18). In the first ninety cases Holt collected, only two abusers were female. Further, 'only 11 of the 77 women in the first 90 victims were abused by husbands, whereas 43 were abused by their sons. Sons-in-law, brothers and grandsons were also among the abusers' (ibid.). Again, the point needs to be made that while there is an increasing recognition that males are likely to be abusers of older women in domestic settings there has been little research or theoretical analysis of this phenomenon. Current research would suggest that sexual abuse of elders, specifically of older women, is carried out by male relatives and frequently by sons. As Jacki Pritchard of Sheffield Social Services Department said: 'A lot of sexual abuse we are coming across is ongoing from incestuous relationships that have been going on 30 or 40 years' (ibid.). The one case of sexual abuse reported in the Northamptonshire study was of a son abusing his older, moderately demented mother. This of course affirms current thinking on sexual abuse in other arenas, such as child sexual abuse, as largely male-executed.

The Northamptonshire study is provisional and suggests the need for a larger-scale study collating information about types of abuse, abuser and abused in domestic settings. It is also indicative of the kinds of abuse professionals in their specific professional context may encounter and will have an awareness of. At the same time, the study offers some indication of the issues that may need consideration as regards domestic elder abuse. These include a recognition of the fact that older women, especially women in their eighties, are likely to be abused and that they are possibly more likely to be abused by their sons than by their husbands. It also includes a recognition that both wives and daughters may be prone to abusing older spouses and parents, and that cohabitation is conducive to abuse. Finally, while outsiders (non-relatives living apart from the abused) may abuse older people financially, when abused and abuser live together, physical violence can gain prevalence.

The Northamptonshire study is in several respects similar to the SSI Report (1992) and can be critiqued on similar grounds (Phillipson, 1992). Its focus was social work professionals rather than the victims of elder abuse. It looked at the occurrence of elder abuse in terms of what cases had come to social workers' attention. This will of necessity skew the findings in particular ways in that it might, for instance, explain why there was quite a high incidence of dementia among those abused – it is possible that Social Services are more likely to be involved with people who have a debilitating condition such as dementia, which in turn might alert them to abuse. The data gathered in this study therefore yield no prevalence figures for the general population; apart from everything else, the sample was too small and too regionally specific.

The findings do not yield information about the severity of the abuse encountered and there is a need to understand better the boundaries between when abuse is reported and when it is tolerated. At present we know nothing of the threshold from non-reporting to reporting. The fact that most of the abusers in this study were male may be significant here and research along the lines of Nazroo's (1995) study is necessary to establish whether or not there is a qualitative difference between abuse by men and abuse by women so that the former is more likely to get reported because it leads to more severely negative consequences than abuse by women. It may also be that abuse by men fits gender stereotypes and is reported because it is 'believable' in terms of dominant socio-cultural expectations regarding gender roles while abuse by women may go unreported because victims may think they will not be believed, especially when the abusing woman also has a caring role.

The Follow-up Study

The Northamptonshire report – and its historical moment has to be borne in mind here – states: 'It was also felt to be significant that a large percentage of professionals reported not knowing, or suspecting, any cases of elder abuse in a year.' Aitken therefore decided to do some follow-up interviews with social workers working with older people in the community to explore further their knowledge of elder abuse and their gendered perspectives. She wanted to follow up the 'awareness raising' element of the working party's findings, partly because of the then imminent launch of the guidelines and training for social workers and other professionals. These workers, as well as the home helps whom they manage, are potentially closest to situations of domestic abuse. As service providers their views on elder abuse of necessity differ from those of abused people and of abusers, but working for Social Services Aitken felt a professional and moral responsibility to ensure that any abusive situation would be investigated and dealt with. This can potentially conflict with interviewing abused people, for example, who for whatever reason do not want social or other services to intervene on their behalf.

Aitken obtained agreement from the social workers' managers for the interviews and then wrote to all twenty-eight workers from the Care at Home service in the south of Northamptonshire, roughly half of the county. Of this total, twenty-two were female, some working part-time, six were male and four were principal social workers (all male). The gender implication here is that most basic-grade social workers are women. But in the supervisory ranks males are over-represented. This may have an effect on where priorities of service provision are placed (see the description of the gender biases informing the working party discussed in Chapter 2, p. 53 ff.). The social workers working with elders are predominantly female.

Replies to Aitken's letters were slow and she reminded unit managers at a meeting to ask their workers to respond, since every unit has at least two social workers. Three units did not respond at all. A total of sixteen social workers responded positively. Only one of these was male; he was the only principal social worker to reply. There was just one negative response, which was from a male social worker who said he had met elder abuse but did not wish to talk about it. In the end, fifteen interviews were arranged, of which thirteen took place, the others having been cancelled by the social workers due to various personal and professional commitments.

The social workers in question were all white, of different ages and from a variety of backgrounds. Some were qualified as social workers. Some had experience of working in a context of residential care for older people which gave an additional (and unexpected) slant to their comments. Some had worked with client groups other than elders and were thus able to make interesting comparisons between these different groups. A few had worked for the Social Services Department for many years, while others were more recent recruits. All had an interest in the issue of elder abuse, which raises the question about the other social workers whom Aitken contacted but who did not respond or participate. As Aitken interviewed only one male social worker no gendered comparisons can be made between female and male social workers' responses. Again, one might want to raise the question why so few men responded to the request for participation in this research. To what extent does this mirror the non-participation of males in the working party Aitken worked with? Aitken had one experience which reinforced the gender stereotyping that pervaded the whole research experience. One of the men she had contacted happened to be in the office when she arrived to interview his female colleague; the off-the-record remark he made to her on the subject of elder abuse was so sexist, ageist and downright offensive that it made her wish very much she was interviewing him, as it might have revealed some very interesting biases in this man's perceptions of elder abuse.

When interviewed, most of the social workers used case examples to illustrate their concept of elder abuse. It was obvious that certain situations of elder abuse stayed very clearly in their minds. Some of the social workers used their files during the interview to remind themselves of events and cases. This was appropriate because the purpose of the interviews was to find out more about the situations of abuse social workers *had* encountered and what they had done about these rather than to establish prevalence figures relating to the abuse. A proportion of occurrences of elder abuse, probably a significant one, will not be known to social workers, either because their services have not been requested or because they have been refused.

It has to be remembered that these interviews were conducted before the guidelines had come into effect and training of social workers had taken place. In the absence of any definitions of elder abuse available from Social Services at the time, and given that Aitken deliberately did not offer any definitions up front so as to see what social workers thought elder abuse was, four of the social workers interviewed did not think they had ever met elder abuse at the start of the interview when what constitutes elder abuse had not been discussed further. However, they all revised their views after about ten minutes. The workers' absence of knowledge was partly due to a lack of understanding of the definitions of elder abuse, a fact which points to the necessity for clear guidance and training. It was also a function of a worrying acceptance of financial abuse by relatives, for example, a point to which we shall return.

All kinds of abuse were mentioned by the social workers. *Physical abuse* usually came first on their agenda (see also SSI, 1992; Phillipson, 1992) and most of these female social workers thought it was likely that this would occur in the form of men doing violence to women, although there was one example of a wife physically abusing her older husband. A contributory factor to the assumption that physical abuse is done by men to women may have been these female social workers' internalization of the stereotypical perception that men do violence to women.

Sexual abuse was suspected by several social workers but often unproven. One worker with experience in the context of residential care was fairly certain that a son was sexually abusing his mother in the privacy of her room in a residential home. For this worker, there was a real conflict between the right to privacy, and the need to protect that woman from her son's abuse. With one exception the situations of sexual abuse all involved a confused older person, and the social worker was uncertain if the older woman's comments which had led to the suspicion of abuse were made as a result of a state of confusion or because sexual abuse had actually occurred. The social workers with whom Aitken spoke had great difficulties in deciding if an elder can be considered to be consenting to sexual activity when he or she suffers from dementia.

There was a very clear acknowledgement among the workers of an older person's right to a sexual life, but this was often not shared by relatives. A complete denial by sons and daughters of sexual abuse within their parent's or parents' relationships was often reported. In this, these relatives are representative of Western society's attitudes to sexuality in later life (see Kaye, 1993).

The social workers Aitken interviewed thought that the crime of rape within marriage was relevant to issues of elder abuse. The one situation of sexual abuse where the abused person was not confused occurred within a fairly recent marriage. In this instance the male abuser was eventually sectioned to a psychiatric hospital, with the rather dubious 'diagnosis' of pathological jealousy. This seemed to be regarded as an appropriate solution in a case where the police were reluctant to take into custody a very elderly man on a possible rape charge. There appeared to be a correspondence here to the 'mad' rather than 'bad' label attached to violent women, not only exemplifying the notion of powerlessness (i.e. this person is no longer capable of committing a crime) in old age but also articulating the stereotype of sexual activity in old age as the expression of a pathological condition. Presumably a fifty-year-old man would not have received the same treatment. Apparently an attempt was made to have the old man under discussion admitted to a residential home which, however, refused to take him because of the numbers of old women present in the home. The upshot of this episode – which has a rather disturbing parallel to what can happen in cases of domestic violence among younger age groups – was that the wife took this man back on discharge as she could not face the alternative, which was her own admission into residential care. This is not dissimilar to the decisions of younger females to remain with their violent partners because they cannot face moving into a refuge for battered women.

Connections are gradually being established between long-term patterns of domestic violence and some forms of elder abuse. There are some studies which indicate that a significant number of abusers are older spouses (Homer and Gilleard, 1990). Interestingly, all the social workers interviewed thought they were at some disadvantage in only coming into people's lives in old age, often not knowing the marital or family history and dynamics of these people's earlier lives which might have gone some way towards explaining some kinds of current abuse. However, given the findings of the questionnaires sent out by Aitken's working party (see p. 107 ff.), it is important to bear in mind that elder abuse between spouses can occur not only as a result of a particular kind of long-term abusive relationship carrying on into old age but also as a result of change in one of the spouses through, for example, the onset of dementia or some other illness.

Abuse by older people of each other was raised in many of the interviews. To her surprise, but also tellingly, Aitken found that one worker who had also worked in residential care remained convinced throughout the interview that elder abuse meant abuse *by* elders rather than *of* them. She provided many examples of old people abusing their carers, an issue discussed elsewhere in the literature, too. Thus Tomlin (1989: 10) writes: 'In the DHSS/NISW [Levin, 1988] study of the supporters of confused elderly people, one in three elderly people was abusive [*sic*] or aggressive towards their supporters and one in five had tried to hit or harm them. The study also found that carers were more likely to hit out at the elderly in their care if the elderly person had previously tried or succeeded in hitting them.'

Financial abuse appeared to be endemic. Every social worker Aitken interviewed had come across examples of it in her working life, so much so, in fact, that few seemed to really consider it abuse unless it involved misappropriation of property. Several of the interviewees thought that more money could have been spent by those responsible for the older person to keep that person in greater comfort instead of using the older person's money for providing minimal services only (presumably in order to secure an inheritance). There was agreement among the interviewees who raised this point that some carers were financially dependent on the older person they cared for, for instance if they were daughters or sons who had never left home, or had lost their jobs. One worker commented that all the elders in her caseload should be receiving the benefits they were entitled to because they had a social worker to advise them in these matters. Others, however, showed a lack of knowledge or a mis-understanding concerning the benefits elders are entitled to. One worker commented: 'It is often difficult to identify abuse by families or others where finance is involved. I would often question what happens to Attendance Allowance payments, but it is hard to find any evidence, and if we are not asked to, it is none of our business anyway.' Since the introduction in the UK of care management financial assessment in 1993 it has been found in Northamptonshire that a large number of elders are not claiming the benefits to which they are entitled. Worryingly, a significant proportion of these people are on social workers' caseloads. The picture may be similar else-where in the UK.

Aitken was alarmed by the culture of acceptance of financial abuse of elders among the social workers she interviewed. The interviewees tended to accompany their acceptance of this type of abusive situa-tion by pointing to gender role stereotypes, maintaining that the present generation of older women did not have a tradition of having their own income, and had looked to husbands and their children to take care of their finances. These interviewees were reproducing gender stereotypes which not only deny the fact that many women, especially in the working and lower middle classes, even of the generation under consideration here, would have had a history of earning their own money, but also propagate the notion that where men have taken care of finances on behalf of women, women are unlikely to take control of their finances if no appropriate male is available to handle them. One might argue that the interviewees were less likely to be critical of abuse which they could read as reinforcing their own gender stereotypes than of abuse which involves behav-iours not socio-culturally sanctioned as part of 'normal' gender role expectations. The female social workers and the male one alike all thought older women's control over their finances might change in their favour in the future, again possibly a case of accepting that more women from diverse class backgrounds work now than did in the past.

Most of the abusive situations which the interviewees reported had been going on for some time. The majority were considered fairly low-key situations which the social workers thought needed monitoring rather than confronting. Many workers felt powerless to intervene because of the limited legal options available to them. Often they were unable to ascertain the wishes of the abused person, and made assumptions that the abused person would wish to remain at home with the abuser rather than be removed or have the abuser removed. To Aitken this assumption occasionally seemed like an avoidance measure on the part of the interviewees, who would offer statements such as 'It will only make matters worse' or 'She/he will refuse to give us access and then we won't know what's happening' as reasons for not confronting the abuse they suspected. In two instances rather dramatic situations had blown up and resulted in the need for police intervention. However, the social workers felt that the police were as unsure as they were of how to proceed. In some cases there had been conflict between the social worker and the doctor dealing with a case of suspected abuse regarding how to intervene effectively and whether or not to invoke measures such as guardianship. All of this is indicative of the fact that diverse professionals may be equally uncertain or divided about how to deal with elder abuse; it also suggests that different professionals tend to work to different and possibly conflicting agendas in such situations.

The information provided by Aitken's interviewees about the abusers they had encountered was consistent with that found in various research studies (Homer and Gilleard, 1990; Steinmetz, 1988). A significant number of the abusers were older spouses, and many were known to have mental health problems, and problems relating to alcohol and/or drug abuse. One worker spoke of a mother and daughter situation where both abused alcohol and had ding-dong fights, but the mother was getting old and frail and was increasingly in real danger of getting hurt. There was a question whether or not this longstanding pattern of violence between mother and daughter, which was known and accepted by neighbours and the home help, had become abusive. Some interviewees gave examples of complex family relationships, with daughters who were actually granddaughters and where they suspected incest and general abuse, exacerbated by frailty and dependence.

Dependency

The interviewees also reported some interesting variations on the issue of dependency, only too often considered a one-way problem with the older person being dependent on their carer. One situation resulted in an older person being denied care in a nursing home because relatives insisted that they could care for her at home although they were clearly unable to do so. Recent research (Eastman, 1994b) has, in fact, increasingly highlighted the mutuality of dependence existing in carer–cared-for situations involving older people. However, it may also be the case that people insist on caring for an older person when they are unable to do so because they wish to retain control over the older person's assets.

When raised, the question of gender and its significance was a surprise to some and a non-issue to others of Aitken's interviewees. Social workers tend on the whole to be very aware of the department's equal opportunities policies in relation to ethnicity, sexuality and disability. Many will have attended specific training on culture and race awareness. However, the importance of gender seems to pass them by. All the social workers interviewed had more women on their caseloads than men and thus deduced that more women would be abused than men. Nonetheless they had often not considered the sex of the abuser other than in the context of sexual abuse. They thought that there would be a large number of women abusers as there are many more female than male carers. In many instances, they had not thought of the possibility of abuse by spouses but had thought of the stereotypical overwrought middle-aged daughter as the classic abuser.

Overall, fewer services were offered to support families who had taken on a caring role than to people living on their own (see also Arber and Gilbert, 1993). Some of the social workers appeared to have the attitude that 'if they do not ask, they must be managing'. According to Jane King (1993), Jill Pitkeathley from the Carers Association maintains that 'guilt is the strongest emotion, the professionals who work with carers mirror that guilt . . . they don't really ask them about the situation because they are frightened of what they are going to hear' (King, 1993: 21).

Social workers who had children of their own, or had worked in child care, were able to draw comparisons, or state the differences between, child abuse and elder abuse. They saw children as becoming gradually more independent and needing less care, with this process being reversed in the case of the elders. They thought that the Social Services Department did not consider elder abuse as a particularly serious problem because of the lack of guidance and procedures, but at the same time they did not want to be constrained by procedures in the way that they saw their colleagues in child care becoming.

The overall picture which emerges from Aitken's interviews with the social workers, conducted in the autumn of 1992 and the spring of 1993, is that the female workers were unevenly informed about elder abuse, that they tended to reproduce conventional gender stereotypes in their perceptions of the kinds of abuse of elders which occur and that they were not as a matter of course confident about how to identify it and what to do when they encountered it. Some forms of abuse (e.g. physical abuse) were regarded as more abusive than others, specifically financial abuse, and a sense of professional powerlessness prevented intervention, including in cases of long-term abuse. The workers seemed not to consider gender as an issue even though they produced gendered narratives of abuse.

The findings of these interviews are not representative in that they relied on a very small, non-random sample, focused on cases of elder abuse which had come to light through particular routes and offered only one perspective: that of a specific group of professionals. We would not wish to make any general claims in respect of these. However, there is clearly room for an investigation of how the establishment and implementation of the elder abuse guidelines which chronologically followed these interviews has impacted on social workers' knowledge and action in the face of elder abuse.

The Role of Dementia in Elder Abuse

One important finding of the Northamptonshire study was the prevalence of dementia among the older women and men who were abused. According to the British Alzheimer's Disease Society (1993), 'Alzheimer's disease is the commonest form of dementia and is responsible for about half to two thirds of all cases.' The prevalence of dementia (Table 5.14) rises steeply in the over-sixty-five-year-old range.

According to this information, one in five of the over-eighty-year-olds, most of whom will be women, suffers from dementia. A survey of people over seventy-five years of age with dementia in Cambridge

Table 5.14   *Prevalence of dementia in population*

Age	Per Hundred
65–70	2
70–80	5
Over 80	20

Source: Alzheimer's Disease Society, 1993

(Pollitt et al., 1991) found that 40 per cent were being cared for by spouses. The oldest carer was aged ninety-one. Slightly more men than women were being cared for. This might be accounted for by the differential mortality rates of women and men. Gender was not considered an issue in this study other than by way of the comment: 'Husbands found new roles at home; wives extended their role to take in areas previously left to their husbands' (1991: 465). The ability to cope varied with the severity of the dementia and whether or not the carer considered that s/he was caring as s/he had always done, caring for physical needs or dealing with a mentally ill partner. For many the use of formal and informal assistance was minimal, sometimes through ignorance of available services, sometimes through choice and a retreat into a cocoon where carer and partner deliberately limit outside contacts. These are situations where abuse can easily occur. Social workers Aitken spoke to were very anxious about couples who had very little contact with the outside world. One social worker rationalized her avoidance of confrontation of an older abuser by saying: 'I was worried that he would then shut the door on us and we would never know what was going on.' Bearing in mind that the Northamptonshire study indicated the specific vulnerability of women in the eighty-year-old age range, it may be women of that age group, living with spouses and/or children, to whom special attention should be paid.

The Alzheimer's Disease Society (1993) maintains that '[dementia] occurs equally across all groups in society and does not appear to be linked to sex, social class, ethnic group or geographical location'. However, prevalence research in this area has produced contradictory results. Thus while Paykel et al. (1994: 325) in their study maintain that 'Rates did not differ significantly by sex, educational level, or social class', other studies have demonstrated higher rates of dementia and Alzheimer's disease in women than men (Bachman et al., 1992; Hagnell et al., 1992; Hofman et al., 1991). Grafstrom et al. (1993) write that 'Abuse of dementia patients by family caregivers is reported to be common in the USA (Hamel et al., 1990). Family members who are caring for relatives with Alzheimer's disease (AD) have been estimated to be at 3 times greater risk of showing violent behaviour towards the demented than other older persons living in the American community (Paveza et al., 1992)' (Grafstrom et al., 1993: 1748). The Northamptonshire study shows that neglect appears to be most closely correlated with dementia although in all other types of reported abuse dementia also played a role in a significant number of cases.

The uneven and sometimes rapid decline of people with Alzheimer's disease, their increasing mental and physical incapacity, places tremendous strain on their families and may lead to abuse in some cases. In *Have the Men Had Enough?* (1989) Margaret Forster describes the slip into old age, the brief trial at a day centre, the assessment for a private people's home, the short stay at a council home and finally the NHS ward. The story is told from the point of view of the family, son, daughter and granddaughter, all trying to cope. The granddaughter says: 'I am sitting in front of Grandma so she can see me and know she is not alone . . . and I look up and stare at Grandma and for a moment she catches my eye and I hold my breath. It is there: sanity. . . . Then Mum drops something, there is a bang, Grandma blinks and she has gone' (Forster, 1989: 42). In Grafstrom et al.'s study, 'Almost all family members who admitted abuse were living alone with the elderly person and reported social isolation and loneliness' (1993: 1748). Bridget Penhale has pointed out that elder abuse may be difficult to detect because 'Elderly people do not lead such public lives and there may be a lack of contact with external agencies, or, indeed, with anyone other than the abuser' (1993a: 105). Grafstrom et al.'s study concluded that abuse of people with Alzheimer's disease might be more common in the early stages of the onset of the disease when carers have to cope with the older person's transition from not having the disease to manifesting it. They also maintain that 'many distressing behavioural symptoms decrease in late dementia' (1993: 1755) and that this might contribute to the fact that their sample did not report abuse two years after they had done so. In contrast to this study, Coyne et al. (1993: 644) found that 'caregivers who abused patients, in comparison to those who did not, had been providing care for more years'. The latter study offered no gender analysis.

The point was made, however, that dementia can lead to violence and aggressive behaviour in the older person, which in turn may provoke violence in the carer. Changes of environment to hospital or day care can increase confusion. Alcohol or drug abuse can also lead to aggression. A major cause of violence in older people can be a sense that their personal autonomy is being interfered with. Institutional regimes in residential care or the same attitudes in other professionals can heighten this risk. Providing choices and explanations can lessen it.

Family Violence

Given that much has been made in recent years of the impact of long-term family dynamics on abusive situations, the issue of reciprocal violence between carer and care receiver has to be considered. Coyne et al. (1993: 645) found that 'Among caregivers who indicated that they were abused by a demented family member, 26.1% directed abuse back at the patient. In contrast, only 4.8% of caregivers who were *not* abused by patients reported abusing patients in their care.' Where there was history of prior abuse, '62.5% of caregivers who had been abused by the patient before his or her illness also had abusive behaviour directed toward them after the onset of dementia.' Clearly, old habits die hard. Abuse prior to the onset of dementia is, however, no certain indicator of abuse in the wake of dementia. Though proportionally more carers and care receivers who had a history of being abused/abusive prior to dementia setting in continued abusing after onset than carers or care receivers who had no history of abuse, the absence of such a history did not protect from the possibility of abuse (Coyne et al., 1993: 645).

We would be reluctant to subscribe wholeheartedly to the conclusion Coyne et al. draw that these findings support 'to some extent, the "cycle of violence" concept, which suggests that abuse or violence within families is a behavioral outcome involving retaliation in addition to imitation' (ibid.: 646). Coyne et al. do suggest that such cycles of violence 'may be amenable to intervention strategies designed to break that cycle'. However, the difficulty with the use of family history as an explanation of possible elder abuse is that it does not account for those who do not commit such violation *despite* such a history or for those who do abuse older people despite *no* such history. Additionally, on a conceptual level it assumes continuity of motivation and in behaviour patterns which may not be warranted. It also implies a construction of the individual as a victim of circumstance and thus not only *not* responsible for their own actions but also beyond the possibility of change. This is not to say that 'cycle of violence' theories do not offer very plausible explanations for *some* abusive situations.

The difficulty remains that people do change over time and that in cases of dementia such change can be fairly drastic. The older person may no longer be able to function in the same role (as mother or wife, for example) they formerly held within the relationship and looking after such a person may be like looking after a stranger. The adjustment required by the spouse or child to cope with this change can be very taxing and may result in abuse as the carer, or indeed the cared-for, attempts to deal with these role changes. Steinmetz (1983: 144–5) describes four stages of increasing dependency which move from a position of a fair degree of independence on the part of the cared-for, through a stage of 'reciprocal dependency' to 'asymmetrical dependency' with the cared-for more dependent than the carer, and a final stage of 'survival dependence' where the older person is very dependent indeed.

Dependence, Power and Powerlessness in Domestic Abuse

Caring for (as opposed to caring about) an older person usually occurs in a context of some dependence on the part of the latter. This raises the issue of power. An imbalance of power in a relationship can be one of the significant causes of abuse, occasioned by a desire not only to exercise power but also to express and exorcize power-lessness. The abusers of women and children often perceive themselves as powerless, either in the relationship or outside it, and abuse to compensate for these feelings (Pillemer and Finkelhor, 1989: 180).

The idea that imbalance of power in a relationship is problematic is an aspect of a culture which refuses dependency and constructs it as negative. The acceptance of this position informs the research which has been done to investigate the need or otherwise for reciprocity in care-giving/-receiving relationships between parents and children, frequently in fact between mothers and daughters (Walker et al., 1990, 1992; Walker and Pratt, 1991). However, contrary to what one might expect (see Steinmetz, 1983), Walker et al.'s work suggests that care-giving by daughters to older mothers arises out of a 'functional solidarity' (1991: 9) characteristic of inter-generational relationships; that daughters, especially where there is a history of a good relationship with the mother, perceive the mother as giving them something of value in return for the daughters' care-giving (though this 'value' does not have to be expressed in material terms – 'love' was mentioned by both mothers and daughters independently and consistently as the main mutual reward; Walker et al., 1992); and that daughters' satisfaction in care-giving was asso-ciated with a prior history of a good relationship with the mother. One might, of course, argue that Walker et al. had read the signs of the times (i.e. pandered to Conservative ideology) in doing this research and are simply reaffirming traditional stereotypes of mother–daughter relationships supposedly functioning on the basis of sym-bolic as well as material exchanges in such a way as to make care-giving, on the whole, a positive and therefore 'worthwhile' activity which does not necessarily require external or additional input. It suggests that it is in the main the family with a history of dysfunction which will succumb to elder abuse as part of a long-standing pattern of relational failure. But clearly this is not always or invariably the case.

Adult children living with parents beyond the age when one is generally expected to move out may experience feelings of power-lessness and in consequence abuse their older parents. Conversely, older parents may retain power over their adult children which enables them to play on the children's feelings for them. Note that either way the perpetrators of the abuse are constructed as hard done by. One social worker described to Lynda Aitken how a disabled woman, whose marriage had broken down, had returned to live with her older mother. Despite the fact that she had married, had a child and had run her own home, her mother wielded the power, made all the decisions and often refused to let her leave the house, saying: 'I am ill, you cannot leave me.' The question which needs to be asked here is why the carer allowed herself to be trapped by this situation. Steinmetz (1983: 137) reported that 'One woman in her late 60s was unable to leave her home to be interviewed because her father, in his 90s, felt that it was his daughter's place to remain at home and answer his demands. When she would leave, he would violently attack any caretaker left with him and would turn the room into a shambles.' In another case an older mother treated her daughter as if she were a teenager, and more than half of the caregivers in Steinmetz's study reported being bothered by not having their privacy respected by the older person they cared for. It is worth noting the victimization of the carers by the cared-for here – the suggestion is that dependency oppresses and leads to abuse both in the carer and in the cared-for.

This can become problematic if carers are dependent on the older person for whom they care for financial and other help, particularly if they have no home of their own or have given up work or lost their job. Such was the case in many abusive situations detailed in the Northamptonshire study. Fay Wright (1986) has looked at single men and women carers living with older mothers, starting from the hypothesis that the mothers would be less dependent on their sons for domestic and personal care. She found that this was so, that 50 per cent of mothers living with sons still did the housework and cooking, compared with only 6 per cent of those living with daughters. The study does not make clear if the cared-for were suffering from a comparable level of disability, nor did Wright comment on the different views of the older generation on the 'genderedness' of tasks.

Wright found some interesting differences in attitudes of employers. Only one son did not have a full-time job, compared with 52 per cent of the daughters who had given up work to care. One man said: 'Of course I have never taken time off work because of my mother. If she is taken bad my sister takes time off her job to look after her' (Wright, 1986: 86). The pressure to give up work came not only from the parent or other family members but also from employers: 'A woman who had been late for work a couple of times because her mother had made such a muddle of getting dressed, was shouted at by the manager and told to give up work if she had those sorts of problems. He was really sympathetic to one of the men who came in late for ages because his child was ill' (Wright, 1986: 80). Sons (55 per cent) were more likely to receive home help than daughters (22 per cent), which could mean that this service was going to older people with a lower level of disability because of the gender of their carer. Many daughters did not realize that they were eligible for such support and did not apply for it, but some had also been turned down, with professionals assuming that housework and personal care would automatically be undertaken by the female.

When carer and cared-for share a living space, power is in part determined by territory and ownership of that territory; both the need for a space and the fear of loss of that space can contribute to abusive behaviour as well as the failure to report it. It is interesting in this context that a survey conducted in the UK in 1993 by Linda Chamberlain found that out of 1,000 employees, 84 per cent did not think the need to look after a loved one would ever affect them. It was suggested that in reality, by the turn of the century, one in five Britons would be carers (Chamberlain, 1993: 2). Estimates such as these vary widely. Some studies include caring responsibilities for children. Many include younger disabled adults as well as frail elders. The overall implication, however, is that in the early 1990s many people were not prepared for the possibility of becoming carers – the fact that they might, and all that that entails, could act as a catalyst for abuse as a way of expressing resistance to being the object of an unforeseen event.

As regards the different care given by women and men it seems that women are more likely to be primary caregivers doing hands-on care and providing care for longer periods than men. Macdonald and Rich (1983) quote Blumenthal, a psycho-geriatrician, as saying: 'My impression is that the family nominates one person, usually a daughter, saying, "This is your job." Interestingly enough, the family usually abandons this one person and doesn't lend a hand any more' (1983: 45). Men delegate more tasks to female members of the family or buy in care. Women are socialized to perform care-giving tasks, although those with the economic means may purchase care-giving. Women do not tend to delegate to male family members. The social workers Aitken interviewed were split as to whether or not this type of gender role stereotyping was changing. Most thought that the 'new man' taking on caring roles did not exist. They thought that there was little comparison between collecting a pension and paying the bills (the tasks given regularly to sons), and toileting and emptying the commode (a task carried out by many daughters).

In 'Caring: A Labour of Love' (1983), Graham explains the motivation of women to care as a combination of psychological and

Table 5.15   *Percentage of total adult population who are carers*

(a) By sex			
Males	12		
Females	15		
All	14		

(b) By Gender and Age	Women	Men	Total
16–29	7	6	8
30–44	16	10	14
45–59	24	16	21
60–74	18	14	17
75 plus	6	10	8

Source: Derived from the GHS 1985 data, in Evandrou, 1991: 24

sociological factors. The psychological ones are based on emotion and assumptions of femininity, the sociological ones on the function of family care within capitalism and patriarchy. The two can be brought together in the position that caring defines the *identity* and *activity* of women (Graham, 1983: 30). This obviously does not account for the women who feel exploited and resentful about caring, let alone male carers.

The 1985 Office of Population Censuses and Surveys' *Informal Carers Survey* offered the analysis of caring in Britain shown in Table 5.15.

A number of issues are immediately apparent from these data:

* Women and men are most likely to be engaged in caring tasks in their middle years (but see Hancock et al., 1995: 1) when they (if living in a partnership which involves children) are also likely to be otherwise committed to caring roles and when women are likely to go through the menopause.
* A significant proportion of carers in all age groups are male.
* Males significantly outnumber females as carers in the over-seventy-five-year age range.

If we consider the likelihood of the last group of carers' diminished health and general physical ability, and bear in mind the finding of the Northamptonshire study that two women in their eighties were neglected by their older husbands, such an occurrence or indeed some form of abuse is not that surprising, given that the older males may have difficulties coping with looking after themselves, never mind someone else. However, the stereotype of the female as carer has meant that, in so far as gender is made explicit within it, comparatively more research has been done on women as carers than on men in that role.

Female vs Male Carers

Arber and Ginn (1990) have done some very detailed work on the OPCS *Informal Carers' Survey*. They point out that identifying carers as a unitary group with a shared problem was derived from feminist writing on the domestic labour of women, with caring being seen as yet another example of women's unpaid domestic labour. In the early 1980s the Equal Opportunities Commission carried out some small scale studies (EOC, 1980, 1982) which emphasized that women's labour market participation was restricted by caring responsibilities and highlighted the gender inequality which at the time prevented women in Britain from claiming the Invalid Care Allowance. Writers such as Finch and Groves (1983) produced texts with titles like *A Labour of Love: Women, Work and Caring* which concentrate on work done by daughters for parents; care by spouses or other relatives received relatively little attention. The identification of feminists with daughters rather than with mothers in the care situation is one indication of how the women's movement has tended to ignore older women. Altogether, this work from the early 1980s reinforced the stereotype of the middle-aged, married woman carer.

Arber and Ginn (1990) looked at gender differences in caring and found that there were a number of discrepancies, for instance in the time spent on caring. A higher proportion of men than women care for under five hours a week, the gender difference increasing 'in favour' of women the greater the time spent caring. Women outnumber men by 50 per cent if the time spent caring is twenty hours a week. The difficulty in researching this kind of situation is that unless you analyse the task and keep a record of the time spent caring, it may appear as if men are doing the same caring tasks as women and men may answer research questionnaires in such a way as to produce this effect even though their effort is in no way comparable to that of the female carer. The disadvantage of using a time threshold as a basis for the caring task analysis is that it does not necessarily relate to the qualitative aspects of the caring role, and time spent as company may be as important as doing the shopping (Keith et al., 1993).

There was limited information about personal care tasks in the OPCS Survey, but it seems that on the whole more women than men undertake personal care of a more intimate nature, the exception being men caring for their wives (Arber and Gilbert, 1993). Some workers have found that there is a hierarchy of obligations in relation to who offers personal care (Finch, 1989: 27), starting with the spouse, followed by a child (usually a daughter), with first call on any child sharing the household. Gender is significant here as daughters or daughters-in-law often give personal care before sons are called upon. Ungerson (1987) suggests, however, that difficulties arise out of the operation of incest taboos and that personal care for kin of the opposite sex can be as much of a problem as personal care for kin of the same sex (1987: 127). 'In a more distant relationship I think it's easier, I feel I could do more personal things for a complete stranger far easier than for a mother-in-law' (ibid.: 119). It is ironic that the supposed advantage of being personally cared for by someone close rather than a paid carer is found to be difficult by some women; it also highlights the assumptions we all tend to make about the facility and willingness of individuals to cope with that kind of situation. Thompson (1994–5: 9) quotes Jill Pitkeathley: 'We have had cases where an elderly carer has been repeatedly physically abused by her schizophrenic son, and times when women have contacted us in great distress because they are being expected to care for a father who sexually abused them when they were children.'

Spousal Caring

Elders caring for each other are often overlooked. Yet a number of male carers in surveys are usually caring for spouses. There is an assumption that spouses will care for each other in old age (Wilson, 1995; Rose and Bruce, 1995) and, in some respects, the 'tradition' of men being older than their female spouses on marriage has promoted that assumption. Younger women sometimes complain that they are always assumed to be prepared to care for sick or disabled husbands as part of their role as a wife. The same assumption is not necessarily made of a husband, particularly one who works, and services to support husbands tend to be readily offered. The social workers Lynda Aitken interviewed did not think that they offered more help to older male carers, so age may blur these differences (see also Wilson, 1995; Rose and Bruce, 1995), but in Aitken's view many older female carers do not ask for help, particularly with personal care tasks for their husbands.

Older people living with others are more at risk of abuse than those living alone, and, ironically, although the bulk of informal care happens within households shared by cared and cared-for, most domiciliary services are provided for older people living alone (Arber et al., 1988: 153). Arber et al. (1988) concluded that there was discrimination by statutory services against women carers, not *per se*, but where there was a younger female spouse or a young married woman in the same household as the cared-for person. This indicates the disadvantaged position of married women who have an older person living with them. The comments by social workers to Aitken that, not surprisingly, they had very few such families 'on their books', reveals more about the policies and prejudices of social workers than about actual need. As the majority of social workers and nurses are female, they reinforce sex roles and related expectations in their professional capacity by failing to recognize the ways in which the services they provide operate selectively to the disadvantage of certain groups and people, often specifically women.

There are considerable expectations, not only by men, that women will continue or take over certain tasks, and here generational differences in assumptions about gender roles come into play. Qureshi (1986) writes of an older woman becoming very upset at her son performing domestic tasks for her rather than her daughter-in-law. Daughters may have difficulty in providing a level of domestic service to their fathers that their own husbands would not expect of them. Aitken has known older men move back in with their mothers (often aged ninety) to be cared for when their wives died. Her own grandfather moved in with his two widowed sisters when her grandmother died as he had no daughters. An interesting fictional version of this type of household is presented in Jane Rule's novel *Memory Board* (1987) in which an older heterosexual man, who has hitherto lived with his children, joins his lesbian retired sister and her lover, who is gradually succumbing to senility, to help his sister look after her partner.

Two types of abusive situation have been identified in the context of spousal caring (Hugman, 1994: 81): where elder abuse is an extension of a history of domestic abuse prior to the onset of old age; and where abuse commences after the onset of old age. Where the former is an expression of long-term relational dysfunctionality, the latter may occur as a result of the onset of dementia in one of the spouses, for example, or of increasing general incapacity leading to neglect.

Black Carers

There is a lack of research on domestic elder abuse in ethnic minority communities which is associated with the generalized socio-cultural and economic marginalization of such groups in British and in other societies. This also means that gender issues in this context remain, in the main, unaddressed. Two recent reports on care in the community and how it affects African/Caribbean and Asian people in North-amptonshire (Wright, 1993; Woolham, 1994), provide some gender-related background information about the older people who were referred for care to the project to improve services offered to African/Caribbean and Asian elders, but these reports do not consider gender beyond saying that a specific percentage of their sample was female or male. The tendency is to use an ascription of ethnic origin as the basis for the homogenization of a group of clients, which obscures the gender issues involved in the care and possible abuse situation that is analysed.

Cameron et al. (1989) refer to a project in Birmingham, UK, looking at the needs of frail elders and disabled people living at home. Black elders tend to have lower incomes, poorer housing, physically demanding jobs and chronic illness that may lead to disability at a younger age than white people (see also Wright, 1993: 2.6–2.15). They may be isolated by limited mobility and language barriers (the latter particularly affecting Asian, as opposed to Afro-Caribbean, elders in Ray Wright's study). Although many black people live as part of an extended family, this does not mean that they do not need services. As Blakemore and Boneham (1994: 83) note:

> It is quite possible to be isolated in a large family group, to be treated in an offhand or condescending way, to be denied freedom of movement and basic rights to one's own money or goods. Such cases do occur and, when occasional physical abuse comes to light, have been reported to social services departments. In addition to this minority of extreme cases of abuse or neglect there is wider evidence, especially among women, of a number who feel trapped and powerless in their family groups.

The stereotype of 'looking after their own' has frequently been used as an excuse for providing Eurocentric services only. This interacts with the white liberal fear of identifying racial differences. It is fostered by the *laissez-faire* attitude that often accompanies notions of multi-culturalism. These assume intra-communal or intra-familial mechanisms for dealing with needs which arise where care of an older person becomes an issue. None of the social workers Aitken interviewed mentioned that they had come across any examples of abuse within black families, and Aitken knows that very few black elders are 'clients' of her Social Services Department. This dovetails with Ray Wright's findings that black people have difficulty accessing statutory services for a variety of reasons, many of them to do with the insufficient sensitivity of the services to diverse needs and with how information about them is disseminated. As Cameron et al. suggest: 'Clearly a system which works ineffectively to meet the needs of the majority white clients is even less likely to begin to address, in a sensitive way, the area of black people's needs, even if this largely "invisible" need were to be presented to it' (1989: 239).

Black and Asian women are usually the carers, rather than men. Some have only recently arrived in Britain and, independently of the cultural sensitivity of the service provided, have no knowledge of how to access community or health services. Additionally, black women are frequently marginalized within their own, often male dominated cultural group. According to Cameron et al., 'For Asian women the new experience of caring for a disabled person, which typifies the individualized response to disability in western society, is often an alien and unanticipated one' (1989: 241).

There was a very small number of male black carers in Cameron's study who faced more problems than female carers in hands-on caring because this can conflict with traditional gendered family roles. In Aitken's experience men fulfilling their traditional role as family spokesperson (rather than as carer) may accompany older women to the GP or hospital and inhibit, as opposed to aid, the expression of personal problems on the part of the cared-for person. If, as has previously been suggested, long-term histories of abuse in a family can act as a predictor of elder abuse, then we may assume that elder abuse occurs in Asian families, for example, who can manifest domestic abuse (Southall Black Sisters, 1994; Griffin, 1995). Ford and Sinclair (1987: 40–4) present the first person narrative of one Asian woman who had arrived in Britain from Kenya and who suffered domestic violence. However, as in her case, so in many others: the abuse is likely to go undetected. If white elders are not very visible, black elders and their carers are even less so.

Problems of Detection of Domestic Elder Abuse

In situations of abuse professionals may have difficulties in identifying the problem and ascertaining the older person's wishes. The reasons for this can be manifold. Penhale (1993a) cites the absence of a generally agreed definition of what constitutes abuse, the prevailing ideology of the family belonging to the private sphere and therefore being beyond external intervention, difficulties of access to the abused person, the ill health of the abused person and the reluctance of victims to report abuse as reasons for why domestic elder abuse goes undetected. This conjoins with professionals' difficulty in identifying abuse and issues about what to do in cases of abuse. Most Social Services departments and the Royal College of Nursing in Britain have by now adopted guidelines on this matter but given the range of unskilled, poorly paid female workers who act as home helps etc. and who are at the forefront of the possibility of detecting or committing abuse, these measures are clearly not enough.

The relationship between informal carers and statutory agencies is often ambiguous and uncertain. Several studies (Ross et al., 1993; Cameron et al., 1989) have pointed to the necessity of statutory agencies and informal carers arriving at some negotiated agreement about roles and tasks in order to provide the best possible care for the care receiver. Carers are not clients or patients. Particularly where older spouses are concerned it is often difficult to judge who the carer is. The tendency in any event is not to care unless an acute crisis occurs, i.e. unless abuse has happened and been brought to public attention.

Elders as a Problem for Women

Finch and Groves's (1983) *A Labour of Love: Women, Work and Caring* is distinguished by its concentration on women as *carers* at the expense of any identification with women who receive care. One may want to consider the extent to which the needs of older and disabled people and those of their carers are as mutually exclusive as this position would suggest. Research of the 1980s tended to view older people as the problem rather than the focus of its enquiry.

Research on carers links with feminist thinking about the position of women in the family and their position in the labour market. Finch and Groves state: 'In practice community care equals care by the family equals care by women' (1983: 494). The work of carers is done out of a complex mixture of love, guilt, a sense of duty and a lack of choice. The needs of those who receive care have never had the same profile. As Keith (1992: 169) writes: 'In wanting to show how difficult and unrecognized is the work of the carer, many have thought it necessary to portray those who may be in need of care as passive, feeble and demanding.' She is critical of Ungerson's account (1987) of why caring is of personal significance to her, which is that 'as an only daughter, my future contains the distinct possibility that I will sooner or later become a carer myself' (Ungerson, 1987: 2). Keith, a disabled feminist, comments on Ungerson's inability to see herself as potentially an older or disabled person needing care: 'It is certainly easier to see ourselves being needed than to image ourselves as dependent' (Keith, 1992: 170).

Another study which, in terms of its front cover alone, reinforces the idea of the 'carer as active, care receiver as dependent and passive' is Lewis and Meredith's (1988) *Daughters Who Care*. Here an older woman sits in her wheelchair, with her daughter/carer doing up her shoelaces. The study highlights some of the conflicts of the caring situation, how some daughters drift into it, and reports some telling interviews in which points such as the following comparison between care-giving and pre-war domestic service are made: 'You don't go anywhere, you don't do anything . . . it's like being in service, I got one evening off, Wednesday evening, and one afternoon a month' (Lewis and Meredith, 1988: 83). There are equally revealing comments by the authors about mothers who 'fail to co-operate in their care' (ibid.: 61), making them sound like naughty children. The opportunity in this study to hear of the mother's experience is almost totally lost. The carer's world is considered the most important to explore. The inferior status of the care receiver is thus reinforced by the importance attached to the views of the carers, as seen in most studies.

Conclusions

Historically, elder abuse in domestic settings has been constructed as a problem between a female abuser and older parents, often an older mother (e.g. Eastman, 1984; Steinmetz, 1988), within a caring context. In the Northamptonshire study detailed in this chapter which correlated types of abuse with the gender of the abuser and the abused most of the abused were very elderly females but their abusers were predominantly male and more likely to be sons than husbands. While spousal abuse has come under increasing scrutiny in recognition both of more older couples caring for each other and of the possibility of long-term patterns of domestic abuse persisting into old age, abuse of older women by sons has received relatively little attention. Further research is needed to establish whether or not this is an idiosyncratic finding, and how this relates to issues of masculinity in the late twentieth century.

Like the SSI Report (1992), the Northamptonshire study confirmed a prevalence of reporting of physical abuse, possibly explicable by the visibility of such abuse relative to other kinds of abuse. As Phillipson (1992) suggests, this may present a very skewed picture of the actual distribution of different kinds of abuse.

There has to be a recognition that women and men may commit abuse including physical, psychological, financial and sexual abuse, as well as neglect. As regards the reporting of such cases, the Northamptonshire study indicates certain patterns.

- Little sexual abuse of either women or men is reported.
- Neglect was equally little reported, though in the reported cases it was by spouses of each other, suggesting possibly the decline in caring ability with increasing age.
- Women were more frequently financially abused than men, which is interesting, given women's generally greater degree of poverty in old age compared with men. Financial abuse appears to be cross-generational rather than intra-generational and a sizeable proportion of abusers do not constitute 'immediate' family.
- Psychological abuse of women and of men was reported but men appeared to be victims of this kind of abuse to a greater extent

than women. This may be a function of gender-stereotypical behaviours and women feeling less able than men to be physically abusive. Most of the psychological abuse was intra-familial involving spouses and children.

- Many more women than men were reported as physically abused, again potentially a function of gender-stereotypical behaviour.
- A sizeable number of abusers were not spouses or children, but either more distant relations or non-relatives. In the past, research on elder abuse in domestic settings has tended to focus on abuse by partners and children. This focus needs to be widened, especially given that the numbers of older people, especially older women, living on their own is rising which means that abuse by people other than immediate family needs to be more closely considered. It also means that the family-centred idea of abuse becomes insufficient as an explanation for what occurs.
- Further investigations are needed to establish the role of dementia as a correlative to elder abuse.
- Elder abuse among elders from ethnic minority groups in general, and gender issues within that specifically, need to be investigated.

When one correlates the findings of the Northamptonshire study with the statements made by the social workers Aitken interviewed, it becomes clear that there is a correspondence between what they perceived to be the case and what was reported. Thus

- physical abuse was high on their agenda, corresponding to the prevalence of reporting of such abuse;
- sexual abuse was suspected but often unproven, hence, possibly the low reporting rate;
- financial abuse was endemic but under-reported in the Northamptonshire study, mirroring the 'acceptance' among social workers of that kind of abuse.

Further research is necessary to establish how social workers' knowledge and perceptions of elder abuse have changed since the establishment of guidelines on the subject. The social workers interviewed by Aitken in 1992 had

- difficulties in knowing what constitutes elder abuse;
- little sense of what gender implications there might be;
- limited knowledge of what to do when confronted with elder abuse and difficulty in deciding on appropriate courses of action.

We need to develop a more sophisticated understanding of what the social relations and care patterns of older people are and how they are changing as part of general demographic trends, because these are the contexts in which elder abuse and neglect occur. At present caring is still predominantly a female task with unequal expectations of women and men as regards their 'obligation' to others, whether or not they should give up jobs to care for another person and what tasks they can be expected to do. This may foster resentment and lead to abuse or neglect. The ageing of carers also has to be considered. Increasing incapacity on their part may underlie cases of neglect.

In general, the relationship between elder abuse and care and between elder abuse and family violence needs to be revisited. Neither care nor family violence by itself offers a sufficient explanation for elder abuse; a more over-arching way of thinking about elder abuse which would also allow an appropriate integration of gender issues would be in terms of power and dependence.

Conclusion: Do We Care? Future Directions for Work on Gender Issues in Elder Abuse

The recognition that we live in a culture in which elder abuse occurs has resulted in a variety of actions designed to combat such abuse. Among these was the establishment in Britain in September 1993 of Action on Elder Abuse, a network whose aim is to prevent elder abuse by promoting changes in policy and practice through raising awareness about elder abuse, providing education in the area, encouraging research and collecting and disseminating information about elder abuse by the publication of regular bulletins and working papers. The first of these working papers was published in 1994 and presented information about work on elder abuse in both the USA and in Britain.

Support Groups for ... ?

As elder abuse has a longer recognition and research history in the USA than in Britain, much of the work that has been done on how to deal with it has come from the United States. This has included the creation of support groups of various kinds, aimed at both abusers and abused. These groups are intended to address factors which have been identified as contributing to the possibility of abuse occurring such as stress, aggression, and social isolation in either abused or abuser. Labrecque et al. (1992), for example, report on a group programme for caregivers of frail older veterans which showed that 'participants experienced significant reductions in subjective burden' as a consequence of attending the support group. As Labrecque et al. suggest, support groups for carers offer a number of benefits: '1) provision of respite for caregivers, 2) reduction of isolation, 3) encouragement to share feelings and experiences in a supportive atmosphere, 4) validation of feelings and experiences related to caregiving, 5) affirmation of the importance of the caregiver role, 6) teaching effective problem-solving and coping strategies, and 7) education about the aging process, effects of chronic health problems, and community resources' (Labrecque et al., 1992: 575). The idea behind support groups is 'to shore up informal care and facilitate adjustment and coping in the caregivers' with the effect that 'the basic pattern and division of care between public and private spheres [goes] largely unexamined' (Aronson, 1990: 62). In other words, programmes and support groups for carers underwrite the need for informal care and embed it in a network of secondary structures aimed to sustain such informal care. This means that the demand for informal care as such, how it is organized and what its effects are, is not subjected to enquiry. Further, if – as has been suggested (Pillemer and Finkelhor, 1989) – elder abuse is not a function of caregiver stress but of particular patterns of familial interaction, then supporting carers will not necessarily alleviate the problems. Additionally, such support groups do not exist for (female) professionals or untrained women workers dealing with elders. Instead, professionals and occasionally unskilled workers tend to be offered training programmes to sensitize them to the possibility of elder abuse, teach them how to detect it and how to intervene. This ignores the fact that paid workers also commit abuse. The question of elder abuse in institutional settings or by paid carers is thus not resolved by the kinds of support group or training currently in existence.

Vaccaro (1992) reports on a social skills training programme for physically aggressive institutionalized elders which aimed at reducing the frequency of aggressive behaviour in elders through a behaviour modification programme which involved the elders in instruction about aggressive behaviour, modelling, role playing and feedback, and staff in recording aggressive or socially acceptable (= non-aggressive) behaviour. Here the benefits of the programme were that 'staff attitudes dramatically changed in that they were more in tune with the subjects' needs and problems . . . the diminution of negative behaviors allowed the subjects to be in less restrictive areas that due to their past behaviors, had been previously "off-limits" . . . and [it] allowed the subjects to be more accepted by their peers, and not viewed as "trouble makers" ' (1992: 286). The two problems with this kind of programme are how aggressive behaviour is defined (which, in an institution, can be *any*, including perfectly reasonable, resistance to impersonal regimes, for example) and the labour-intensive nature of such work. As was indicated in Chapter 4, it is much more cost effective to medicate or sedate when older people's behaviour is interpreted as disruptive than to deal with such behaviour through sustained personal/personnel engagement. There is therefore an economically driven question of the extent to which institutions will be prepared to support such programmes.

Clare Wenger's work on social networks, self-help and mutual aid in Wales detailed five types of support network among elders: (a) local family dependent, (b) locally integrated, (c) local self-contained, (d) wider community focused, and (e) private restricted.

Wenger suggested that three factors influenced which networks are available to any given individual: the extent and size of their family; migration; and personality. With all three factors there is a question of how much control the individual has over them. Wenger concludes by suggesting that 'policies which reinforce migration (mobility of labour; retirement villages/developments) or lead to a concentration or ghettoization of elderly people effectively undermine mutual aid and thus the capacity of the community to provide informal support and care' (Wenger, 1993: 38). Here, as elsewhere, the emphasis is on how to sustain elders in the community and enable them to retain autonomy in the face of increasing incapacity.

The support groups we encountered all seem to serve the function of reinforcing existing policies concerning the treatment of elders rather than rethinking or changing them. Significantly, we did not come across a support group for older victims of abuse, though in the autumn of 1995 a helpline for victims came into operation in the UK, initially in four pilot areas (Action on Elder Abuse Bulletin No. 10, March/April 1995: 1). This is useful for those older people who have access to and can handle a telephone and who are willing to disclose that they have been or are being abused. It does little for the confused or demented elders (who in many studies have been the largest number of abused people; e.g. Homer, 1994) who may be the objects of abuse but are not in a position to tackle the problem directly themselves.

Helping Professionals: Guidelines for Action in Cases of Elder Abuse

The extent to which gender issues in elder abuse still remain one of the hidden agendas is evident in the ways in which guidelines on elder abuse by and for Social Services and health services departments in the UK have been constructed. In 1995 Action on Elder Abuse published *Everybody's Business! Taking Action on Elder Abuse* which contained the results of a survey they had done in 1994 on the policies and procedures in all local authority social services departments, health authorities and National Health Service trusts in England and Wales. They found that three-quarters of the 79 per cent of the Social Services departments who replied had fully implemented policies on elder abuse, that just over one in five of health authorities who replied (response rate 51 per cent) had such a policy and that of responding National Health Service trusts (rate 71 per cent) just under one in four had a policy (Table 6.1). In other words, Social Services departments were the ones most likely to have a policy in place. While all responding Social Services departments

Table 6.1 *Authorities with policies on elder abuse in England and Wales, 1994*

	No. of returned questionnaires	No. with policies in place
Social Services departments	92	66
Health authorities	72	17
National Health trusts	187	41

Source: Derived from Action on Elder Abuse, 1995

agreed on the need to have such a policy, not all health trusts or health authorities did.

The questionnaires sent out by Action on Elder Abuse did not specifically ask if gender was addressed in the policies adopted by the various services and authorities but it did ask if the gender of the abuser and that of the abused were recorded as part of the monitoring process. While the gender of the victim was recorded in most cases, the gender of the abuser was monitored in slightly fewer (Action on Elder Abuse, 1995: 9).

There was disturbing evidence of lack of joint work and multi-agency policies in Social Services departments, health authorities and the police (Valios, 1995: 8). Action on Elder Abuse recommended that both the police and housing departments should be involved. Clearly, lack of co-operation can not only make the detection of elder abuse more difficult but can also delay or prevent effective intervention. It thus feeds into the 'helplessness' model which some professionals adopt in the face of evidence of abuse and which we shall discuss below.

The guidelines on elder abuse that we looked at pay no or very scant regard to gender issues. Most miss the opportunity to point out that the victim, especially in the very elderly age range, is likely to be female and that, contrary to what one might expect, both women and men are abusers, including in the older age ranges. Where gender surfaces in guidelines on elder abuse, it tends to reinforce stereotypes which have been questioned by the research into elder abuse over the last few years. Rochdale Metropolitan Borough Council focus extensively on the put-upon informal carer, exonerated from abuse by the trying situation to which most likely she, but possibly he, is exposed. This council falls into the trap of characterizing the carer as a menopausal woman (n.d.: 10), ignoring the fact that in many instances older spouses and male children care. Similarly, the *Guidelines for Action* produced by Age Concern et al. (n.d.) imply that the carer, and therefore the potential abuser, is a married woman when they cite as sources of stress '[having] other dependants and responsibilities that are making demands, e.g. children, *husband*, own home or work' (our emphasis). The only reference made to gender in the Northamptonshire guidelines is in the context of the initial assessment of abuse where it is suggested that 'One of the workers should be the same sex/culture as the older person [the abused] if at all possible' (1994: 3b). The only guidelines we came across which mentioned gender in relation to the victim were those from the Royal College of Nursing which state that the victims are 'classically . . . over 75, *female*, roleless within the family, functionally impaired, unable to fulfil activities of daily living, lonely, fearful, living at home with or near to adult children' (1991: 1; our emphasis).

Overall, then, the situation in the UK is that while many Social Services departments and health authorities have developed guidelines for professionals, a significant proportion have not done so and those who have, pay insufficient or no attention to the issue of gender as it is relevant to elder abuse.

Elders as a Menace

We live in a culture in which elders seem to be increasingly viewed as an insidious menace threatening to overwhelm the rest of the population both in sheer numbers and in terms of the 'drain' they are on resources. In 1979 Robert A. Kalish described this phenomenon as 'The New Ageism and the Failure Models'. The former referred to people's tendency to stereotype elders based on the least capable, least healthy, regarding them as helpless and dependent and therefore in need of support services. New ageism, Kalish maintained, 'produces an unrelenting stream of criticism against society in general and certain individuals in society for their mistreatment of the elderly, emphasizing the unpleasant existence faced by the elderly' (1979: 398). Kalish distinguished between two failure models: the Incompetence Failure Model and the Geriactivist Model. Both are models of lobbying for money and services for elders; the former *on their behalf* on the basis of the elders' incompetence, the latter *by* elders, those who are fit enough, themselves. Both models, according to Kalish, imply that 'the older person is not only victimized, but is also impotent and powerless to have any significant impact on the society and/or individuals who perpetrate the victimization. The built-in assumption is that change is governed from without' (ibid.: 400). Kalish described his piece as a polemic, his intention being to highlight the fact that older people are not a homogeneous group and are not to be viewed in such terms.

Kalish may claim that his is a polemic; others simply straightforwardly admit that 'older people . . . are stereotypically seen, in western society, as being burdensome' (Penhale, 1993a: 104). At the point where such positions are reinforced, in part through the very homogenization Kalish seeks to decry, phrases like 'the elderly' are commonly used because they allow the depiction of an undifferentiated dehumanized mass. However, the people who are being referred to here are, in large measure, *women*, especially in the oldest age group. It is this age group who now also represent a big drain on the public health purse because they have the chronic illnesses which, rather than the acute ones of previous times, now characterize old age (Fries, 1980). Mortality due to acute illness has been much reduced with the elimination or pharmaceutical control of many infectious diseases. Morbidity due to chronic illness has taken over as the major medical expense and concern in Western society. Where once a woman might have died of childbed fever or consumption, she is now more likely to be a long-term sufferer of arthritis or osteoporosis. Fries (1980) maintains that health policies need to be directed at the prevention and management of chronic illnesses which are cost intensive and affect women in particular.

Women's demands on the public purse as a result of chronic illness in old age have to be considered in a context where women have traditionally been assigned to the private, non-direct income earning sphere and where, even if they are in the employment market as is increasingly the case, they earn significantly less than their male counterparts (Morris, 1995). Women therefore, either by virtue of not earning or by virtue of earning less than men, do not contribute as much directly to the public purse as men do. However, those who decide what to do with the public purse are all men. Put crudely, a situation has arisen where those who contribute least to the public purse need most out of it as they age. This is as true for the situation of ageing *per se* as it is for abuse in that situation. For the willingness to deal with abuse also needs an acknowledgement of the fact that investments will have to be made in order to research, prevent and intervene in elder abuse. The question thus arises: why should men bother to spend on something which does not seem to concern them? As Fries tellingly puts it in a medical context:

> High-level medical technology applied at the end of a natural life span epitomizes the absurd. The hospice becomes more attractive than the hospital. Human interaction, rather than respirators and dialysis and other mechanical support for failing organs, is indicated at the time of the 'terminal drop.' Anguish arising from the inescapability of personal choice and the inability to avoid personal consequences may become a problem for many. (1980: 135)

One can see how substituting 'home' for 'hospice', 'female informal care' for 'human interaction' and so on can redraw this picture to provide a rationale for the privatization of care for elders, the ghettoization of older women and of older couples who are expected to self-manage. Such privatization – which comes together with the bourgeois ideology of the private as an intervention-free zone where every person is his own little sovereign – operates on several different levels, as is made plain in Fries's statement and, indeed, in his article. It begins with the devolution of health costs to the individual, whose ability to pay determines the care he or she receives. It leads to the establishment of private nursing and residential homes which, due to the very fact that they are 'private', escape public scrutiny and therefore the barrier to abuse which such scrutiny can constitute. It demands that individuals take responsibility for themselves, even unto – as Fries suggests – death and deciding, in a sense, when to die. Hence the anguish which will be a problem for many. All these measures effectively countermand the possibility of dealing appropriately with the abuse of older women. We would suggest that the attitudes inherent in the low level of general interest in and concern about elder abuse are, in fact, part of the late twentieth-century backlash against women (Faludi, 1992; French, 1992). It seems to us significant, for example, that those articles which most vociferously adopt economistic terminology to discuss what happens in relationships, in abusive and in caring situations, are written by men (e.g. Fries, 1980; Blank et al., 1993).

Women: Abused and Abusers

There is resistance to dealing with what might be perceived as women's issues (Lynda Aitken's experience of the multi-agency group working on guidelines on elder abuse is evidence of this), and elder abuse can in many ways be viewed (and dismissed) as a women's issue, not only because most of the abused are women but also because some perpetrators are women. This statement could be widened to suggest that there is little political will to investigate and improve the position of disempowered groups in Western society; the fact that so little is known about elder abuse in ethnic minority groups indicates that. It is further supported by the fact that elders across all races represent an economically disempowered group (Hugman, 1994: 83–4, 141–2) whose relative poverty reduces their political clout. As we write (May 1995), debates are raging in Britain about the (ab)use of pension funds and the power of shareholders to intervene in company decisions. This debate was initiated as a result of the misappropriation of pension funds by private companies which left pensioners threatened with financial ruin. Significantly, in the current debates institutional shareholders who have the most shares also wield the most decision-making power while individual shareholders and elders as beneficiaries of the pension funds look on helplessly as their financial support is eroded. As Hugman puts it: 'In consumer-oriented society disposable resources are as much a basis of social power as the ownership of property: poverty is socially disempowering as well as personally demeaning. It is known also that poverty is greater, proportionally, among women and members of ethnic minorities and this compounds the issue, linking ageism with sexism and racism' (1994: 84).

Poverty as a factor which disadvantages specific groups of individuals and which lays individuals open to victimization and abuse is related to class issues, a concern which – with the demise of socialism in Britain and the decline of communism in Eastern Europe – has been relegated to the backburner. However, according to Hancock et al. (1995: 5), 'Men and women in social classes I and II [are] less likely to be carers than those in other social classes.' They suggest that people in the higher classes may be less willing to leave their jobs and in a better financial position to afford formal care than those from other classes. If there is a significant correlation between domestic elder abuse and care (and despite some evidence to the contrary, this book still assumes that there is, although care is not the only precondition for abuse), then more domestic elder abuse inflicted by kin is likely to occur in certain social classes simply because less formal care will be bought in. The significance of class in the context of elder abuse needs to be re-examined.

While there has been some engagement with women as victims of abuse, little has been done to investigate women as abusers other than to suggest that stressed carers, either as middle-aged daughters or as older spouses, may be prone to abuse. Penhale (1993a: 97–8) points out that

> the gender of the abuser is related to the type of abuse . . . where physical abuse was found to be most common . . . the abusers were predominantly male. Miller and Dodder (1989) . . . concluded that whilst men were more likely to be physically abusive, women were more involved in neglectful acts . . . a high proportion of spouse abuse in later life concerned women abusing their male partners. Although in this sample there were more men than women who were abused, female victims were subjected to more severe forms of abuse.

Apparently men, being men and therefore more physically abusive, do what men have to do while women, 'as usual', offer passive resistance in the form of neglect. This representation of elder abuse reinforces gender stereotypes, sidelining the more disturbing elements ('more men than women were abused') into dependent clauses and relegating them to secondary concerns. As such it acts to disarm the incentive for action for, if the status quo has been preserved, what is there to worry about? As Penhale states, 'Further research may help to clarify the significance of such findings' (1993a: 98). Further research urgently needs to address the question of women as abusers, of sons as abusers and of abuse by non-relatives and in institutions. It also, perhaps as a first step, needs to be clear about the ways in which research has tended to reproduce gender stereotypes in its lines of enquiry.

Rethinking Dependence

Much of the writing on elder abuse is informed by a sense of the dependence of older people on others. Here dependence is negatively valued. As Steinmetz (1983: 147) puts it: 'we are a society which values independence. To be dependent on someone is an indication of failure. It is with reluctance that an older person must resign himself [*sic*] to being dependent on someone for whom a few decades ago he felt responsible.' Aronson (1990: 61) eloquently discusses the contradiction older women experience, caught 'between the cultural imperative to be unburdensome and independent and their wish for security [and need of support]'. Research into caregiving and care receiving (e.g. Walker et al., 1990; Walker and Pratt, 1991; Blank et al., 1993) tends to be premised on the need for balance in a caring relationship. This assumes that power imbalances resulting from differential degrees of dependence between caregiver and care receiver will facilitate abuse.

Debates about autonomy and dependence are longstanding within feminist research (e.g. Chodorow, 1978; Gilligan, 1982). Based on theories of psychosexual development, feminist writers have suggested that women value dependence differently from men due to the former's ongoing attachment to their primary love object, the mother, in the course of their development. Men, in contrast, supposedly have to differentiate themselves from their mothers to achieve a masculine identity. In consequence, women are relationally rather than self-oriented and cope with dependence better than men. It is, of course, possible that this explanation simply fosters stereotypes of femininity and masculinity which suggest dependency in women and autonomy in men. However, in the debate of autonomy versus dependence in the context of elder abuse, a gendered agenda exists which seemingly privileges one position – autonomy – over the other, dependence. This privileging is politically underwritten by the demand that individuals take care of themselves rather than rely on the state or voluntary agencies for support, and by the tendency for reactive rather than proactive policies in this matter.

While the notion of dependency in the context of elder abuse tends, on the whole, to be based on the assumption that it is the abused person who is dependent, this does not necessarily reflect the reality of the situation. Not only can abuse arise out of a state of perceived or actual dependence on the abused person on the part of the abuser (Pillemer and Finkelhor, 1989), a dependence which may temporarily be 'alleviated' in the act of abuse, but, further, it is quite simply not the case that only the abused person is dependent even if it is only in the 'victim' that we recognize – and decry – such dependence. Many of the preventive measures that have been taken to deal with elder abuse, for instance, suggest and encourage dependence. They include support groups, guidelines to which practitioners can refer, respite care, medication, etc. All of these indicate that people, no matter who they are, do not exist in a state of autonomy relative to the rest of the world. Rather, they are part of a large and complex network of interdependencies in which certain dependencies have a 'higher status' and are more acceptable than others. Thus it is more 'acceptable' for a stressed carer to be dependent on respite care than it is for an older person to need care in the first instance. While the issue of how 'dependence' is constructed in Western culture urgently needs rethinking, the idea of autonomy has been useful in refiguring domestic abuse (of which elder abuse might be deemed a variety) as a human rights issue.

Reviewing Power/lessness

Dependence is associated with an imbalance of power. There is, however, considerable difference between the powerlessness which abused and abusers may experience, and the powerlessness *vis-à-vis* elder abuse manifested by some professionals who are, in fact, in a position to intervene. 'Helplessness' in the face of adversity or unpleasant facts is a common response. It is easier to assume a position which does not require one to act than to take responsibility when confronted with elder abuse and act upon it. Penhale (1993a: 100) lists a number of reasons why professionals when faced with elder abuse fail to intervene. They include a lack of knowledge about abuse, a lack of clarity about procedures, treatments, referral systems, a tendency to prioritize the idea of privacy, (knowledge of) inadequate resources and the biases and attitudes both professional and personal which militate against the acknowledgement of elder abuse. In a recent Action on Elder Abuse Bulletin (1995: 3) Phil Slater raised the issue of professional power, pointing out that professionals have the power to define clients, assess needs, manage services, 'protect' individuals and campaign for enhanced statutory powers.

Slater argues for user involvement in policy making, demands that 'power imbalances institutionalized in existing "elderly" services [be] explicitly highlighted and challenged' and that 'current proposals for reform need to be re-evaluated in terms of their likely impact on existing power differentials'. His position implies that professionals at all levels who are involved in situations of elder abuse need to recognize their potential for action and activate it. Unlike the present authors, he does not consider the power differential he perceives to be tied, *inter alia*, to issues of gender but this is clearly one area in which and through which power differentials in society are played out. As suggested in Chapter 3, older people, and in particular women, are constantly encouraged to accept their own powerlessness through the images of old age with which they are daily confronted and the implicit and explicit disregard in which they are held. Transcending this potential and actual victim status is doubly difficult for abused old:r women. Women as abusers may consider their underprivileged status a shield from investigation (being 'invisible' anyway, nobody will detect their activities) and a justification for their abuse of another, equally disenfranchised woman.

Gender Issues in Elder Abuse in Domestic Settings

Much of the research on elder abuse has focused on abuse within what is, sometimes unintentionally ironically, described as a 'caring relationship'. It may well be that this is because the caring relationship can involve outside professionals who might notice and/or intervene in abuse situations. Against this has to be set the fact that professionals, as discussed in Chapter 4, are frequently not the ones to detect or notify abuse. It may be that the political imperative to focus on care in the community has resulted in the perception that the caring family is both desirable and a source of risk. This ignores the possibility that family members may be or become abusive without 'care' being involved. It has been suggested that 'the bulk of abuse is not from stressed carers . . . It occurs in families with multiple problems such as mental illness and drug abuse . . . you have to look at the pattern of family relationships' (Cohen, 1993: 19). The notion that the context of care is central to the possibility of elder abuse also ignores one of the findings of the Northamptonshire study detailed in Chapter 5, namely that in a sizeable number of cases of abuse, the abuse was committed by non-relatives. Thus a significant number of non-relatives abused women physically (see Table 5.8, p. 112 in this volume), and noticeably more women than men were financially abused by non-relatives. With the rise of single person households containing older people, and in particular older women (see Chapter 2), abuse by non-relatives has to become more of a focus for attention. At present, little attention is paid to who these abusing non-relatives are, or to those living *alone* who may be the objects of abuse. As Esther Oxford asks: 'What can be done about the 73-year-old man living in a council flat, whose house is pelted with mud and whose door-bell never stops ringing, when the culprits are neighbourhood kids?' (1995: 21). More research needs to be carried out to establish the extent of abuse of single household occupants, meaning in the main women living on their own, and of their abusers.

At the same time, the question of intra-familial abuse needs to be reframed to include the issue of gender. The Northamptonshire study suggests that sons tend to abuse mothers, especially physically, and in one case sexually. Malcolm Holt's research (Neate, 1993) seems to indicate that sons also feature significantly in the sexual abuse of their older mothers. Jacki Pritchard (Neate, 1993: 18) asserts: 'A lot of sexual abuse we are coming across is ongoing from incestuous relationships that have been going on 30 or 40 years.' Apparently, 'she has known cases where a mother and son have had an incestuous relationship for many years, and the mother has become dependent and withdrawn sexual consent, after which the son has become violent' (ibid.). Such an abuse pattern supports the idea that abuse arises out of long-term relationship patterns. A 1993 survey published by Durham County Council on intra-familial elder abuse indicated that 'three-quarters of the victims had been mistreated for months or years' (Oxford, 1995: 21). Again, more research is needed to investigate this.

At present, the abuse of elderly mothers and fathers on which research exists is presented in gendered scenarios which reinforce existing gender stereotypes. Typically, daughters will be thought of as abusive in consequence of the stress they suffer due to caring, while sons' abuse remains unexplained except for some suggestions that their dependence on a parent in adulthood undermines their sense of self-worth or that they may have suffered abuse from the parent as a child and therefore are revenging themselves, a version of the dysfunctional family reproducing itself. Sons' physical and sexual abuse of elders, relative to, for instance, daughters' neglect or (minor?) physical violence against an older parent fit prevalent stereotypes of masculinity and femininity and thus implicitly suggest that while these instances are regrettable, they are intelligible within commonsensical explanations of gendered behaviour. The prevalence of these conventionally gendered images of abuse may blind us to abuse which fails to fit into these images, specifically women's abuse of women and women's abuse of men, as well as inter-generational abuse of mothers by sons.

Culturally, we seem at present not ready to engage with the idea of the abusing female other than by making her exceptional, 'mad' or 'bad'. Such selective viewing is encouraged by the way in which both the media and professionals tend to treat the occurrence of elder abuse in terms of individual cases which require a response to that one situation and no more. This not only helps to explain some authorities' reluctance to adopt guidelines for elder abuse situations; it also indicates a further reason why the research in the field has been so circumscribed. Hugman (1994: 80) asserts that elder mistreatment and neglect 'are constructed as individual, interpersonal problems' which he interprets 'partly as a reflection of general social ideologies of the family . . . and partly as the outcome of public policy which "residualizes" welfare provision'. The upshot of this is a 'focus on individuals within families, pathologizing actions which may be grounded in contradictory social circumstances' (Hugman, 1994: 81). These may include the expectation of care versus the inability to resource or fulfil that expectation, the demands of the care receiver versus those of other family members, the need to care versus the need to maintain an income, etc. Importantly, such pathologizing of individuals and actions ('she lost her temper and hit the old woman because she has to put up with so much from her husband') ignores the continuities between the violence of everyday behaviour and the violence occurring in elder abuse. It also frequently serves both to reinforce the status quo of gendered role distributions and expectations (women care – men do jobs around the house; men commit active physical and sexual violence, women passively neglect), and of the intelligibility of elder abuse within that status quo.

This situation is noticeable in the fairly recent recognition that spousal abuse occurs among older couples. The Northamptonshire study clearly indicated that older men are abused by wives and daughters, and that older women are abused by sons and husbands. Neglect in older couples where both are decreasingly capable to cope with the daily activities of living seems not to be uncommon and suggests that more help needs to be directed at such couples. Other forms of abuse, as well as their motivation, need further research. Both long-term dysfunctional relational histories and recent personality changes in one partner due to dementia have been presented as reasons for physical, sexual and other kinds of partner abuse. Beyond the issue of motivation, further thought needs to be given to how best to detect and to intervene in such situations of abuse. According to Malcolm Holt, 'The message I get from front line workers, time and time again, is that they don't feel empowered to assess and confront abuse. The management structures and the decision making of an organization can disempower workers' (Francis, 1993c: 19).

Gender Issues and Elder Abuse in Institutional Settings

At present it is difficult to make comparisons between the likelihood of the occurrence of elder abuse in institutional as opposed to domestic settings. We know too little about the former. Bennett (1994) paints a pretty horrific picture of the daily routines of abuse apparently common in institutional settings for elders. What research has been done in this arena has tended to concentrate on small groups of professionals, usually nurses, and their attitudes towards elders. We have not come across work that looks at the vast numbers of semi-skilled and unskilled women working in nursing and residential homes, or, indeed, on their wardens. Nor is there much, outside topics such as the use of reminiscence therapy, by way of first person accounts of older people in institutional settings. It is as if, once these older people who are of course predominantly older women have arrived in the institution, their last 'home' before death, they have become non-persons, are already dead. It is the profoundest and most shocking indictment of the ageism that pervades our culture.

The silence which surrounds elder abuse in institutions is exacerbated by three facts: that in institutional abuse we are dealing to a very large extent with abuse of women by women; the recognition that homes for elders are the public way of dealing with what is constructed as a social problem which has, however, due to the expectation of the imminent death of elders, a terminal point to it; and the increasing privatization of the sector and the ideological implications of this.

As suggested in the context of talking about elder abuse in domestic settings, the absence of a public discourse to encompass women's abuse by women other than through the notion of individual pathologies forecloses the recognition of women's abuse of women as part of the violence of everyday behaviour in women. Thus significantly the Action on Elder Abuse survey *Everybody's Business!* reported that '*One* health trust was monitoring abuse by nurses. This was stated to be in response to the Department of Health letter CNO PL 94 (6) (1994) issued after the Beverly Allitt case' (1995: 10; our emphasis). Whether one is familiar with this case or not, the fact that a single case promoted a Department of Health letter which in turn made one health trust (and seemingly one only) respond by monitoring nurses indicates both the sustained individualization of occurrences of abuse in institutions and the impact which such a single case can nevertheless have.

What to do with older people once they can no longer care for themselves is increasingly considered a problem both socially and economically. Dealing with 'many people living beyond their economically productive years' (Steinmetz, 1983: 135) has become an 'embarrassment' in a society in which economic productivity is the only measure of human worth and in which absence of this productivity results in loss of identity, 'status, power and prestige' (Steinmetz, 1983: 135) and general disenfranchisement. Families may well continue to take an active interest in the older relative whom they have had to put into a home or institution and visit on a regular basis (Ross et al., 1993) but as was indicated in Chapter 4, this does not necessarily mean that they have a clear insight into the workings of the home or institution in question. If, additionally and as is likely to be the case, the older person is confused or demented, she may have difficulty in communicating her situation.

Even for those who can communicate there is always the question of who to talk to. This is particularly the case with privately run institutions, the numbers of which are steadily increasing and which, in the UK at least, are still largely unregulated. The very idea of privacy inherent in the concept of the private nursing or residential home militates against intervention from outside. Bennett (1994: 18) found that in smaller homes, 'life is organized on the model of a household'. This of course combines with the idea of privacy to establish a 'home' which, like the private domestic setting, escapes public scrutiny unless a criminal act occurs. The staff can come to act as symbolic authority figures with virtually complete control over all aspects of residents' lives (Blank et al., 1993: 279–80). The resultant disempowerment or infantilization of residents is in itself a form of abuse. Bennett (1994: 18) refers to one older woman who came to a smaller residential home to avoid being put in a council home where she expected to be treated 'as a child'. Another resident saw her co-residents 'as my relations, you know, family' (ibid.). For her this provided relief and company, but as Bennett found: 'A disparate family, however. The residents are civil to one another, but it is hard to imagine that anything but age and infirmity would have brought them all together' (ibid.). The random assemblage of older women which characterizes many residential homes and denies the residents' need to be with like-minded people is one of the many ways in which older women's rights are undermined when they need to go into institutional care: 'homes [make] no effort to facilitate or sustain friendships ... they only [notice] relationships between residents when they [become] "problematic" ' (Bennett, 1994: 20).

Elder Abuse as a Human Rights Issue

It is because of the dangers of seeing women's violation, whatever form it takes, as a private issue occurring in private settings between economically apparently relatively unimportant people that feminists have begun to call for a review of violence against women as a public rather than a private issue and as a matter of human rights rather than of gender-oriented specific laws. As Jane Maslow Cohen, calling for a sense of public obligation, explains: 'The inquiries done to abused women within the privacy of home and intimate relationship must . . . be understood not as atomistic events of no acknowledged meaning to the social order but, rather, as class-based wrongs that help, the way that gender-based workplace harassment and gender-stratified career options and wage scales help, to define the place of women in that order' (Maslow Cohen, 1994: 351). The systematic subjection of women across the world serves, among other things, to legitimize their abuse and is enhanced by the construction of the home (as 'family' home and as private institution) as a 'realm free from state intervention' (ibid.: 360). The result has been a 'lack of coherent organizing strategies' (ibid.: 361), evidenced in the context of elder abuse in the limited number of multi-agency guidelines on how to deal with elder abuse.

Beasley and Thomas (1994) argue that for a problem to be recognized as a human rights issue, i.e. as one affecting the rights of the individual to autonomy and freedom, it has to be shown that the state systematically fails to prosecute abuses committed by its agents or by private individuals due to a failure to enforce laws equitably across, for instance, gender lines. In Chapter 3 of this volume we indicated that there have been suggestions, for instance in the *Guidelines* of the Royal College of Nursing, that elder abuse might involve violations of human rights by failing to meet individuals' needs. In so far as the abuse of women, whether these are older or not, is tolerated by states which fail to prosecute such violation, these states fail to afford women equal protection of the law against those abuses.

One of the noticeable aspects of domestic abuse as it is addressed by feminists is that it has, without this being directly expressed, separated out older women from women of other age groups. Whenever domestic abuse is referred to, it is assumed that this relates to adult women up to some invisible age barrier beyond which lies elder abuse. This means that older women at present have no lobby in the human rights forum as addressed by feminists. Yet many feminists see the way forward in combating domestic abuse as utilizing the human rights forum to demand interventions from the state in cases of domestic abuse. Given the evidence of abuse of older women by women and men, there is an urgent need to review the idea of domestic violence, or 'private violence' as it is sometimes called, to explicitly include older women. If 'the concept of human rights is one of the few moral visions ascribed to [*sic*] internationally', we would argue, with Beasley and Thomas (1994: 323), that '[elder abuse] violates the principles that lie at the heart of this moral vision: the inherent dignity and worth of all members of the human family, the inalienable right to freedom from fear and want, and the equal rights of men and women (Universal Declaration 1948)'.

Bibliography

Action on Elder Abuse (1994) *Working Paper No. 1*. London: Action on Elder Abuse.

Action on Elder Abuse (1995) *Everybody's Business! Taking Action on Elder Abuse.* London: Action on Elder Abuse.

Age Concern (1986) *The Law and Vulnerable Old People*. London: Age Concern.

Age Concern (1987) *Celebrating Age: What is Ageism?* London: Age Concern.

Age Concern (n.d.) *Abuse of Elderly People: Guidelines for Action*. London: Age Concern.

Alexander, George (ed.) (1992) *International Perspectives on Aging*. Dordrecht, Netherlands: Martinus Nijhoff.

Allen, Hilary (1987) 'Rendering Them Harmless: The Professional Portrayal of Women Charged with Serious Violent Crimes', in P. Carlen and A. Worral (eds), *Gender Crimes and Justice*. Milton Keynes: Open University Press. pp. 81–95.

Alzheimer's Disease Society (1993) *Information Sheet No. 1*. London: Alzheimer's Disease Society, June.

Arber, Sara and Gilbert, Nigel (eds) (1992) *Women and Working Lives: Divisions and Change*. London: Macmillan.

Arber, Sara and Gilbert, Nigel (1993) 'Men: The Forgotten Carers', in Joanna Bornat et al. (eds), *Community Care: A Reader*. Houndsmill: Macmillan. pp. 134–42.

Arber, Sara and Ginn, Jay (1990) 'The Meaning of Informal Care: Gender and the Contribution of Elderly People', *Ageing and Society*, 10: 429–54.

Arber, Sara and Ginn, Jay (1991) *Gender and Later Life: A Sociological Analysis of Resources and Constraints*. London: Sage.

Arber, Sara and Ginn, Jay (eds) (1995) *Connecting Gender and Ageing*. Buckingham: Open University Press.

Arber, Sara, Gilbert, G. Nigel and Evandrou, Maria (1988) 'Gender, Household Composition and Receipt of Domiciliary Services by Elderly Disabled People', *Journal of Social Policy*, 17 (2): 153–75.

Arnold, June (1979) *Sister Gin*. London: Women's Press.

Aronson, Jane (1990) 'Women's Perspectives on Informal Care of the Elderly: Public Ideology and Personal Experience of Giving and Receiving Care', *Ageing and Society*, 10: 61–84.

Association of Directors of Social Services (1991) *Adults at Risk: Guidance for Directors of Social Services*. Stockport: ADSS.

Bachman, D.L., Wolf, P.A., Linn, R. et al. (1992) 'Prevalence of Dementia and Probable Senile Dementia of the Alzheimer Type in the Framingham Study,' *Neurology*, 42: 115–19.

Baker, A.A. (1975) 'Granny Battering', *Modern Geriatrics*, 5 (8): 20–4.

Balarajan, R., Yuen, P. and Raleigh, Soni V. (1989) 'Ethnic Differences in General Practice Consultations', *British Medical Journal*, 299: 958–60.

Barker, Pat (1982) *Union Street*. London: Virago.

Barker, Pat (1986) *The Century's Daughter*. London: Virago.

Barrett, Michèle and McIntosh, Mary (1982) *The Anti-Social Family*. London: Verso.

Beasley, Michele E. and Thomas, Dorothy Q. (1994) 'Domestic Violence as a Human Rights Issue', in Martha Albertson Fineman and Roxanne Mykitiuk (eds), *The Public Nature of Private Violence*. London: Routledge. pp. 323–46.

Bennett, Catherine (1994) 'Ending Up', *Guardian Weekend*, 8 October: 12–14, 18, 20.

Bennett, Gerry (1990) 'Action on Elder Abuse in the '90s: New Definition Will Help', *Geriatric Medicine*, April: 53–4.

Bennett, Gerald and Kingston, Paul (1993) *Elder Abuse: Concepts, Theories and Interventions*. London: Chapman and Hall.

Bennett, Gerry and Ogg, Jim (1993) 'Researching Elder Abuse', in Claudine McCreadie (ed.), *Elder Abuse: New Findings and Guidelines*. London: Age Concern Institute of Gerontology. pp. 3–7.

Biggs, Simon, Phillipson, Chris and Kingston, Paul (1995) *Elder Abuse in Perspective*. Buckingham: Open University Press.

Birmingham BASE (British Association for Service to the Elderly) (1988) *Old Age Abuse: A West Midlands Perspective*. Birmingham: BASE.

Blackhurst, Chris (1995) 'Long-stay Patients Ejected by Hospital "Lost Will to Live"', *Independent on Sunday*, 19 March.

Blakely, B.E., Dolon, Ronald and May, Douglas D. (1993) 'Improving the Responses of Physicians to Elder Abuse and Neglect: Contributions to a Model Program', *Journal of Gerontological Social Work*, 19 (3/4): 35–47.

Blakemore, Ken (1983) 'Ethnicity, Self-Reported Illness and Use of Medical Services by the Elderly', *Postgraduate Medical Journal*, October (59): 668–70.

Blakemore, Ken and Boneham, Margaret (1994) *Age, Race and Ethnicity*. Buckingham: Open University Press.

Blank, Thomas O., Levesque, Maurice J. and Winter, Georgie P. (1993) 'The Triad of Control: Concepts and Applications to Caregiving', *International Journal of Behavioral Development*, 16 (2): 261–86.

'Bleeper Plan to "Spy On" Over-55s', *Guardian*, 4 October 1994: 5.

Block, M. and Sinnott, J. (eds) (1979) 'The Battered Elder Syndrome: An Exploratory Study'. Unpublished Manuscript, University of Maryland.

Blundy, Anna (1995) 'More Families Dump Granny for Christmas', *Sunday Times*, 1 January: 9.

Blythe, Ronald (1969) *Akenfield: Portrait of an English Village*. London: Allen Lane.

Bornat, Joanna, Pereira, Charmaine, Pilgrim, David and Williams, Fiona (eds) (1993) *Community Care: A Reader*. Houndsmill: Macmillan.

Boult, Chad, Dowd, Bryan and McCaffrey, David (1993) 'Screening Elders for Risk of Hospital Admission', *Journal of the American Geriatrics Society*, 41 (8): 811–17.

Braid, Mary (1994) 'Life for Teenage Killer Who Preyed on Elderly', *Independent*, 28 September: 3.

Briggs, Anna and Oliver, Judith (eds) (1985) *Caring: Experience of Looking after Disabled Relatives*. London: Routledge and Kegan Paul.

Briggs, Simon and Phillipson, Chris (1992) *Understanding Elder Abuse: A Training Manual for Helping Professions*. Harlow: Longman.

Brindle, David (1992) 'Nurses to get Guidance on Withdrawing Care', *Guardian*, 1 May: 2.

Brindle, David (1994) 'More than 90pc of Pensioners in Poll Back Voluntary Euthanasia', *Guardian*, 29 November: 3.

British Geriatrics Society (1990) *Abuse of Elderly People: Guidelines for Action for Those Working with Elderly People*. London: Age Concern.

Brown, Hilary (1992) 'An Abuse of Power', *Community Care*, 29 October: 15–17.

Brown, Hilary and Smith, Helen (1993) 'Women Caring for People: The Mismatch between Rhetoric and Women's Reality?' *Policy and Politics*, 21 (3): 185–93.

Browne, Colette V. (1995) 'Empowerment in Social Work Practice with Older Women', *Social Work*, 40/3 (May): 358–64.

'Bully Nurse Escapes Ban' (1992) *Northampton Chronicle and Echo*, 6 June: 4.

Burston, G.R. (1975) 'Granny Battering', *British Medical Journal*, 3: 592.

Bytheway, Bill (1995) *Ageism*. Buckingham: Open University Press.

Callahan, J.J. (1988) 'Elder Abuse: Some Questions for Policy Makers', *The Gerontologist*, 28 (4): 453–8.

Cameron, Elaine et al. (1989) 'Black Old Women, Disability and Health Carers', in Margot Jeffreys (ed.), *Growing Old in the 20th Century*. London: Routledge. pp. 230–47.

Campbell, Duncan (1995) 'Violence Tops Crime Fear', *Guardian*, 3 January: 5.

Carey, Tanith (1994) 'Gran's Ordeal: My Night of Terror at Hands of Killer', *Daily Mirror*, 28 September: 5.

Carlen, Pat (1988) *Women, Poverty and Crime*. Milton Keynes: Open University Press.

Carr-Hill, Roy and Rudat, Kai (1995) 'Unsound Barrier', *Health Service Journal*, 9 February: 28–9.

Carrington, Lucie (1993) 'Taking Care', *Community Care*, 25 (14–20 July): 26–7.

Central Statistical Office (1989) *Social Trends*. London: HMSO.

Cervi, Bob (1993) 'HomeCare Agencies will Self-regulate', *Community Care*, 1 July: 2.

Challis, David (1992) 'Providing Alternatives to Long Stay Hospital Care for Frail Elderly Patients: Is It Cost-Effective?', *International Journal of Geriatric Psychiatry*, 7: 773–81.

Challis, D., Chesterman, Jack, Darton, Robin and Traske, Karen (1993) 'Case Management in the Care of the Aged: The Provision of Care in Different Settings', in J. Bornat, C. Pereira, D. Pilgrim and F. Williams (eds), *Community Care: A Reader*. Houndsmill: Macmillan. pp. 184–203.

Chamberlain, Linda (1993) 'Report Warns of Gags for Elderly People', *Community Care*, 6 May: 2.

Chambers, Ruth (1991) 'The Power and the "Gory" of Private Care Homes', *Care of the Elderly*, September: 356.

Chodorow, Nancy (1978) *The Reproduction of Mothering*. Berkeley: University of California Press.

Cixous, Hélène (1981) 'The Laugh of the Medusa', in E. Marks and I. de Courtivron (eds), *New French Feminisms*. Brighton: Harvester Press. pp. 245–64.

Code, Lorraine (1991) *What Can She Know? Feminist Theory and the Construction of Knowledge*. Ithaca, NY: Cornell University Press.

Cohen, Phil (1993) 'A Matter of Judgment', *Community Care*, 10 June: 18–19.

Comfort, A. (1977) *A Good Age*. London: Mitchell Beazley.

Commission for Racial Equality (1987) *Ethnic Origins of Nurses Applying for and in Training: A Survey*. London: CRE.

Cook, J. and Watts, S. (1987) 'Racism, Women and Poverty', in C. Glendenning and J. Millar (eds), *Women and Poverty in Britain*. London: Tavistock.

Counsel and Care (1993) *People not Parcels*. London: Counsel and Care.

'Counting the Cost of Caring' (1994) *Guardian*, 20 September 1994: 12–13.

Coyne, Andrew C., Reichman, William E. and Berbig, Lisa J. (1993) 'The Relationship between Dementia and Elder Abuse', *American Journal of Psychiatry*, 150 (4 April): 643–6.

Craft, Ann (1994) 'The Vulnerable Adults Who Need Protection from Their Carers', *Parliamentary Brief*, November: 72.

Daly, Mary (1978) *Gyn/ecology*. Boston, MA: Beacon Press.

Daly, Mary with Caputi, Jane (1988) *Webster's First Intergalactic Wickedary of the English Language*. Dublin: Attic Press.

Dant, Tim and Gearing, Brian (1993) 'Key Workers for Elderly People in the Community', in J. Bornat, C. Pereira, D. Pilgrim, and F. Williams (eds), *Community Care: A Reader*. Houndsmill: Macmillan. pp. 296–303.

Day, Liz (1986) 'Time to Value the Golden Age', *Nursing Times*, 15 October: 67–9.

De Beauvoir, Simone (1972) *Old Age*. London: André Deutsch.

Decalmer, Peter (1993) 'Clinical Presentation', in P. Decalmer and F. Glendenning (eds), *The Mistreatment of Elderly People*. London: Sage. pp. 35–61.

Decalmer, Peter and Glendenning, Frank (eds) (1993) *The Mistreatment of Elderly People*. London: Sage.

Delphy, Christine and Leonard, Diana (1992) *Familiar Exploitations: A New Analysis of Marriage in Contemporary Western Societies*. Cambridge: Polity Press.

Department of Health (1986) *The Health of the Nation: A Strategy for Health in England*. London: HMSO.

Department of Health (1989) *Caring for People: Community Care in the Next Decade and Beyond*. London: HMSO.

Department of Health (1992) *The Health of the Nation*. London: HMSO.

Department of Health (1995) *The Patient's Charter and You*. London: HMSO.

Diessenbacher, Hardy (1989) 'Neglect, Abuse and the Taking of Life in Old People's Homes', *Ageing and Society*, 9: 61–71.

Dobash, R. Emerson and Dobash, Russell P. (1992) *Women, Violence and Social Change*. London: Routledge.

Donaldson, L.J. (1986) 'Health and Social Status of Elderly Asians: A Community Survey', *British Medical Journal*, 293 (25 October): 1079–82.

Douglass, R.L., Hickey, T. and Noel, C. (1980) *A Study of the Maltreatment of the Elderly and Other Vulnerable Adults*. Michigan: Institute of Gerontology, University of Michigan.

Drabble, Margaret (1981) *The Middle Ground*. Harmondsworth: Penguin.

Dugan, Elizabeth and Kivett, Vira R. (1994) 'The Importance of Emotional and Social Isolation to Loneliness among Very Old Rural Adults', *The Gerontologist*, 34 (3): 340–6.

Eastman, Mervin (1984) *Old Age Abuse*. London: Age Concern.

Eastman, Mervin (1988) 'Granny Abuse', *Community Outlook*, October: 15–16.

Eastman, Mervin (1993) 'Fighting it Right', *Community Care*, 6 May: 20.

Eastman, Mervin (ed.) (1994a) *Old Age Abuse: A New Perspective*. London: Chapman and Hall.

Eastman, Mervin (1994b) 'The Victims: Older People and Their Carers in a Domestic Setting', in Mervin Eastman (ed.), *Old Age Abuse: A New Perspective*. London: Chapman and Hall. pp. 23–9.

Equal Opportunities Commission (1980) *The Experience of Caring for the Elderly and Handicapped Dependants*. Manchester: Equal Opportunities Commission.

Equal Opportunities Commission (1982) *Caring for the Elderly and Handicapped: Community Care, Policies and Women's Lives*. Manchester: Equal Opportunities Commission.

Evandrou, Maria (1991) 'Challenging the Invisibility of Carers: Mapping Informal Care Nationally', *Community Care*, 25 April: 24.

Faludi, Susan (1992) *Backlash: The Undeclared War against Women*. London: Chatto and Windus.

Family Policy Studies Centre (1984) *The Forgotten Army: Family Care and Elderly People*. London: FPSC.

Fentiman, Ian S. (1995) 'Gap in Health Care for Older Women', *The Times*, 1 February: 15.

Fentiman, I.S. et al. (1990) 'Cancer in the Elderly: Why So Badly Treated?' *The Lancet*, 28 April: 1020–2.

Finch, Janet (1989) *Family Obligations and Social Change*. Cambridge: Polity Press.

Finch, Janet and Groves, Dulcie (eds) (1983) *A Labour of Love: Women, Work and Caring*. London: Routledge and Kegan Paul.

Finch, Janet and Mason, Jennifer (1993) 'Filial Obligations and Kin Support for Elderly People', in Joanna Bornat et al. (eds), *Community Care: A Reader*. Houndsmill: Macmillan. pp. 96–106.

Fineman, Martha Albertson and Mykitiuk, Roxanne (eds) (1994) *The Public Nature of Private Violence: The Discovery of Domestic Abuse*. London: Routledge.

Fitzherbert, Claudia (1992) 'Old Bones and Fresh Bruises', *Daily Telegraph*, 23 October: 21.

Ford, Janet and Sinclair, Ruth (1987) *Sixty Years On: Women Talk about Old Age*. London: Women's Press.

Forster, Margaret (1989) *Have the Men Had Enough?* London: Chatto and Windus.

Foucault, Michel (1989) *The Birth of the Clinic*. London: Routledge. First published 1973.

Foucault, Michel (1977) *Discipline and Punish: The Birth of the Prison*. Harmondsworth: Penguin.

Francis, Joy (1993a) 'Call the Register', *Community Care*, 8 July: 16–17.

Francis, Joy (1993b) 'The Distress of Disclosure', *Community Care*, 17 June: 18–19.

Francis, Joy (1993c) 'Where Do You Draw the Line?', *Community Care*, 20 May: 18–19.

Francis, Joy (1994) 'Pain Killer', *Community Care*, 15–21 December: 22–3.

Frank, Helen (1992) 'No Sex Please, We Live in an Old People's Home', *Independent*, 9 June: 13.

French, Marilyn (1992) *The War Against Women*. London: Hamish Hamilton.

Freud, Sigmund (1905) *On Psychotherapy*. London: Hogarth Press.

Friedan, Betty (1993) *The Fountain of Age*. London: Vintage.

Fries, James F. (1980) 'Aging, Natural Death and the Compression of Morbidity', *New England Journal of Medicine*, 303 (3): 130–5.

Fulmer, T. and O'Malley, T.A. (1987) *Inadequate Care of the Elderly: A Health Care Perspective on Abuse and Neglect*. New York: Springer.

Garrett, Gill (1991) 'Caring in the UK Today', in Gill Garrett (ed.), *Healthy Ageing: Some Nursing Perspectives*. London: Wolfe Publishing.

George, Julie and Ebrahim, Shah (eds) (1992) *Health Care for Older Women*. Oxford: Oxford University Press.

Giancola, Peter R., and Zeichner, Amos (1993) 'Aggressive Behavior in the Elderly: A Critical Review', *Clinical Gerontologist*, 13 (2): 3–22.

Gibbs, J., Evans, M. and Rodway, S. (1987) *Report of the Enquiry into Nye Bevan Lodge*. London: Borough of Southwark.

Gillam, S.J. et al. (1989) 'Ethnic Differences in Consultation Rates in Urban General Practices', *British Medical Journal*, 299: 953–7.

Gilligan, Carol (1982) *In a Different Voice*. Cambridge, MA: Harvard University Press.

Glasse, Lou and Hendricks, Jon (eds) (1992) *Gender and Ageing*. New York: Baywood.

Glendenning, Frank (1993) 'What is Elder Abuse and Neglect?', in P. Decalmer and F. Glendenning (eds), *The Mistreatment of Elderly People*. London: Sage. pp. 1–34.

Glendenning, F. and Pearson, M. (1988) *The Black and Ethnic Minority Elders in Britain: Health Needs and Access to Services*. Working Paper No. 6, University of Keele.

Glendinning, Caroline and Millar, Jane (eds) (1992) *Women and Poverty in Britain in the 1990s*. Hemel Hempstead: Harvester Wheatsheaf.

Goddard, Eileen and Savage, David (1994) *People aged 65 and over: A Study Carried out on behalf of the Department of Health as Part of the 1991 General Household Survey*. London: HMSO.

Godkin, Michael A., Wolf, R.S. and Pillemer, K.A. (1989) 'A Case Comparison Analysis of Elder Abuse and Neglect', *International Journal of Ageing and Human Development*, 28 (3): 207–25.

Goffman, Ervin (1968) *Asylums*. Harmondsworth: Penguin.

Golden, James (1993) 'Staying Power of the Asian Happy Families', *Daily Mail*, 5 June.

Gordon, David S. and Easton, Norman (1991) 'Patterns of Caring: Case Studies in Informal Care', *Practice*, 6 (1): 16–24.

Grafstrom, Margareta, Norberg, Astrid, and Hagberg, Bo (1993) 'Relationships between Demented Elderly People and Their Families: A Follow-up Study of Caregivers Who Had Previously Reported Abuse When Caring for Their Spouses and Parents', *Journal of Advanced Nursing*, 18: 1747–57.

Graham, Hilary (1983) 'Caring: A Labour of Love', in Janet Finch and Dulcie M. Groves (eds), *A Labour of Love: Women, Work and Caring*. London: Routledge and Kegan Paul. pp. 13–30.

Grant, Linda (1994) 'Why Do Young Men Rape Elderly Women? And Why Does Nobody Care?', *Independent on Sunday*, 23 January: 21.

Green, H. (1988) *Informal Carers*. OPCS, Series GH5 No. 15. Supplement A. London: HMSO.

Greenhalgh, Trisha (1995) 'Ethnic Groups and a Question of Health', *The Times*, 9 February: 17.

Greer, Germaine (1991) *The Change: Women, Ageing and the Menopause*. London: Penguin.

Griffin, Gabriele (1995) 'The Struggles Continue – An Interview with Hannana Siddiqui', in G. Griffin (ed.), *Feminist Activism in the 1990s*. London: Taylor and Francis.

Grimley Evans, J. (1991) 'Ageing and Rationing', *British Medical Journal*, 303, 12 October: 869–70.

Groves, Dulcie (1992) 'Occupational Pension Provision and Women's Poverty in Old Age', in Caroline Glendinning and Jane Millar (eds), *Women and Poverty in Britain – the 1990s*. Hemel Hempstead: Harvester Wheatsheaf. pp. 176–92.

Gunaratnam, Yasmin (1993) 'Breaking the Silence: Asian Carers in Britain', in Joanna Bornat et al. (eds), *Community Care: A Reader*. Houndsmill: Macmillan. pp. 114–23.

Hagnell, O., Ojesjo, L. and Rorsman, B. (1991) 'Incidence of Dementia in the Lundby Study', *Neuroepidemiology*, 11 (suppl. 1): 61–6.

Hamel, M., Gold, D.P. and Andres, D. et al. (1990) 'Predictors and Consequences of Aggressive Behavior by Community-based Dementia Patients', *The Gerontologist*, 30 (2): 206–11.

Hancock, Ruth and Jarvis, Claire (1994) *The Long Term Effects of Being a Carer*. London: HMSO.

Hancock, Ruth, Jarvis, Claire and Mueller, Ganka (1995) *The Hidden Carers*. London: The Princess Royal Trust for Carers.

Hek, Gill (1991) 'Contact with Asian Elders', *Journal of District Nursing*, 10 (6): 13–15.

Hen Co-op (1993) *Growing Old Disgracefully*. London: Piatkus Books.

Hennessy, Rosemary (1993) *Materialist Feminism and the Politics of Discourse*. London: Routledge.

Hess, Beth (1992) 'Gender and Ageing: The Demographic Parameters', in Lou Glasse and Jon Hendricks (eds), *Gender and Ageing*. New York: Baywood. pp. 20–35.

Hicks, Cherrill (1988) *Who Cares? Looking after People at Home*. London: Virago.

Hill, Aletta Olin (1986) *Mother Tongue, Father Time: A Decade of Linguistic Revolt*. Bloomington: Indiana University Press.

Hilldrew, Mary Ann (1991) 'New Age Problem', *Social Work Today*, 22 August: 15–17.

Hofman, A., Rocca, W.A., Brayne, C., et al. (1991) 'The Prevalence of Dementia in Europe: A Collaborative Study of 1980–1990 Findings', *International Journal of Epidemiology*, 20: 734–48.

Holland, Patricia (1987) 'When a Woman Reads the News', in Helen Baehr and Gillian Dyer (eds), *Boxed In: Women and Television*. London: Pandora. pp. 133–50.

Hollows, Belinda (1996) 'Public Relations, Private Hell: Lesbian Domestic Violence', in Nicola Godwin, Belina Hollows and Sheridan Rye (eds), *Assaults on Convention: Essays on Lesbian Transgressors*. London: Cassell. pp. 128–42.

Holt, Malcolm (1993) 'Elder Sexual Abuse in Britain', in Claudine McCreadie (ed.), *Elder Abuse: New Findings and Guidelines*. London: Age Concern Institute of Gerontology. pp. 16–18.

Holt, Malcolm (1995) 'Looking After Uncle Sam', *Community Care*, 16–22 March: 22–3.

Home Office (1984) *Statement of Changes in Immigration Rules Laid before Parliament on 9 Feb. 1983 under Section 3(2) of the Immigration Act 1971*. London: HMSO.

Homer, Ann (1994) 'Prevalence and Prevention of Abuse', in Mervin Eastman, (ed.), *Old Age Abuse: A New Perspective*. London: Chapman and Hall. pp. 31–50.

Homer, Ann C. and Gilleard, C. (1990) 'Abuse of Elderly People by Their Carers', *British Medical Journal*, 301: 1359–62.

hooks, bell (1984) *Feminist Theory: From Margin to Center*. Boston: South End Press.

Hope, Christopher (1992) *Serenity House*. London: Macmillan.

Hudson, Robert B. and Gonyea, Judith G. (1992) 'A Perspective on Women in Politics: Political Mobilization and Older Women', in Lou Glasse and Jon Hendricks (eds), *Gender and Ageing*. New York: Baywood. pp. 129–37.

Hugman, Richard (1994) *Ageing and the Care of Older People in Europe*. Houndsmill: Macmillan.

Hurrell, Ian (1992) 'Age and Outrage', *Northampton Chronicle and Echo*, 13 May: 12.

Itzin, Catherine (1984) 'The Double Jeopardy of Ageism and Sexism: Medical Images of Women', in D.B. Bromley (ed.), *Gerontology: Social and Behavioural Perspectives*. London: Croom Helm. pp. 170–83.

Jack, Raymond (1994) 'Dependence, Power and Violation: Gender Issues in Abuse of Elderly People by Formal Carers', in M. Eastman (ed.), *Old Age Abuse: A New Perspective*. London: Chapman and Hall. pp. 77–92.

Jenkins, Ginny (1993) 'Accidents Will Happen', *Health Service Journal*, 7 October: 31.

Johnson, Mark R.D. (1991) 'Health and Social Services: Chartering for Black Citizens' Rights', *New Community*, 18 (2): 316–25.

Johnson, Norman (1995) 'Domestic Violence: An Overview', in P. Kingston and B. Penhale (eds), *Family Violence and the Caring Professions*. London: Macmillan. pp. 101–26.

Johnson, Julia and Slater, Robert (eds) (1993) *Ageing and Later Life*. London: Sage.

Johnson, Tanya F., O'Brien, James G. and Hudson, Margaret F. (1985) *Elder Neglect and Abuse: An Annotated Bibliography*. Westport, CT: Greenwood Press.

Jones, E. Ann (1993) 'News Women – New Women? The Sidelining of Older Women Newsreaders in the UK.' MA dissertation, Nene College, Northampton.

Jones, Helen (1993) 'Altered Images', *Nursing Times*, 89 (5): 58–60.

Jukes, Adam (1993) *Why Men Hate Women*. London: Free Association Books.

Julian-Allen, R. (1993) 'Attitude Problem', *Health Service Journal*, 10 June: 35.

Kalish, Richard A. (1979) 'The New Ageism and the Failure Models: A Polemic', *The Gerontologist*, 19 (4): 398–402.

Kappeler, Susanne (1995) *The Will to Violence: The Politics of Personal Behaviour*. Cambridge: Polity Press.

Kauffman, Linda (ed.) (1989) *Gender and Theory: Dialogues in Feminist Criticism*. Oxford: Basil Blackwell.

Kaye, Richard A. (1993) 'Sexuality in the Later Years', *Ageing and Society*, 13: 415–26.

Keith, Lois (1992) 'Who Cares Wins? Women, Caring and Disability', *Disability, Handicap and Society*, 7 (2): 167–75.

Keith, Pat M., Schafer, Robert B. and Wacker, Robbyn (1993) 'Outcomes of Equity/Inequity among Older Spouses', *International Journal of Aging and Human Development*, 36 (3): 187–97.

Kelman, H. (1973) 'Violence without Moral Restraint', *Journal of Social Issues*, 29: 30–41.

King, Jane (1993) 'Walking a Tightrope', *Community Care*, 24 June: 18–19.

Kingston, Paul and Penhale, Bridget (eds) (1995) *Family Violence and the Caring Professions*. Basingstoke: Macmillan.

Kirsta, Alix (1994) *Deadlier than the Male: Violence and Aggression in Women*. London: HarperCollins.

Kohner, Nancy (1988) *Caring at Home*. Cambridge: National Extension College.

Kosberg, Jordan I. (ed.) (1983a) *Abuse and Maltreatment of the Elderly*. Boston: John Wright, PSG.

Kosberg, Jordan I. (1983b) 'The Special Vulnerability of Elderly Parents', in Jordan I. Kosberg (ed.), *Abuse and Maltreatment of the Elderly*. Boston: John Wright, PSG. pp. 263–75.

Kramarae, Cheris and Treichler, Paula A. (1992) *Amazons, Bluestockings and Crones*. London: Pandora.

Kurrle, S.E. et al. (1991) 'Elder Abuse in Australian Case Series', *Medical Journal of Australia*, 155 (3): 150–3.

Labrecque, Mark S., Peak, Terry and Toseland, Ronald W. (1992) 'Long-Term Effects of a Group Program for Caregivers of Frail Elderly Veterans', *American Journal of Orthopsychiatry*, 62 (4): 575–88.

Lau, E. and Kosberg, Jordan I. (1979) 'Abuse of the Elderly by Informal Care Providers', *Ageing*, 229–300, September–October: 10–15.

Laurance, Jeremy (1994) 'Abuse of the Elderly More Than Doubles', *The Times*, 15 June.

Law Commission (1993a) *Mentally Incapacitated Adults and Decision Making: A New Jurisdiction*. Consultation Paper No. 128. London: HMSO.

Law Commission (1993b) *Mentally Incapacitated Adults and Decision Making: Medical Treatment and Research*. Consultation Paper No. 129. London: HMSO.

Law Commission (1993c) *Mentally Incapacitated and Other Vulnerable Adults: Public Law Protection*. Consultation Paper No. 130. London: HMSO.

Lee, Luke T. (1992) 'Aging: A Human Rights Approach', in George J. Alexander (ed.), *International Perspectives on Aging*. Dordrecht: Martinus Nijhoff. pp. 1–14.

Leroux, T.G. and Petrunik, M. (1990) 'The Construction of Elder Abuse as a Social Problem: A Canadian Perspective', *International Journal of Health Services*, 20 (4): 651–3.

Lessing, Doris (1984) *The Diaries of Jane Somers*. London: Michael Joseph.

Levin, E. (1988) *The Supporters of Confused Elderly People: Problems, Strains and Services*. London: National Institute of Social Work.

Lewis, Jane and Meredith, Barbara (1988) *Daughters Who Care: Daughters Caring for Mothers at Home*. London: Routledge.

Lobel, Karen (1986) *Naming the Violence: Speaking Out about Lesbian Battering*. Seattle: Seal Press.

Luker, Karen and Waters, Karen (1993) 'The Six O'Clock Shock', *Health Service Journal*, 22 April: 20–2.

McCreadie, Claudine (1991) *Elder Abuse: An Exploratory Study*. London: Institute of Gerontology.

McCreadie, Claudine (1993) *Elder Abuse: New Findings and Policy Guidelines*. London: Age Concern Institute of Gerontology.

McCreadie, Claudine (1994) 'Introduction: The Issues, Practice and Policy', in M. Eastman (ed.), *Old Age Abuse*. London: Chapman and Hall. pp. 3–22.

McCreadie, Claudine and Tinker, Anthea (1993) 'Review: *Abuse of Elderly People in the Domestic Setting. A UK Perspective*', *Age and Ageing*, 22: 65–9.

Macdonald, Victoria (1995) 'Battered Husbands Afraid to Seek Help', *Sunday Telegraph*, 29 January.

Macdonald, Barbara and Rich, Cynthia (1983) *Look Me in the Eye: Old Women, Ageing and Ageism*. London: Women's Press.

McEwen, Evelyn (ed.) (1990) *Age: The Unrecognised Discrimination*. London: Age Concern.

McNabb, P. (1964) 'Social Structure', in J. Newman (ed.), *The Limerick Rural Survey 1958–1964*. Tipperary: Muintir na Tire Rural Publications.

Mahoney, Martha R. (1994) 'Victimization or Oppression? Women's Lives, Violence, and Agency', in Martha Albertson Fineman and Roxanne Mykitiuk (eds), *The Public Nature of Private Violence*. London: Routledge. pp. 59–92.

Marchant, Catriona (1993) 'Out in the Cold', *Community Care*, 27 May: 24–5.

Marshall, Mary (1990) 'Proud to be Old: Attitudes to Age and Ageism', in Evelyn McEwen (ed.), *Age: The Unrecognised Discrimination*. London: Age Concern. pp. 28–42.

Maslow Cohen, Jane (1994) 'Private Violence and Public Obligation: The Fulcrum of Reason', in Martha Albertson Fineman and Roxanne Mykitiuk (eds), *The Public Nature of Private Violence*. London: Routledge. pp. 349–81.

Mawby, R.I. (1983) 'Crime and the Elderly: Experience and Perceptions', in D. Jerrome (ed.), *Ageing in Modern Society*. London: Croom Helm.

Mawby, R.I. (1988) 'Age, Vulnerability and Crime', in M. Maguire and J. Pointing (eds), *Victims of Crime: A New Deal?* Milton Keynes: Open University Press. pp. 101–11.

Medical Research Council (1994) *The Health of the UK's Elderly People*. London: Medical Research Council.

Mehta, Gita (1993) 'The Ethnic Elderly', *Journal of Community Nursing*, March: 16–20.

Midwinter, Eric (1991a) *The British Gas Report on Attitudes to Ageing*. London: Centre for Policy on Ageing.

Midwinter, Eric (1991b) 'Forgotten Army: Ageism and the Media', *Social Work Today*, 7 November: 18–19.

Milan Women's Bookstore Collective (1990) *Sexual Difference: A Theory of Socio-Symbolic Practice*. Bloomington: Indiana University Press.

Miller, Casey and Swift, Kate (1981) *The Handbook of Non-Sexist Language*. London: Women's Press.

Miller, R.B. and Dodder, R.A. (1989) 'The Abused–Abuser Dyad: Elder Abuse in the State of Florida', in R. Filinson and S.R. Ingman (eds), *Elder Abuse: Practice and Policy*. New York: Human Sciences Press.

Mills, Jane (1991) *Womanwords*. London: Virago.

Milne, Derek et al. (1993) 'Evaluation of a Carer Support Scheme for Elderly People: The Importance of Coping', *British Journal of Social Work*, 23: 157–68.

Miskelly, Frank (1993) 'No Placement like Home', *Health Service Journal*, 15 July: 30.

Montgomery, Rhonda et al. (1992) 'Women and Men in Care-giving Roles', in Lou Glasse and Jon Hendricks (eds), *Gender and Ageing*. New York: Baywood. pp. 59–67.

Moon, Ailee and Williams, Oliver (1993) 'Perceptions of Elder Abuse and Help-Seeking Patterns among African-American, Caucasian American and Korean-American Elderly Women', *The Gerontologist* 33 (3): 386–95.

'More Will Die Alone, Report Says' (1994) *Independent*, 2 December: 5.

Morgan, David (1981) 'Men, Masculinity and the Process of Sociological Enquiry', in Helen Roberts (ed.), *Doing Feminist Research*. London: Routledge and Kegan Paul. pp. 83–113.

Morris, Jenny (1993) 'Voices for Social Change', *Community Care*, 20 May: 30–1.

Morris, Lydia (1995) *Social Division: Economic Decline and Social Structural Change*. London: UCL Press.

Murray, Nicholas (1993) 'Legal Clout', *Community Care*, 1 July: 16–17.

Naffine, Ngaire (1987) *Female Crime: The Construction of Women in Criminology*. London: Allen and Unwin.

Nazroo, James (1995) 'Uncovering Gender Differences in the Use of Marital Violence: The Effect of Methodology', *Sociology*, 29/3 (August): 475–94.

Neate, Polly (1993) 'No Escape', *Community Care*, 27 May: 18.

Neustatter, Angela (1993) 'Of Misogyny and Men', *Daily Mail*, 12 July: 8.

'NHS Suffering from "Ageism" ' (1994) *Health Service Journal*, 29 September: 13.

Nichol, Jenny (1993) *Working with Elderly Survivors of Sexual Abuse*. Norwich: Social Work Monographs, No. 125.

'No Problem' (1993) *Community Care*, 6 May: 13.

Norman, Alison (1985) *Triple Jeopardy: Growing Old in a Second Homeland*. London: Centre for Policy on Ageing.

Northamptonshire County Council Social Services Department et al. (1994) *Guidelines for Responding to the Abuse of Older People in Domestic Settings*. Northampton.

Nundy, Julian (1994) 'Mellow Bardot Drops her Pout as She Turns 60', *Independent*, 28 September: 9.

Oakley, Ann (1981) 'Interviewing Women: A Contradiction in Terms', in Helen Roberts (ed.), *Doing Feminist Research*. London: Routledge and Kegan Paul. pp. 30–61.

'OAPs Tied to Bedpost' (1992), *Northampton Chronicle and Echo*, 11 May: 1.

Office of Population Censuses and Surveys (OCPS) (1985) *General Household Survey: Informal Carers*. Series THS No. 15. London: HMSO.

Ogg, Jim (1993) 'International Perspectives on Elder Abuse', in Claudine McCreadie (ed.), *Elder Abuse: New Findings and Policy Guidelines*. London: Age Concern Institute of Gerontology. pp. 19–24.

Ogg, Jim and Bennett, Gerry (1991a) 'Elder Abuse: Providing Answers to Some of the Questions', *Geriatric Medicine*, October: 15–16.

Ogg, Jim and Bennett, Gerry (1991b) 'Community Care: Identifying Risk Factors for Elderly Abuse', *Geriatric Medicine*, November: 19.

Ogg, Jim and Bennett, Gerry (1992a) 'Elder Abuse in Britain', *British Medical Journal*, 305: 989–9.

Ogg, Jim and Bennett, Gerry (1992b) 'Elder Abuse: An American Perspective', *Geriatric Medicine*, June: 22.

Ogg, Jim and Munn-Giddings, Carol (1993) 'Researching Elder Abuse', *Ageing and Society*, 13: 389–413.

O'Malley, H. et al. (1979) *Elder Abuse in Massachusetts: A Survey of Professionals and Paraprofessionals*. Boston, MA: Legal Research and Services for the Elderly.

OPCS (1985) *Informal Carers Survey*. London: HMSO.

OPCS (1990) *Population Trends, 61*. London: HMSO.

OPCS (1991) *1991 Census County Report: Northamptonshire (Part 1)*. London: Government Statistical Office.

OPCS (1992) *General Household Survey in 1990 Monitor SS92/93*. London: HMSO.

Owen, David (1993a) *Ethnic Minorities in Great Britain: Settlement Patterns*. 1991 Census Statistical Paper No. 1. Coventry: University of Warwick, Centre for Research in Ethnic Relations.

Owen, David (1993b) *Ethnic Minorities in Great Britain: Age and Gender Structure*. 1991 Census Statistical Paper No. 2. Coventry: University of Warwick, Centre for Research in Ethnic Relations.

Owen, David (1993c) *Ethnic Minorities in Great Britain: Housing and Family Characteristics*. 1991 Census Statistical Paper No. 4. Coventry: University of Warwick, Centre for Research in Ethnic Relations.

Oxford, Esther (1995) 'Cruelty to Elderly People: Do We Care?', *The Times*, 19 April: 21.

Pain, Rachel H. (1995) 'Elderly Women and Fear of Violent Crime: The Least Likely Victims?', *British Journal of Criminology*, 35 (4): 584–98.

The Patient's Charter and You (1995) London: Department of Health.

Paveza, G.J., Cohen, D., Eisdorfer, C. et al. (1992) 'Severe Family Violence and Alzheimer's Disease: Prevalence and Risk Factors', *The Gerontologist*, 32 (4): 493–7.

Paykel, Eugene S., Brayne, Carol, Huppert, Felicia A., et al. (1994) 'Incidence of Dementia in a Population Older than 75 Years in the United Kingdom', *Archives of General Psychiatry*, 51: 325–32.

Pedrick-Cornell, Claire and Gelles, Richard J. (1982) 'Elder Abuse: The Status of Current Knowledge', *Family Relations*, 31: 457–65.

Penhale, Bridget (1993a) 'The Abuse of Elderly People: Considerations for Practice', *British Journal of Social Work*, 23 (2): 95–112.

Penhale, Bridget (1993b) 'Abuse on the Map', *Community Care*, 10 June: 20–1.

Penhale, Bridget (1993c) 'Local Authority Guidelines and Procedures', in Claudine McCreadie (ed.), *Elder Abuse: New Findings and Policy Guidelines*. London: Age Concern Institute for Gerontology. pp. 8–15.

Perkins, Elizabeth R. (1991) 'Screening Elderly People: A Review of the Literature in the Light of the New General Practitioners' Contract', *British Journal of General Practice*, 41: 382–5.

Phillipson, Chris (1992) 'Confronting Elder Abuse: Fact and Fiction', *Generations Review*, 2/3 (September): 2–3.

Pijil, Marja (1992) 'Netherlands Politics for Elderly People', *Social Policy and Administration*, 26 (3): 201–8.

Pillemer, K.A. (1994) 'Methodological Issues in the Study of Elder Abuse'. Action on Elder Abuse Working Paper No. 1. London: Action on Elder Abuse: 1–10.

Pillemer, K.A. and Finkelhor, D. (1988) 'The Prevalence of Elder Abuse: A Random Survey Sample', *The Gerontologist*, 28 (1): 51–7.

Pillemer, K.A. and Finkelhor, D. (1989) 'Causes of Elder Abuse: Caregiver Stress versus Problem Relatives', *American Journal of Orthopsychiatry*, 59 (2): 179–87.

Pillemer, K.A. and Wolf, R.S. (1986) *Elder Abuse: Conflict in the Family*. New York: Auburn House.

Pillemer, K.A. and Wolf, R.S. (1989) *Helping Elderly Victims*. New York: Columbia University Press.

Pitkeathley, Jill (1989) *It's My Duty, Isn't it? The Plight of Carers in Our Society*. London: Souvenir Press.

Plante, David (1984) *Difficult Women: A Memoir of Three – Jean Rhys, Sonia Orwell, Germaine Greer*. London: Futura.

Polity Press (ed.) (1994) *The Polity Press Reader in Gender Studies*. Cambridge: Polity Press.

Pollitt, P.A., Anderson, I. and O'Connor, D.W. (1991) 'For Better or for Worse: The Experience of Caring for an Elderly Dementing Spouse', *Ageing and Society*, 11: 443–69.

Pritchard, Jacki (1992) *The Abuse of Elderly People: A Handbook for Professionals*. London: Jessica Kingsley.

Pritchard, Jacki (1993) 'Gang Warfare', *Community Care*, 8 July: 22–3.

Probyn, Elspeth (1993) *Sexing the Self: Gendered Positions in Cultural Studies*. London: Routledge.

Pugh, Helena and Moser, Kath (1990) 'Measuring Women's Mortality Differences', in Helen Roberts (ed.), *Women's Health Counts*. London: Routledge. pp. 93–112.

Qureshi, Hazel (1986) 'Responses to Dependency: Reciprocity Affect and Power in Family Relationships', in Chris Phillipson et al. (eds), *Dependency and Interdependency in Old Age: Theoretical Perspectives and Policy Alternatives*. London: Croom Helm. pp. 167–79.

Ramazanoglu, Caroline (1989) *Feminism and the Contradictions of Oppression*. London: Routledge.

Rathbone-McCuan, E. (1980) 'Elderly Victims of Family Violence and Neglect', *Social Casework: The Journal of Contemporary Social Work*, 61 (4): 296–304.

Renzetti, Claire (1992) *Violent Betrayal*. Thousand Oaks, CA: Sage.

'A Report on Elder Abuse in Domestic Settings in Northamptonshire, November 1991–October 1992' (1992). Unpublished Report, Northampton: Northamptonshire County Council Social Services Department.

Riley, Joan (1987) *Waiting in the Twilight*. London: Women's Press.

Robb, Barbara (1967) *Sans Everything: A Case to Answer*. London: Thomas Nelson.

Roberts, Helen (ed.) (1981) *Doing Feminist Research*. London: Routledge and Kegan Paul.

Roberts, Lynn and Nolan, Mike (1993) 'Elder Abuse: Raising the Awareness of Nurses Working in A. and E. Units', *British Journal of Nursing*, 2 (3): 167–71.

Rochdale Metropolitan Borough Council (n.d.) *Working Together: Guidelines for Staff to Follow when the Abuse of Older People is Suspected or Confirmed*. Rochdale.

Rose, Hilary and Bruce, Errollyn (1995) 'Mutual Care but Differential Esteem: Caring between Older Couples', in S. Arber and J. Ginn (eds), *Connecting Gender and Ageing*. Buckingham: Open University Press. pp. 114–28.

Ross, Margaret M., Rosenthal, Carolyn J., and Dawson, Pamela G. (1993) 'Spousal Caregiving Following Institutionalization: The Experience of Elderly Wives', *Journal of Advanced Nursing*, 18: 1531–9.

Royal College of Nursing (1991) *Guidelines for Nurses: Abuse and Older People*. London: Royal College of Nursing.

Rule, Jane (1987) *Memory Board*. London: Pandora.

Sadler, Catharine (1990) 'Breaking Point', *Nursing Times*, 86/24 (13 June): 21.

Saveman, Britt-Inger, Hallberg, Ingalill Rahm and Norberg, Astrid (1993) 'Identifying and Defining Abuse of Elderly People, as seen by Witnesses', *Journal of Advanced Nursing*, 18: 1393–400.

Scheman, Naomi (1993) *Engenderings: Constructions of Knowledge, Authority and Privilege*. London: Routledge.

Schlesinger, Benjamin and Schlesinger, Rachel (1988) *Abuse of the Elderly: Issues and Annotated Bibliography*. Toronto: University of Toronto Press.

Scrutton, S. (1990) 'Ageism: The Foundation of Age Discrimination', in E. McEwen (ed.), *Age, The Unrecognised Discrimination: Views to Provoke a Debate*. London: Age Concern. pp. 12–27.

Sengstock, Mary C. and Hwalek, Melanie (1987) 'A Review and Analysis of Measures for the Identification of Elder Abuse', *Journal of Gerontological Social Work*, 10 (3–4): 21–36.

Showalter, Elaine (1987) *The Female Malady*. London: Virago.

Sidell, Moyra (1992) 'The Relationship of Elderly Women to their Doctors', in Julie George and Ebrahim Shah (eds), *Health Care for Older Women*. Oxford: Oxford University Press. pp. 179–94.

Slater, Phil (1995) 'Elder Abuse and Professional Power', *Action on Elder Abuse Bulletin*, 10 (March/April): 2–3.

Smith, Jef (1992) *What If They Hurt Themselves?* London: Counsel and Care.

Social Services Inspectorate (1992) *Confronting Elder Abuse*. London: HMSO.

Southall Black Sisters (eds) (1994) *Domestic Violence and Asian Women*. London: Southall Black Sisters.

Spender, Dale (1980) *Man Made Language*. London: Routledge and Kegan Paul.

Stammers, Trevor (1992) 'What is the Root of Ageism?' *Care of the Elderly*, July: 288–90.

Stanley, Liz and Wise, Sue (1993) *Breaking Out Again*. London: Routledge.

Stearns, P. (1977) *Old Age in European Society: The Case of France*. London: Croom Helm.

Stearns, P. (1986) 'Old Age Family Conflict: The Perspective of the Past', in K. Pillemer and R. Wolf (eds), *Elder Abuse*. Dover: Auburn House.

Steinmetz, Suzanne K. (1983) 'Dependency, Stress, and Violence between Middle-Aged Caregivers and their Elderly Parents', in J. Kosberg (ed.), *Abuse and Maltreatment of the Elderly*. Boston: John Wright, PSG. pp. 134–49.

Steinmetz, Suzanne K. (1988) *Duty Bound: Elder Abuse and Family Care*. Sage Library of Social Research. Vol. 166. London: Sage.

Stevenson, Olive (1989) *Age and Vulnerability: A Guide to Better Care*. London: Edward Arnold.

'S.W.D. Found Guilty' (1993) *Community Care*, 7 January: 2.

Taylor, R. and Ford, G. (1983) 'Inequalities of Old Age: An Examination of Age, Sex, and Class Differences in a Sample of Community Elderly', *Ageing Society*, 3: 183–208.

Thomas, K. (1977) 'Age and Authority in Early Modern England', *Proceedings of the British Academy*. Vol. 62, pp. 205–48.

Thompson, Audrey (1994–5) 'Call for Debate to Stop Elder Abuse', *Community Care*, 22 December–5 January: 8–9.

Thone, Ruth Raymond (1992) *Women and Aging: Celebrating Ourselves*. New York: Haworth Press.

'Thugs Attack Woman, 83' (1992) *Northampton Chronicle and Echo*, 6 November: 1.

Tomlin, Sara (1989) *Abuse of Elderly People: An Unnecessary and Preventable Problem*. London: Centre for Policy on Ageing.

Townsend, Peter (1962) *The Last Refuge*. London: Routledge and Kegan Paul.

Townsend, Peter (1981) 'The Structured Dependency of the Elderly: Creation of a Social Policy in the Twentieth Century', *Ageing and Social Policy*, 1 (1): 5–28.

Treharne, Gwyneth (1990) 'Attitudes towards the Care of Elderly People: Are They Getting Better?' *Journal of Advanced Nursing*, 15: 777–81.

Trollope, Joanna (1992) *The Men and the Girls*. London: Bloomsbury.

Tulloch, A.J. (1991) 'Preventive Care of Elderly People: How Good Is Our Training?', *British Journal of General Practice*, September: 354–5.

Twigg, J. et al. (1990) *Carers and Services: A Review of Research*. London: HMSO.

Twycross, R. (1992) 'Euthanasia: Killing for Convenience', *British Medical Association News Review 1992*, January: 25.

Ungerson, Clare (1987) *Policy is Personal: Sex, Gender and Informal Care*. London: Tavistock.

Vaccaro, Frank (1992) 'Physically Aggressive Elderly: A Social Skills Training Program', *Journal of Behavioral Therapy and Experimental Psychiatry*, 23 (4): 277–88.

Valios, Natalie (1995) 'Elder Abuse Needs United Approach', *Community Care*, 6–12 April: 8–9.

Wagner, G. (1988) *Residential Care: A Positive Choice*. London: National Institute for Social Work/HMSO.

Walby, Sylvia (1986) *Patriarchy at Work*. Cambridge: Polity Press.

Walker, Alan (1992) 'The Poor Relation: Poverty among Older Women', in Caroline Glendinning and Jane Millar (eds), *Women and Poverty in Britain – the 1990s*. Hemel Hempstead: Harvester Wheatsheaf. pp. 163–75.

Walker, Alexis J. and Pratt, Clara C. (1991) 'Daughters Help to Mothers: Intergenerational Aid versus Caregiving', *Journal of Marriage and the Family*, 53 (February): 3–12.

Walker, Alexis J., Shin, Hwa-Yong and Bird, David N. (1990) 'Perceptions of Relationship Change and Caregiver Satisfaction', *Family Relations*, 39: 147–52.

Walker, Alexis J., Pratt, Clara C. and Oppy, Nancy Chun (1992) 'Perceived Reciprocity in Family Caregiving', *Family Relations*, 41: 82–5.

Ward, Linda (1994) 'Outlining the Need for a Practical Agenda for Action', *Community Care*, 15–21 December: 29.

Wardhaugh, J. and Wilding, P. (1993) 'Towards an Explanation of the Corruption of Care', *Critical Social Policy*, 37: 4–31.

Warwick University Centre for Research in Ethnic Relations (1993) *Ethnic Minorities of Great Britain: Housing and Family Characteristics*. Warwick: Commission for Racial Equality.

Waterhouse, Rosie (1994) 'Screw Tightens on NHS Geriatric Care', *Independent*, 26 August: 5.

Weale, Sally (1993) 'Why Granny is Down in the Dumps', *Guardian*, 19 May: 13.

Wenger, G. Clare (1993) 'The Formation of Social Networks: Self Help, Mutual Aid, and Old People in Contemporary Britain', *Journal of Aging Studies*, 7 (1): 25–40.

White, A.E. (1986) 'Health Visiting and Elderly People', in Sally J. Redfern (ed.), *Nursing Elderly People*. Edinburgh: Churchill Livingstone. pp. 458–63.

Whittaker, Terri (1995) 'Violence, Gender and Elder Abuse: Towards a Feminist Analysis and Practice', *Journal of Gender Studies*, 4 (1): 35–45.

'Who Cares for Carers?' (1991) *Community Care*, 25 April: 24–5.

Wilkinson, Sue and Kitzinger, Celia (eds) (1994) *Women and Health: Feminist Perspectives*. London: Taylor and Francis.

Wilson, Gail (1994) 'Abuse of Elderly Men and Women among Clients of a Community Psychogeriatric Service', *British Journal of Social Work*, 24: 681–700.

Wilson, Gail (1995) '"I'm the Eyes and She's the Arms": Changes in Gender Roles in Advanced Old Age', in S. Arber and J. Ginn (eds), *Connecting Gender and Ageing*. Buckingham: Open University Press. pp. 98–113.

Windsor, Valerie (1986) *Effie's Burning*. London: Samuel French.

Wolf, Naomi (1990) *The Beauty Myth*. London: Chatto and Windus.

Wolf, R.S. and K.A. Pillemer (1989) *Helping Elderly Victims: The Reality of Elder Abuse*. New York: Columbia University Press.

Woolham, John (1994) *Care Management for Ethnic Minority Groups: A Report of an Evaluation of Projects for African/Caribbean and Asian People in Northampton-shire*. Research Report No. 38. Northampton: Northamptonshire County Council.

Wright, Fay D. (1986) *Left to Care Alone*. Aldershot: Gower.

Wright, Ray (1993) *Care in the Community: How it Affects Black Communities in Northamptonshire*. Northampton: Northamptonshire County Council.

Zdorkowski, R. Todd and Galbraith, Michael W. (1985) 'An Inductive Approach to the Investigation of Elder Abuse', *Ageing and Society*, 5 (4): 413–29.

Appendix: Elder Abuse Questionnaire

RESPONDENT DETAILS

1. Which organization do you work for? _____

2. What is your job title/profession? _____

3. Have you suspected or known any cases of elder abuse?   YES/NO

If YES continue with questionnaire

If NO please return form anyway

CASE DETAILS

4. Type of abuse

Case no.	Details of person abused							Details of abuser				Abuse	
	Type of abuse Enter code		Were any of the abused suffering from dementia?			Gender	Age	Relationship to abused	Do abused and abuser live together? Y/N	Gender		Suspected	Confirmed
Case	Code	Number	Mild	Moderate	Severe								
1													
2													
3													
4													
5													
6													

Codes for question 4

Physical (PH)	Code no.
Hitting/punching/pushing	PH1
Unexplained bruising	PH2
Pattern of falls	PH3
Confined/locked in	PH4
Stabbing	PH5
Burns/cigarette/scalding	PH6

Medication (M)	
Medication withheld	M1
Over-medicated	M2

Psychological (PS)	Code no.
Verbally abusive/aggressive	PS1
Threatening/frightening behaviour	PS2
Humiliating or taunting	PS3
Making unreasonable demands	PS4
Ignoring/not communicating	PS5
Told to confine movements	PS6

Sexual (S)	
Made to engage in unwanted sexual activity	S1

Financial (F)	Code no.
Extracted money reg. from A/C	F1
Took pension book/bankbook	F2
Attempted to get house	F3
Stole furniture/jewellery	F4
Withheld money due	F5

Neglect (N)	Code no.
Insufficient food	N1
Insufficient warmth	N2
Ineffective shelter	N3
Left unclean deliberately	N4
Left in pain deliberately	N5
Denied access to services	N6

5. In how many cases were other agencies involved? _____

Index